FROM GENERATION *to* GENERATION

Devotional Thoughts Drawn from the Past

Peter Kennedy
with
Brenda Colby
and
Lorraine Espinosa

BARBOUR
PUBLISHING, INC.
Uhrichsville, Ohio

Published by Barbour Publishing, Inc., P.O. Box 719, Uhrichsville, Ohio 44683 http://www.barbourbooks.com

ecpa Member of the
Evangelical Christian
Publishers Association

Printed in the United States of America.

INTRODUCTION

When Moses met God in the burning bush, he was afraid no one would believe it had happened. Over the centuries and millennia others have had this same fear. In fact, just like Moses, you may have once been reluctant to tell other people about an encounter with the Lord, or your faith in Jesus Christ, or your love of God. But notice what God said to Moses: "Say to the Israelites, 'The LORD, the God of your fathers—the God of Abraham, the God of Isaac and the God of Jacob—has sent me to you.' This is my name forever, the name by which I am to be remembered from generation to generation" (Exodus 3:15).

God was saying this: "Moses, I am the God of human beings; the God of real people like Abraham, Isaac, and Jacob. For all time, I want to be remembered like this." Yes, God is the Creator, the sovereign King of the universe, the all-powerful, entirely righteous One. But God is also yours. God is involved with real people from one generation to the next and desires to always be remembered in this way.

This book provides a year of daily devotional readings which will help you to recall that God's name is "The God of Abraham, the God of Isaac, and the God of Jacob"; that God is intimately involved in the human race. It will even remind you that God is involved in your own life, day by day. There is nothing to fear in a God who is so close. In fact, knowing this we can join all the generations who sing Psalm 79:13:

We your people, the sheep of your pasture,
will praise you forever;
from generation to generation
we will recount your praise.

Day 1
JUST AS I AM

Now then, why do you try to test God by putting on the necks of the disciples a yoke that neither we nor our fathers have been able to bear? No! We believe it is through the grace of our Lord Jesus that we are saved, just as they are.
Acts 15:10–11

*C*harlotte Elliott's health started to fail her when she turned thirty. Soon she was an invalid. As her physical health deteriorated, her sweet disposition soured. Dr. Cesar Malan, a famous Swiss minister, visited the Elliott home one evening. "If God loved me, he would not have treated me this way," Charlotte cried to him.

Dr. Malan patiently responded, "You are tired of yourself, aren't you?"

"What do you mean?" she asked.

"You are holding to your hate and anger because you have nothing else in the world to cling to," he said. He went on to explain the wonderful grace of God through Jesus Christ. He told her to go to Christ just as she was. There she would find salvation.

"I would come to God just as I am. . .is that right?" she wondered.

That evening, Charlotte gave her life to Jesus Christ. And fourteen years later, on the anniversary of her new birth, she penned the words to the favorite hymn, "Just As I Am."

We cannot tidy up our lives before we go to the Lord. Are you tempted to add good works to your salvation? Today in prayer praise Jesus Christ that it is only through the grace of your Lord that you are saved—just as you are.

Just as I am, without one plea, but that thy blood was shed for me, and that thou bidd'st me come to thee, O Lamb of God, I come.

—Charlotte Elliott

Day 2
A NEW CREATURE

*You, however, are controlled not by the sinful nature but by
the Spirit, if the Spirit of God lives in you. And if anyone
does not have the Spirit of Christ, he does not belong to Christ.*
Romans 8:9

In January 1956 American missionary pilot Nate Saint
and four missionaries flew into the jungle of Ecuador to make
contact with the Auca Indians, an isolated people who distrusted the outside world. The missionaries cautiously dropped
gifts and gospel leaflets. After a few days they reported that
they had contacted three Aucas. Nothing more was heard
from the missionaries. Later a search party found the five men
dead and floating in the Curaray River. All had been killed by
Auca arrows and lances. Nate had been killed by a lance
wrapped with a gospel tract.

The men's widows continued their husbands' work. Eleven
months after the massacre they made contact with the Aucas.
The women feared for their lives but God provided protection. The Aucas admitted they had killed the missionaries to
preserve their way of life. Through the years the valiant women
translated the Scriptures into the Auca language. Then a miracle occurred in the heart of one Aucan warrior. Iketa was
fierce. He had lanced Nate Saint. But after hearing the Word
of God, Iketa gave his life to Christ. His faith made him a
new creature controlled by God's Spirit.

No one is beyond the love of God. Do you know someone who needs the life-changing salvation of Jesus Christ?
Today pray for that person that they may find faith.

> Souls in which the Spirit dwells, illuminated by the
> Spirit, themselves became spiritual and send forth
> their grace to others.
>
> —Basil of Caesarea

Day 3
TO DESCRIBE THE INDESCRIBABLE

Thanks be to God for his indescribable gift!
2 Corinthians 9:15

The indescribable gift of God is salvation through Jesus Christ. One person has attempted a description of this good news using John 3:16:

For God. . .the greatest Lover
. . .so loved. . .the greatest degree
. . .the world. . .the greatest number
. . .that he gave. . .the greatest act
. . .his one and only Son,. . .the greatest Gift
. . .that whoever. . .the greatest invitation
. . .believes. . .the greatest simplicity
. . .in him. . .the greatest Person
. . .shall not perish. . .the greatest deliverance
. . .but. . .the greatest difference
. . .have. . .the greatest certainty
. . .eternal life. . .the greatest possession

The Lord cared so much for you that He gave you Himself. Thank Christ that through Him you have eternal life—His wonderful, indescribable gift.

Let us forget how much we have done for God, and remember what he has done for us in Christ, and what he is continuing to do for us everyday.
—George R. Hendrick

Day 4
TEMPORAL BUILDING VS. TRUE SECURITY

*I undertook great projects: I built houses for myself and
planted vineyards. I made gardens and parks and
planted all kinds of fruit trees in them.*
Ecclesiastes 2:4–5

A. J. Gordon was a leading evangelical Christian
minister at the end of the nineteenth century and founded
what is now known as Gordon College and Gordon-Conwell
Seminary. He helped compile two hymnals and wrote the
favorite hymn "My Jesus I Love Thee."

Once he noticed that if you tear down a sparrow's nest the
little bird will build again in the same place. However if you
pull the nest down several times the bird will catch on and seek
a new location less vulnerable to attack. Gordon observed that
Christians are not always so wise. They form dwelling places of
happiness and hope that are built on the values of this world
only to see them "pulled down" time and time again. Yet after
each brief interval of destruction they rebuild in the same
manner and make no significant changes in their lives. They
fail to realize that through their disappointments the Lord is
calling them to put their security in Him; to set their sights
heavenward.

Building gives us a sense of accomplishment and security,
but even the grandest monuments on earth are temporal and
vulnerable. Our true security rests with Jesus Christ and the
truth of the Bible. Are you spending too much energy on projects that one day will rust or decay? Today in prayer give
thanks to Christ that you can securely rest in Him.

It is not enough to be busy. . .the question is: what
are we busy about?

—Henry David Thoreau

10

Day 5
SPONTANEOUS COMBUSTION

Words from a wise man's mouth are gracious,
but a fool is consumed by his own lips.
Ecclesiastes 10:12

The following is a definition of spontaneous combustion as given by John Machnick, an engineer for the Travelers Insurance Company: "Under a variety of conditions, the temperature of certain materials can increase without drawing heat from surroundings. If the temperature of the material reaches its ignition temperature, spontaneous ignition is said to occur. In most cases, spontaneous heating occurs when a material reacts with oxygen from the air. . . .

"Cotton rags soaked in linseed oil are very susceptible to spontaneous ignition. This is because the reaction of oxygen and linseed oil (oxidation) is fairly rapid and evolves considerable heat. Spontaneous ignition of the cotton rags can be prevented by restricting the amount of oxygen reaching the rags (placed in sealed metal container) or by providing sufficient ventilation (hanging on a clothesline) to quickly dissipate the heat."

Spontaneous combustion can occur if you let sin soak into your life. Only the foolish fail to deal with sin. Are you allowing sin to soak into your life? Today confess any sin to Christ and ask Him for His gracious forgiveness.

Sensible talk meets with approval in a stable society,
but there is a destructive talk that degrades.
—J. Stafford Wright

Day 6
THE NATURE OF LIGHT

But everything exposed by the light becomes visible, for it is light that makes everything visible. This is why it is said: "Wake up, O sleeper, rise from the dead, and Christ will shine on you."
Ephesians 5:13–14

For centuries people have struggled to explain the nature of light. For Aristotle light was a state or a quality of an object which was acquired all at once from a luminous object. Descartes believed that the propagation of light was instantaneous. In his view light was beyond speed. Fermat refuted Descartes and proposed that light traveled in time. Light did move but extremely fast beyond measure.

Isaac Newton theorized that light is particles—big particles were red and little particles were purple and the other colors were made of particles that varied in size between the big red particles and the little purple particles. Christian Huygens postulated that light was composed of waves. He believed that light was ripples in a medium that could be detected by the eye. The long waves were red and the short waves were purple and the other colors were made of waves that varied in size between the long red wave and the short purple waves.

Albert Einstein declared that the speed of light is the same for all inertial observers regardless of the motion of the source. In Einstein's theory the speed of light is a constant and is more fundamental than time or space.

We may have difficulty understanding the nature of light but we know that Jesus Christ is the light of the world. In Him all things are made visible and judged. Are you letting the light of Christ shine in your life? Today in prayer give thanks that God has taken away the darkness and provided true light.

Light reveals what the darkness conceals. Darkness is not driven away by preaching at it; darkness is dissipated by the presence of light.

—J. Vernon McGee

Day 7

THE NAME ABOVE ALL NAMES

For to us a child is born, to us a son is given, and the government will be on his shoulders. And he will be called Wonderful Counselor, Mighty God, Everlasting Father, Prince of Peace.
Isaiah 9:6

The Guinness Book of Records lists some interesting facts about names. The oldest recorded personal name outside of the Bible is Sekhen—a predynastic king in Upper Egypt about 3,050 B.C. The longest name to appear on a birth certificate is Rhoshandiatellyneshiaunneveshenk Koyaanisquatsiuth Williams who was born September 12, 1984, to Mr. and Mrs. James Williams of Beaumont, Texas. Three weeks later Mr. Williams filed an amendment that expanded his daughter's first name to 1,019 letters and he added thirty-six letters to her middle name.

A. Lindup-Badarou of Truro, England as of March 1995 had a total of 3,530 first names registered as his full name. And Zachary Zzzzzzzzzzra wanted to ensure he was the last name in the San Francisco telephone book.

Jesus Christ was given a name which exceeds all other names. He is Wonderful Counselor, Mighty God, Everlasting Father, Prince of Peace. There is no other name in heaven or on earth that is more wonderful, more beautiful, more mighty than that of Jesus Christ. Today thank Him for His name.

The name Jesus is the combination of all the Old
Testament titles used to designate the Coming one
according to his nature and his work.

—Keil and Delitzsch

Day 8

REMEMBERING HIM
UNTIL HE COMES AGAIN

For whenever you eat this bread and drink this cup,
you proclaim the Lord's death until he comes.
1 Corinthians 11:26

In January 1777 the American Revolutionary War
was entering its first winter. General George Washington's army
made its winter camp in the heights surrounding Morristown,
New Jersey, an excellent strategic position for a four-month
encampment.

One of the few comforts Washington sought for himself
was to attend a church when it celebrated the Lord's Supper.
He heard that a local Presbyterian church was going to have
communion. He visited the home of the Rev. Dr. Jones, pastor of the church, and asked him, "Doctor, I understand that
the Lord's Supper is to be celebrated with you next Sunday: I
would learn if it accords with the canons of your church to
admit communicants of another denomination?" Rev. Dr.
Jones responded, "Most certainly; ours is not the Presbyterian
table, General, but the Lord's Table; and hence we give the
Lord's invitation to all His followers, of whatever name."

Washington was relieved and replied, "I am glad of it: that
it is as it ought to be; but as I was not quite sure of the fact, I
thought I would ascertain it from yourself, as I propose to join
with you on that occasion. Though a member of the Church
of England, I have no exclusive partialities." The next Sunday

14

General Washington joined the congregation of the Presbyterian church for worship and communion.

It is a Christian's privilege to remember Christ at His table. Today give thanks to Him for this celebration and seek to celebrate it regularly.

> It is a pledge of the Lord's return. As it points backward to his death, so does it also point forward to that marriage supper where He, the returning Bridegroom, will entertain his bride clothed in white array.
> —Johann Peter Lange

Day 9

THE HAND OF PRAYER

I want men everywhere to lift up holy hands in prayer,
without anger or disputing.
1 Timothy 2:8

A hand can be clenched in anger or used for prayer. The index finger represents those who point the way to Christ. This would include ministers and pastors, missionaries and Sunday school teachers. The middle finger is the tallest of the fingers and represents those who have authority. This finger represents the president, Congress, the governor, and all who are our leaders throughout the world. The third finger, sometimes called the ring finger, is the weakest of the three larger fingers. We are to remember those who are helpless, homeless, ill, poor, and less fortunate than us. The smallest finger represents my own needs and those of my family, friends, and neighbors. The one digit that can easily touch all of the fingers is the thumb. The thumb represents prayer. As the thumb touches each of the different fingers, we can remember to pray for those who Christ has brought to mind.

The next time you feel your hands clenching into a fist, extend them to Jesus Christ instead. Which "finger" is causing the anger? Touch it with your thumb and pray. Christ is faithful to give you wisdom.

No man can think clearly when his fists are clenched.
—George Jean Nathan

Day 10
A FULL LIFE OF CONTENTMENT

But godliness with contentment is great gain. For we brought nothing into the world, and we can take nothing out of it. But if we have food and clothing, we will be content with that.
1 Timothy 6:6–8

Henry Martyn was born in 1781, studied at Cambridge and at age twenty was the top undergraduate in mathematics. However, the awards and recognition he received from mathematics left him with a hollow feeling. Charles Simeon, the vicar of Holy Trinity Church, encouraged Martyn to become a missionary. After reading of the life of David Brainerd, he resolved to go to India as a missionary.

Arriving in India at age twenty-four, Martyn prayed, "Lord, let me burn out for You." Before his death at age thirty-one, Henry Martyn had translated the New Testament into Hindi and Persian. He also revised an earlier Arabic version of the New Testament, translated the Book of Psalms into Persian, and the *Anglican Book of Common Prayer* into Hindi. In 1812 Henry Martyn died. In his diary he expressed a deep love and devotion to Jesus Christ and a contentment in serving God.

We come into the world with nothing and we leave in the same manner. Today in prayer turn your life over to Jesus Christ. Know that He will provide the necessities of food, clothing, and shelter. Ask Him to grant you contentment as you live a full life for Him.

> Contentment makes much of little; greed makes little of much. Contentment is the poor man's riches and desire the rich man's poverty.
> —John Quincy Adams

Day 11
PURSUE RIGHTEOUSNESS

Flee the evil desires of youth, and pursue righteousness, faith, love and peace, along with those who call on the Lord out of a pure heart.
2 Timothy 2:22

Joe E. Brown was a talented entertainer, a gifted athlete, and comedian. His boyhood heroes were the baseball player Ty Cobb and the politician William Jennings Bryan. He was invited to try out with the New York Yankees and he said, "Naturally I tried to play baseball like Ty Cobb, but actually I played it like Bryan."

Joe was in the 1935 version of Shakespeare's "A Midsummer Night's Dream" with James Cagney and the 1951 Rogers and Hammerstein classic "Showboat" with Ava Gardner. In 1941 Brown started visiting military installations throughout Alaska and the South Pacific. For his tireless work at providing wholesome entertainment to the troops during World War II, Joe E. Brown was presented the U.S. Army's highest civilian award, the Bronze Star.

Once while entertaining troops in the South Pacific, Brown was asked to tell some dirty jokes. Brown responded, "Son, a comedian like me lives for applause and laughter. . . . But if telling a dirty story is the price I must pay for your laughter, then I'm not interested. I've never done an act that I couldn't perform before my mother and I never will." The troops cheered Brown's response.

With all of the wonderful choices Christ has given to us, why would we ever want to strike out on our own? Today in prayer ask Christ to give you a pure heart that desires to pursue righteousness, faith, love, and peace.

> When God says, "Don't," you know he has other, even
> better provisions to give you if you will obey him.
> —Josh McDowell

Day 12
HUNGER FOR THE BIBLE

Therefore, rid yourselves of all malice and all deceit, hypocrisy, envy, and slander of every kind.Like newborn babies, crave pure spiritual milk, so that by it you may grow up in your salvation, now that you have tasted that the Lord is good.
1 Peter 2:1–3

When Mary Jones was ten years old, she began saving for something special. She baby-sat, tended neighbors' gardens, and sold eggs from her own chickens. By the time she was sixteen, she had accumulated enough money to get what she so desperately wanted.

Was it a new car? A fresh wardrobe? A computer? No. Mary Jones was saving for a Bible. But there was no place to buy one in her tiny Welsh village in 1800. So Mary, now age sixteen, walked twenty-five miles to Bala. There a preacher named Thomas Charles had one Bible to sell. After some convincing he sold it to her.

Because of Mary's hunger for the Bible, Charles and others

began discussing the need for making the scriptures more readily available. The British and Foreign Bible Society was started and during the next 100 years it had distributed more than 200 million copies of God's Word worldwide. To Mary no book was more important than the Bible and her persistence paid huge spiritual dividends.

Do you have that same craving for God's Word as when you first accepted Christ? Today ask God to give you a hunger for spiritual growth in Him which can only be satisfied by taking in His Word.

> If a man's Bible is coming apart it is an indication
> that he himself is fairly well put together.
> —James E. Jennings

Day 13
THE DEATH OF AN EYEWITNESS

We did not follow cleverly invented stories when we told you
about the power and coming of our Lord Jesus Christ,
but we were eyewitnesses of his majesty.
2 Peter 1:16

Werner Moelders, a colonel in the German Luftwaffe, was the first German fighter ace in World War II to reach 100 air victories and is credited with shooting down a total of 115 enemy aircraft. He was awarded the Knight's Cross of the Iron Cross, one of his country's greatest honors. He said, "The most important thing for a fighter pilot is to get his first victory without too much shock."

But Moelders received a shock one day. His aircraft was riddled with bullets and he cried out, "God, God Almighty in heaven, You alone can save me." Miraculously, he was able to land his fighter and walk away. Shaken, Moelders returned to his quarters. His mind went back to his godly parents, his pastor, and the teaching he had received about Jesus Christ. That night he gave his life to the Lord.

Werner Moelders spoke out against the Nazi's euthanasia program that killed older adults and the mentally and physically disabled. This angered the nation's leaders. He also told his fellow aviators about the love of Jesus Christ and how he was saved by His redeeming grace. On November 22, 1941, while on a noncombat flight, the *Heinkel He-111* aircraft Moelders was flying mysteriously crashed. Both engines had failed.

Even though today you are not an eyewitness of Jesus Christ, you will one day see the Lord face-to-face. Today in prayer give thanks! One created you, knows you, loves you, and saves you—Jesus Christ.

> The sense of being led by an unseen hand which takes mine, while another hand reaches ahead and prepares the way, grows upon me daily.
> —Frank Laubach

Day 14
THE WRITTEN PROMISE

*I write these things to you
who believe in the name of
the Son of God so that you may know
that you have eternal life. 1 John 5:13*

A man once told H. A. Ironside, "I won't go a foot further until I know I am saved, or else know it is hopeless to seek to be sure of it."

Ironside asked the man if a happy feeling or the voice of an angel would give him the needed assurance. The man initially said yes. Ironside answered, "What if the devil gave you that happy feeling or transformed himself into an angel? Then on your deathbed Satan visited you and said 'I gave you that happy feeling. I was that angel. You are lost forever.' " The man agreed that an inner feeling or the voice of an angel would not give him assurance of eternal life.

Ironside went on, "God has given us something better than happy feelings, something more dependable than the voice of an angel. He has given His Son to die for your sins, and He has testified in His own unaltered Word that if you trust in Him all your sins are gone. Do you believe on the name of the Son of God?"

"I do, sir, I do indeed! I know He is the Son of God, and I know He died for me." That night the man had full assurance of eternal life.

God's promise is not found in feelings or miraculous visions. It is found in the Bible. Today give thanks that not only did Jesus die to give you eternal life, but He gave you the Bible so you will forever have that assurance.

> Jesus and I shall never part for God is greater than my heart.
>
> —Nathan Cole

Day 15
THE HIGHEST RANK

You are all sons of God through faith in Christ Jesus,
for all of you who were baptized into Christ
have clothed yourselves with Christ.
Galatians 3:26–27

Theodore Roosevelt, Jr. grew up under the shadow of a large man. His father was the hero of San Juan Hill and president of the United States. The pressure to excel often caused him problems, but Teddy, Jr. went on to be a highly decorated Brigadier General during World War II, receiving the Medal of Honor for heroism. He was also the Governor General of the Philippines, Governor of Puerto Rico, and Assistant Secretary of the Navy.

During World War II, while waiting for a flight at an airport, Teddy, Jr. saw a sailor step to a ticket window and ask for a ticket. "I want to see my mother," the sailor explained. "I don't have much time."

The indifferent woman at the ticket window was not impressed by the sailor's sense of urgency, "There's a war on, you know," she rudely replied.

At this point, Roosevelt, who had overheard the conversation, stepped to the ticket window and told her to give the sailor his seat. A friend of the general spoke in surprise, "Teddy, aren't you in a hurry too?"

"It's a matter of rank," he replied. "I'm only a general; he's a son!"

Sons of God. What a marvelous name! This is what the Bible calls everyone who trusts in Christ. Do you sometimes forget you have the rank of a son? Today give thanks that you have been bestowed with this high rank.

Abba, Father, we approach thee in our Savior's precious name. We the children of your mercy bow before your throne today.

—James G. Deck

Day 16
DO GOOD IN HIM

Let us not become weary in doing good, for at the proper time
we will reap a harvest if we do not give up. Therefore, as we
have opportunity, let us do good to all people, especially to
those who belong to the family of believers.
Galatians 6:9–10

Many obstacles had to be overcome to bring electric lighting to everyday life. One of the most important was the design of the light bulb. For years Thomas A. Edison worked. Yet every step closer to the goal was accompanied by a setback. Finally, in October 1879 Edison discovered the correct electrical resistance for light bulbs. He then began to work feverishly testing materials for the right filament. Edison patiently tested every possible material: fish line, cotton, cardboard, coconut hair, hickory shavings. He had to find a material that would burn bright and not burn out.

On November 1 Edison filed a patent application for a carbon filament lamp. However his lamp could only produce light for fourteen hours. Francis Upton, one of his assistants, remarked that Edison was "always sanguine, and his valuations are on his hopes more than on the realities." By November 16 excitement grew when a bulb lasted sixteen hours. Around-the-clock testing began. Two weeks later, carbonized filaments attached to platinum lamps produced sixteen candlepower and did not burn out! On November 28, 1879, Edison wrote, "My light is perfected."

The Lord leads us to times when we are stretched beyond normal limits. He gives us much to do and little time to do it. Are you making the most of every opportunity to do good? Today in prayer thank Christ for every opportunity to live for Him.

Do good, and leave behind a monument of virtue. Write your name in kindness, love, and mercy on the hearts of all you come in contact with; you will never be forgotten.

—Thomas Chalmers

Day 17
MIND THE DETAILS

Whoever can be trusted with very little can also be trusted with much, and whoever is dishonest with very little will also be dishonest with much.
Luke 16:10

The Panama Canal is a fifty-one-mile-long waterway linking the Gulf of Mexico with the Pacific Ocean. In 1878 a French company secured a ninety-nine year lease to operate the canal.

Thousands of men were brought into the jungle of Panama to begin construction. But the project was derailed by diseases spread by mosquitoes. Yellow fever and malaria claimed twenty thousand lives in eight years of construction. The French invested over $100 million but were forced to abandon their equipment to the jungle.

So the United States resumed the canal project. Dr. William Gorges was the senior officer in charge of sanitation in the canal zone area. Gorges invested over four million dollars into window screens, mosquito insecticide, landscaping, trash collecting, and vaccinations. He built quarantine stations and carefully watched over every detail to eradicate mosquitoes in the canal zone. By 1906, less than three years after he began, Dr. Gorges had eliminated yellow fever from the canal zone. The Panama Canal opened for business in 1914.

Eliminate the mosquitoes in your life and God may entrust to you monumental projects. It is the little details in your life, things as small as mosquitoes, which can prevent you from effectively serving God. Today give thanks to Christ for what He has given you. Ask Him for wisdom to be mindful of the details.

> As a person of wealth entrusts part of his estate to his son to test him before giving him the whole inheritance, so God tests our fitness for the "true riches" of heaven in our use of material possessions.
> —Donald G. Miller

Day 18
REPENTANCE AND CHANGE

John said to the crowds coming out to be baptized by him, "You brood of vipers! Who warned you to flee from the coming wrath? Produce fruit in keeping with repentance. And do not begin to say to yourselves, 'We have Abraham as our father.' For I tell you that out of these stones God can raise up children for Abraham."
Luke 3:7–8

Patrick Neff attended Baylor University and received his law degree from the University of Texas. He became a prosecuting attorney in Waco then went on to be a member of the Texas House of Representatives and finally served as governor of Texas for two terms. He was a Christian who loved peace and reconciliation.

Once, when he was serving as governor, he visited the state penitentiary and spoke to the assembled convicts. He told them that if any man wanted to talk to him that day he would gladly listen. He further announced that he would listen in confidence—nothing a man said would be used against him.

When the general meeting was over a large group of men remained to talk to the governor. One by one they told him that they were there because of an injustice or a frame-up. All of them proclaimed their innocence. Finally one man came to the governor and said, "Mr. Governor, I just want to say that I am guilty. I did what they sent me here for. But I believe I have paid for it and if I were granted the right to go out I would do everything I could to be a good citizen and prove myself worthy of your mercy."

The governor realized the man's sincerity and granted him a pardon.

With the true sorrow of repentance comes a desire to change. Today give thanks to Christ that when you bring your life to Him, He brings change to your life.

> Regeneration is a beginning, but there is much more yet to come. The manifestations of this spiritual ripening are called "fruit of the Spirit." They are the direct opposite of the fruit of the old nature, the flesh.
> —Millard J. Erickson

Day 19
NOT A PRINCE BUT A SINNER

But the tax collector stood at a distance. He would not even look up to heaven, but beat his breast and said, "God, have mercy on me, a sinner."
Luke 18:13

Edward, the Duke of Kent, was the fourth son of King George III and father of Queen Victoria. The duke fell into debt early in life and never recovered from it. He lived beyond his means and his father refused to bail him out. He spent time in the British Army where he was known as a tyrannical officer with his only redeeming trait being his bravery on the field of battle. He was an intelligent man and believed in a "practical Christianity" that could be lived out seven days a week through good works. He detested drunkenness, never told a lie, and disapproved of gambling. During his lifetime he lent his name to over fifty charities.

In 1819, at age fifty-two, Edward suddenly came down with a high fever and pain in his chest. He started bleeding and had trouble breathing. His doctor visited him on January 22, 1820, and told the Duchess of Kent, "Human help can no longer avail." The physician tried to ease the duke's mind by speaking of his respectability and honorable conduct in the distinguished situation in which Providence had placed him. The duke stopped him short saying, "No; remember, if I am to be saved, it is not as a prince, but as a sinner."

We come to Christ only as a sinner who needs mercy. Today praise God for His wonderful mercy towards you.

> Lord, save me from that evil man—myself.
> —Augustine of Hippo

Day 20
THE RIGHTEOUS LIFE

Therefore do not let sin reign in your mortal body so that you obey its evil desires. Do not offer the parts of your body to sin, as instruments of wickedness, but rather offer yourselves to God, as those who have been brought from death to life; and offer the parts of your body to him as instruments of righteousness.
Romans 6:12–13

Cooperstown, home of the Baseball Hall of Fame, is located in the hills of central New York State. Established in 1939, the Hall honors baseball's greatest players and memorializes its outstanding moments. But "Shoeless" Joe Jackson is not represented there.

Jackson, a member of the Chicago White Sox, had a career batting average of .356 and was an excellent fielder. Gamblers influenced Jackson's teammates to throw the 1919 World Series in order to collect on bets. Jackson himself played to the best of his ability but his teammates did not. Jackson was acquitted of any wrongdoing but baseball banned him for life for his failure to report his teammates' association with gambling.

If you visit Cooperstown you'll see Joe Jackson's glove and bat—remembrances of great moments of the game. But their owner—a great baseball player—is disqualified because he failed to protect the integrity of the game. He compromised good judgment and lost his place of honor.

A Christian is born again with the life of the righteous God. So we reflect the goodness of Jesus. Today give thanks that you will receive honor from God because of the obedience and righteousness of Jesus Christ.

> Sin, therefore, is no more to have dominion over a Christian, who does not live under the law, but under grace, than death dominion over Christ.
> —Hermann Olshausen

Day 21
THE AMAZING TRANSFORMATION

And we, who with unveiled faces all reflect the Lord's glory, are being transformed into his likeness with ever-increasing glory, which comes from the Lord, who is the Spirit.
2 Corinthians 3:18

It is difficult to believe that the exquisite winged creatures called butterflies were once crawling caterpillars. Such caterpillars are transformed through a process called metamorphosis.

This involves four stages: egg, larva (caterpillar), pupa

(chrysalis), and adult. The butterfly begins life as an egg on a plant leaf. A caterpillar forms in the egg, grows, and eventually breaks out of its shell. It eats plants and grows. As it grows, it sheds its outer skeleton four or five times. When this caterpillar is full grown it spins a silk button on a solid object, clings to the button, and molts for the last time. As it sheds its skin a naked pupa appears and a hard, golden shell called a chrysalis forms over the pupa. During this in-active stage an amazing transformation takes place inside the chrysalis—the pupa's body tissues break down into a semiliquid and reassemble into the parts of a butterfly. When the wet adult frees itself from the chrysalis it fans its soft, limp wings until they expand and harden. Within a few hours the butterfly is ready to fly off in search of a mate.

Christians are transformed too. When you believe in Christ the Holy Spirit begins to change you inwardly, making you more and more like Jesus. How has God changed you since you began following Jesus? Today thank the Lord that one day you will be like Him because of the Spirit's progressive and continuous transforming work.

> Under the new covenant, not one man alone, but all Christians behold and then reflect the glory of the Lord.
>
> —Murray J. Harris

Day 22
TAKE THE LORD AT HIS WORD

Now Stephen, a man full of God's grace and power,
did great wonders and miraculous signs among the people.
Acts 6:8

George Müller founded the Scriptural Knowledge Institute for Home and Abroad. It sent out over 160 missionaries from Britain, distributed 111 million gospel tracts, supported 2,000 orphans in five orphanages, and trained 121,000 students.

Müller believed that his material needs would be supplied by God through prayer alone. He relied on gifts for his ministry and personal support, but only the Lord knew of the needs. One day a man arrived at one of Müller's orphanages. A woman opened the door and said, "Have you brought the bread?"

The man replied, "What bread?"

"The bread for the children. It is five minutes before mealtime."

He found many children waiting patiently for breakfast. In a few minutes the woman came back saying, "The bread has come." A cart of bread had been delivered in answer to prayer.

Later the man learned they needed about twenty-five thousand dollars that day by noon. Mr. Müller confessed, "I don't know where a penny of it is coming from, but it is certainly coming." A letter from India arrived and was opened in the visitor's presence. It contained a draft for the exact amount needed.

Over $500,000 was given to the Institute. Müller gave away most of it and left a personal estate valued at less than one thousand dollars.

Are you looking to the Lord for the needs in your life? In prayer give thanks to Jesus Christ—the supplier of every good thing. Let Him know your needs.

Jesus was himself the one convincing and permanent miracle.

—Ian MacLaren

Day 23
ENCOURAGEMENT AND LOVE

*They preached the good news in that city and won a large
number of disciples. Then they returned to Lystra, Iconium
and Antioch, strengthening the disciples and encouraging
them to remain true to the faith. "We must go through
many hardships to enter the kingdom of God," they said.
Paul and Barnabas appointed elders for them in each
church and, with prayer and fasting, committed them
to the Lord, in whom they had put their trust.*

Acts 14:21–23

When Billy Graham was in his first semester at Bob Jones
College in 1936 he felt he did not fit in and considered leaving
the school. Graham wrote to his mother, "I know I've been converted. I know that I know Jesus Christ, but I've lost my feeling.
I can't seem to get anywhere in prayer. I don't feel anything."

She wrote back, "Son, God is testing you. He tells us to
walk not by feeling but by faith, and when you don't feel
anything, God may be closer to you than ever before. Through
the darkness and through the fog, put your hand up by faith.
You'll sense the touch of God."

During Christmas vacation Graham joined his family and
relatives vacationing in Florida. There he visited the Florida
Bible Institute, applied to the school, and was accepted. Unbe-
knownst to Graham, every day after lunch his parents prayed
for him on their knees.

At the new college Graham's enthusiasm for the Lord
returned. He preached at every opportunity and noticed that
people accepted Christ after hearing his sermons. He sensed
the Lord was calling him to be an evangelist. In May 1938
Graham began to preach full-time.

Have you encouraged a family member or friend lately?
Today ask Jesus to show you how you can give hope, courage,

or confidence to someone in your home, workplace, church, or neighborhood.

> One of the highest duties of a Christian is the duty of encouragement.
> —William Barclay

Day 24
LIBERTY VS. TEMPTATION

Therefore, if what I eat causes my brother to fall into sin, I will never eat meat again, so that I will not cause him to fall.
1 Corinthians 8:13

Marco Polo was the son of a Venetian merchant. In 1270, when he was fifteen years old, Polo and his father made an overland journey to China to trade with Kublai Khan. Khan was overjoyed with their arrival and requested that Polo's father be his ambassador to Rome and presented Marco's father with numerous expensive gifts.

Later the Polos returned to China through Baghdad to the edge of the Gobi Desert. There they rested at a town called Lop to pick up supplies and camels to cross the desert. In Lop they heard strange stories of people who had tried to cross the desert and had died. The arduous crossing of the desert with its heat, lack of water, and constant swirling winds caused delirium. Many strayed away from their caravans enticed by the sound of a wind which sounded like voices of their friends. The people of Lop warned: "Do not stray from your caravan. You will hear false voices that will call out your names as though they were your friends calling you. Following these voices you will be led in the wrong direction and hopelessly lost." The voices of those whom we think are our friends can lead us into dangerous temptations.

You may have liberty. But do not let that liberty lead someone else into sin. Are you considerate in your liberty to ensure that others will not fall into sin? Today ask God for wisdom in your conduct.

> There are many forms of recreation which in themselves might be honorable, but they have become associated with worldliness and godlessness and have proved to be snares to many a young heart. The law of love leads me to avoid them and in no way encourage others to participate in them.
>
> —A. B. Simpson

Day 25
THE SUPREME COMMANDER

Your kingdom come, your will be done on earth as it is in heaven.
Matthew 6:10

In 1968 the U.S. naval vessel U.S.S. *Pueblo* was taken captive by the North Korean government. Its crew of eighty-three men were held eleven months before being released. The crew prayed more and more as their captivity dragged on. At mealtime the men would bow their heads ever so slightly and thank God for the food before them. But when the Communist guards would spot them they would scream, "This is not a church! This food is a gift from the Democratic People's Republic of North Korea!" At night they dared not kneel because of the beatings they would have to endure. Instead the men prayed on their backs in their bunks. The men addressed God as COMM-WORLDFLT which stands for Commander of the World's Fleets. In prayer they made contact with the Supreme Commander of all things and were under His protection and care.

Modern thinking associates democracy with freedom.

When the will of the people is heard, freedom is the reward. But there is a greater freedom than that of democracy. It is the freedom found in the Kingdom of God. When you elect Jesus Christ as Lord of your life He is in total control. Jesus is King. His Kingdom is without end. His will will be done. In today's prayer acknowledge that Jesus is Lord and is in control of all as your Supreme Commander.

> O Lord, you know what is best for me. Let this or that be done, as you please. Give what you will, how much you will and when you will.
>
> —Thomas à Kempis

Day 26
THE HIGH COST OF A FREE RIDE

*For it is by grace you have been saved, through faith—
and this not from yourselves, it is the gift of God—
not by works, so that no one can boast.*
Ephesians 2:8–9

G. Campbell Morgan had no formal education but was a popular preacher because he was able to use ordinary situations to demonstrate biblical truths. Never dramatic, Morgan appealed to facts to get a point across.

Once a coal miner said to Morgan, "I would give anything to believe that God would forgive my sins but I cannot believe that He will forgive them if I just ask Him. It is too cheap." Morgan asked, "My dear friend, have you been working today?"

"Yes," the man replied. Morgan continued, "How did you get out of the pit? Did you pay?" The man answered, "Of course not. I just got into the cage and was pulled to the top." Morgan pressed, "Were you not afraid to entrust yourself to that cage? Was it not too cheap?"

"Oh, no," said the miner, "it was cheap for me but it cost the company a lot of money to sink the shaft to make the transport cage." Suddenly the man understood. Salvation had cost him nothing but it had not come cheap to God who sent the Son to rescue fallen humanity. Forgiveness was his if he would "get into the cage" by faith and let the work of Christ pull him out of the pit.

Salvation is a free gift but it isn't a cheap gift. It came at the extreme cost of Christ's death on the cross. Today in prayer give thanks to Jesus Christ that He paid the full price for your salvation.

Works without faith is idolatry.

—Martin Luther

Day 27
SHORTCUTS TO DISASTER

At this, the administrators and the satraps tried to find grounds for charges against Daniel in his conduct of government affairs, but they were unable to do so. They could find no corruption in him, because he was trustworthy and neither corrupt nor negligent.
Daniel 6:4

On January 27, 1967, NASA technicians and a crew of three astronauts were conducting ground tests of the Apollo One spacecraft. Astronauts Gus Grissom, Ed White, and Roger Chaffee were aboard when Apollo Systems Engineer John Tribe heard the cry, "Fire!" come from inside the module. The next words Tribe recalls hearing were something like, "Get us out! We're burning up. We've got a fire in the cockpit." The fire caused pressure to increase and the exit hatch sealed tight. By the time it could be opened all three astronauts had been killed.

NASA had instituted a "zero-defects" policy for the Apollo One project. But an investigation after the fire revealed that every company involved had fallen short of that standard. Over 100 items could not stand up to the heat, pressure, speed or vibration during space flight. In space, the cockpit fire could have been smothered by releasing a valve that would suck all the oxygen and fire into the vacuum of space. The astronauts would breathe from the oxygen in their space suits. Everyone overlooked the fact that on the launch pad no vacuum existed to evacuate the fire from the cockpit.

The temptation to take shortcuts can lead to disaster. Today in prayer ask the Lord to make you aware of any defects in your life and thank Him that He can make you flawless.

There is only one way to improve one's work—love it.
—Phillips Brooks

Day 28
THE CELESTIAL NAVIGATOR

*Not that we are competent in ourselves to claim anything
for ourselves, but our competence comes from God.*
2 Corinthians 3:5

For centuries humanity has been fascinated with magnetism. Socrates wrote, "There is a divinity moving you, like that contained in the stone which Euripides calls a magnet." The Chinese called magnetic rocks, known today as lodestones, "loving stones" because of their property to attract iron.

In 1600, William Gilbert wrote a groundbreaking work, *De Magnete*. In this book Gilbert posits that the earth is itself a giant magnet. From this Robert Norman developed the first compass called a dip needle.

When Robert Peary was endeavoring to reach the North Pole he ran into navigation problems. His charts of Greenland located Cape Morris Jessup on the northern tip of Greenland some twelve miles from its actual location. Peary trusted his magnetic compass for direction not knowing that magnetic compasses are useless near the North Pole. In 1906 Perry pushed north for three weeks. But he also drifted westward. When Peary finally took accurate celestial measurements he found himself seventy miles off course. He had trusted in a magnetic compass instead of the tried and true methods of celestial navigation.

We are not competent in ourselves to navigate through life. Our only true direction comes from God in the Person of Jesus Christ. Do you look to Christ for life's direction? Today thank the Lord that He is your celestial navigator.

> We know what God is like because we know the character of Jesus Christ.
>
> —George Hodges

Day 29
LIVING WITH THE WORD

Let the word of Christ dwell in you richly as you teach and admonish one another with all wisdom, and as you sing psalms, hymns and spiritual songs with gratitude in your hearts to God.
Colossians 3:16

As an infant Fanny Crosby was blinded through a physician's negligence. Yet she is one of the church's most prolific hymn writers. Her hymns are characterized by excellent theological content and wonderful rhyming meter. In her autobiography Crosby tells this story:

"Mrs. Hawley, a kind Christian lady, in whose house we resided, and who had no children of her own, became deeply interested in me, and under her supervision I acquired a thorough knowledge of the Bible. She gave me a number of chapters each week to learn. . .and so at the end of the first twelve months I could repeat a large portion of the first four books of the Old Testament and the four gospels.

"At Sunday school the children would stand in the aisles and repeat some of the passages that they had committed during the previous week. . . . I often hunted among the records of my memory for the longest and most involved verses with the idea of showing my elders what a little blind girl could do and they, in turn, flattered me with compliments and presented me with a fine Bible. . . . Had my growing pride been unchecked by my friends at home, it might have proven a stumbling block in after years. . . ."

Where did Fanny Crosby receive her theological training? In part through memorizing scripture. You may never write two thousand hymns, but by memorizing scripture you will be able to recall the truth of the gospel. Today ask the Lord to give you a heart to memorize His Word.

Though troubles assail and dangers affright, though friends should all fail and foes all unite; Yet one thing assures us, whatever betide, the scripture assures us the Lord will provide.

—Fanny Crosby

Day 30
TAKE A STAND FOR CHRIST

I am not ashamed of the gospel, because it is the power of God for the salvation of everyone who believes: first for the Jew, then for the Gentile.
Romans 1:16

Frederick the Great, King of Prussia between 1740 and 1786, was known as the "enlightened despot" yet was a confirmed atheist. He strengthened the Prussian economy by promoting industry and agriculture and conducted three wars during his reign. One of his most loyal and capable generals was Hans von Zieten. Slight in stature, feeble in voice, with a brilliant military mind, and valiant in battle, von Zieten held the respect of Frederick the Great.

Once Frederick invited von Zieten and others to dine with him. Von Zieten declined the invitation so that he could attend church. Later at another banquet the king and his guests mocked the general for his Christian beliefs. Von Zieten rose, placed conviction over safety, and with respect addressed Frederick, "My lord, there is a greater King than you, a King to whom I have sworn allegiance even unto death. I am a Christian man and I cannot sit quietly as the Lord's name is dishonored and His character belittled."

Everyone was silent. They expected Frederick's temper to erupt. Would von Zieten be imprisoned? Executed? But Frederick grasped the hand of his courageous general, asked for his forgiveness, and requested that he remain at the dinner. The king promised he would never again belittle Christianity.

Take a stand for Jesus Christ. There is no shame in this. Christ hung on the cross for you. Now you can stand on your convictions and tell others the good news of salvation. Today thank Christ for your salvation and for the courage to share the gospel.

Oh, that I might never through shame or fear disown him who has already acknowledged me!
—George Swinnock

Day 31
A COMFORTABLE LIFE

Give thanks in all circumstances,
for this is God's will for you in Christ Jesus.
1 Thessalonians 5:18

Matthew Henry was a biblical scholar who lived in England from 1662 to 1714. He is best known for the Bible commentary which bears his name. After being robbed one day Henry recorded this in his diary: "Let me be thankful. First, because I was never robbed before. Second, because although they took my wallet, they did not take my life. Third, because although they took my all, it was not much. Fourth, because it was I who was robbed, not I who robbed."

Later in life, Henry suffered a stroke. Once his friend Illidge helped the dying man get to a bed. Henry said to him, "You have been used to take notice of the sayings of dying men—this is mine: That a life spent in the service of God and communion with Him is the most comfortable and pleasant life that one can live in the present world."

If you can give thanks during the difficult times in your life you will tend to be thankful when things are not going well. Gratitude toward Christ and thanksgiving in difficult circumstances indicate Christian maturity. Thanksgiving during tough times brings growth in Christ. Today give thanks to the Lord not because of your circumstances but in spite of them.

When I find a great deal of gratitude in a poor man,
I take it for granted there would be as much generosity if he were rich.

—Alexander Pope

Day 32
IN THE PRESENCE
OF THE ENEMY

I plead with Euodia and I plead with Syntyche
to agree with each other in the Lord.
Philippians 4:2

Napoleon's fleet was gathering off the coast of Spain. Britain immediately dispatched her best admiral, Lord Horatio Nelson, to command their fleet in battle.

In a letter prior to arriving off of Trafalgar, Nelson wrote his friend Admiral Collingwood: "My dear Coll: I shall be with you in a very few days, and I hope you will remain as second-in-command. You will change the Dreadnought for the Royal Sovereign, which I hope you will like."

Collingwood was unhappy with this change and argued openly with the captain of his flagship. Nelson implored them, "In the presence of the enemy all men should be brothers. We are one and I hope always will be." Prior to the battle, Nelson addressed his fleet: "In our several stations we must all put our shoulders to the wheel, and make the great machine of the fleet, entrusted to our charge, go on smoothly." On October 21, 1805, the British fleet scored a resounding victory at Trafalgar. Not all of those in Nelson's fleet agreed with each other, but they followed his encouragement to fight together against a greater enemy.

Often disagreements occur within the church. But we must remember that there is a much larger battle going on for the souls of men and women. Are you in a disagreement with another Christian? Ask the Lord for wisdom so you can find common ground to spread the good news about Jesus Christ.

Yet far from letting the disagreement harm the outreach of the gospel, God providentially used it to

double the missionary force, with Barnabas taking
Mark and returning to Cyprus.

—Richard N. Longenecker

Day 33
WORDS OF THE LOST

*Several days later Felix came with his wife Drusilla, who was
a Jewess. He sent for Paul and listened to him as he spoke
about faith in Christ Jesus. As Paul discoursed on righteousness,
self-control and the judgment to come, Felix was afraid and
said, "That's enough for now! You may leave.
When I find it convenient, I will send for you."*
Acts 24:24–25

Consider the following statements:

You may offer like Cain (Genesis 4:3),

Leave Sodom like Lot's wife (Genesis 19:26),

Weep like Esau (Genesis 27:38),

Take part in worship like Korah (Numbers 16:19),

Desire to die the death of the righteous like Balaam
(Numbers 23:10),

Prophesy like Saul (1 Samuel 10:9–10),

Have a godly father as did Rehoboam (2 Chronicles
12:13–14),

Read God's word like Jehoiakim (Jeremiah 36:1, 23),

Seek the advice of believers like King Belshazzar (Daniel
5:13),

Be a seeking soul like the rich young ruler (Matthew 19:16),

Make long prayers like the Pharisees (Matthew 23:14),

Hate blasphemy like Caiaphas (Matthew 26:57, 65),

Be a disciple like Judas (Acts 1:25),

Make a gift to the church like Ananias and Sapphira (Acts
5:1–10),

Be afraid like Felix (Acts 24:25),
Be almost a Christian like Agrippa (Acts 26:28),
And still be lost!

Only by faith in Christ are we saved—by nothing else but faith in the finished work of Jesus Christ. Do you know someone who has not put their faith in the Lord? Today pray for that person and ask the Lord for the opportunity to share with them the truth of the gospel.

Because he is aware that he must speak in the name
of Christ, Paul does not submit to human authority;
but, as if from a higher level, he carries out the mission entrusted by God.

—John Calvin

Day 34
THE UNSHAKABLE KINGDOM

*Therefore, since we are receiving a kingdom that cannot
be shaken, let us be thankful, and so worship God
acceptably with reverence and awe.*
Hebrews 12:28

Dave Dravecky was a pitcher for the San Francisco Giants when it was discovered that he had a cancerous tumor in his pitching arm. He underwent surgery to remove the tumor and half of the surrounding muscle. His remarkable return to the major leagues ended when he broke his arm in the middle of a pitch. Dravecky described what went through his mind immediately after his arm snapped, "As odd as it sounds, I wasn't discouraged as I lay there, because with the excruciating pain came a strange sense of exhilaration, a sense that God wasn't finished with the story He was trying to tell with my life. It was weird. There I was gritting my teeth, biting back, and I was thinking, 'Okay, God, what's the next chapter gonna be?' Then suddenly I became overwhelmed at what God was doing in my life, and I realized what He was doing was much bigger than baseball."

Are you overwhelmed by physical pain or heartache? Is it a struggle to get through the day? Pain is inevitable in this world and it is sometimes easy to forget that God is good and that we can trust Him completely. Today give thanks that Christ's kingdom is unshakable. He does not always prevent pain or heartache from entering our lives. But He is faithful to bring us closer to Him and His unshakable kingdom.

> Thank God that faith does not depend on any joy that we manufacture. But with humility let's also thank God that here and there he lets us feel again some of the wonder of his grace, which descends to lift up a desolate people.
>
> —Cornelius Plantinga, Jr.

Day 35
FULL DEVOTION

If I had cherished sin in my heart,
the Lord would not have listened.
Psalm 66:18

In 1495 Leonardo da Vinci was commissioned to paint the mural "The Last Supper" in the dining hall of the monastery of Santa Maria delle Grazie in Milan, Italy. Leonardo studied the Bible as he painted the personalities of the different disciples into the fresco. He used friends and acquaintances to be his models for the disciples. The only thing lacking in the mural were the faces of Jesus and Judas. Leonardo found it impossible to conceive of the beauty and grace of God incarnate. He also found it difficult to paint the man who had benefited so much from Christ's love only to betray him. The prior of the monastery gently urged da Vinci to finish the work, but da Vinci was unable to visualize the two faces. The artist painted the face of one of his enemies on the body of Judas. He soon repented of this unkind act and searched in the thieves' quarter of the city until he found the face of a stranger who was to bear the image of Judas. It was only then that Leonardo da Vinci was able to visualize Christ and finish the fresco.

Jesus Christ wants us to cherish Him alone. He wants our full devotion. If you are clinging to any sin or have not forgiven someone, make things right today. Your vision of Christ will become clearer for it.

> God hears no more than the heart speaks; and if the heart be dumb, God will certainly be deaf.
>   —Thomas Brooks

Day 36
WORK IS NOT LIFE'S MEANING

What does a man get for all the toil and
anxious striving with which he labors under the sun?
All his days his work is pain and grief;
even at night his mind does not rest.
This too is meaningless.
Ecclesiastes 2:22–23

*R*obert G. Ingersoll was a famed agnostic in the nineteenth century. He told this story of a Vermont farmer: "When I was a boy I heard them tell of an old farmer in Vermont. He was dying. The minister at his bedside asked if he was a Christian, if he was prepared to die. The old man answered that he had made no preparation, that he was not a Christian, and that he had never done anything but work. The preacher said that he could give him no hope unless he had faith in Christ.

"The old man was not frightened. He was perfectly calm. In a weak and broken voice he said: 'Mr. Preacher, I have no fear of the future, no terror of any other world. There may be such a place as hell—but if there is you never can make me believe that it's any worse than old Vermont.' Sadly both the farmer and Mr. Ingersoll thought nothing was beyond the work of this world or there was anything worse than the life they had endured."

Americans tend to worship their work, work at their play, and play at their worship. Though we live under the sun our life can only be found in the Son of God, Jesus Christ. Are you striving too much at work? Today give thanks to Christ that life has meaning because of Him.

> They intoxicate themselves with work so they won't
> see how they really are.
>
> —Aldous Huxley

Day 37
BREAD ON THE WATER

Cast your bread upon the waters,
for after many days you will find it again.
Give portions to seven, yes to eight, for you do not know
what disaster may come upon the land.
Ecclesiastes 11:1–2

𝒞harles Spurgeon allowed newspapers to reprint his sermons worldwide and did not receive any compensation. In 1882, Charles' son Thomas Spurgeon assumed a pastorate in Auckland, New Zealand. While there he wrote his mother and enclosed a portion torn off an old Australian paper with the following particulars:

"This scrap of newspaper has been given me by a town missionary here, who regards it as a very precious relic. It came to him from a man who died in the hospital, and bequeathed it to his visitor as a great treasure. It is a portion of the Melbourne Argus, and of Father's sermon "Loving Advice for Anxious Seekers" (No. 735). The man found it on the floor of a hut in Australia, and was brought by its perusal to a knowledge of the truth as it is in Jesus. He kept it carefully while he lived (for it was discolored and torn when he found it), and on his deathbed he gave it to the missionary as the only treasure he had to leave behind him. [The missionary's] desire [is], that I should send it home, that the dear preacher might be encouraged."

To cast bread on the water looks like a waste of bread but the Lord has purposes beyond your comprehension. Are you giving freely of your time and talents? Thank Christ that He alone can multiply our gifts!

It is one of the most beautiful compensations of this life that no man can sincerely try to help another without helping himself.
— Ralph Waldo Emerson

Day 38
THE SAFETY OF SALVATION

Then these men went as a group and found Daniel praying and asking God for help.
Daniel 6:11

Cyrus Ingerson Scofield studied law in St. Louis, served in the Kansas Legislature, and was appointed United States District Attorney for Kansas. In 1874 Scofield began to drink heavily. Then a YMCA worker led Scofield to a personal

47

knowledge of the Lord Jesus.

Scofield often told this story: "Shortly after I was saved, I passed by the window of a store in St. Louis where I saw a painting of Daniel in the lion's den. That great man of faith, with his hands behind his back and those wild beasts circling him. . . . Only a few days had passed since I, a drunken lawyer, had been converted; and no one had yet told me anything about the keeping power of Jesus Christ. I thought to myself, there are lions all about me too, such as my old habits and sins. But the one who shut the lions' mouths for Daniel can also shut them for me! I knew that I could not win the battle in my own strength. The painting made me realize that while I was weak and helpless, my God was strong and able. He had saved me, and now he would also be able to deliver me from the wild beasts in my life. O what a rest of spirit that truth brought me!"

When life's battles find you, how do they find you? Today in prayer give the battles of your life over to the Lord Jesus Christ. In His hands you are safe.

> I have held many things in my hands, and I have lost them all; but whatever I have placed in God's hands, that I still possess.
>
> —Martin Luther

Day 39
HE WAS LIKE US

Therefore the Lord himself will give you a sign:
The virgin will be with child and will give birth to a son,
and will call him Immanuel.
Isaiah 7:14

Joseph Damien went as a missionary to the Hawaiian Islands in 1864. In 1873, he volunteered to minister at the leper colony on the island of Molokai. In Molokai there was no doctor, nurse, clergy or even grave digger. The island was a place of quarantine for people with leprosy. Damien built a small chapel on the island but few came to worship. After twelve long years of unfruitful ministry Joseph Damien decided to leave Molokai in 1885.

Standing on the pier waiting for his ship to take him home to his native Belgium, Damien looked down at his hands and noticed white spots—he had contracted leprosy.

The news of the missionary's disease spread quickly and hundreds of lepers gathered outside of Joseph Damien's hut. The people could identify with his pain and despair. The following Sunday the little chapel was filled to overflowing because the people knew that Joseph Damien could now identify with their condition. In the next four years, before his death at age forty-nine, Joseph Damien shared Christ's love in a way he never could before his leprosy.

Jesus Christ humbled Himself to be a man. Though He did not sin, He took on the sins of the world. He became part of the human race so we could accept Him. Thank Christ today that He humbled Himself for you so you could be with Him.

> A sign shall be given. A virgin shall conceive. A human baby bearing undiminished deity. The glory of the nations, a light for all to see, and hope for all who will embrace this warm reality.
>
> —Michael Card

THE EXPECTATION OF FAITH

*She had suffered a great deal under the care of many doctors and
had spent all she had, yet instead of getting better she grew worse.
When she heard about Jesus, she came up behind him in the
crowd and touched his cloak, because she thought, "If I just touch
his clothes, I will be healed." Immediately her bleeding stopped
and she felt in her body that she was freed from her suffering.*
Mark 5:26–29

*C*harles Spurgeon began his ministry at age seventeen in
1851. In two and a half years the membership of his first
church grew from forty to one hundred. At age nineteen he
assumed the pastorate of New Park Street Chapel, formerly
one of London's leading churches. His first sermon was to
eighty people in the church's twelve hundred-seat auditorium.
Within months the auditorium was too small and the church
had to rent a ten thousand-seat auditorium. By 1861 New
Park Street Chapel had built the Metropolitan Tabernacle. For
thirty- one years, attendance there averaged five thousand people in the morning and evening services.

One day a young preacher came to Spurgeon and said
"Sir, my sermons are well-prepared, by I am unable to get the
fire into my congregation as you do."

"You don't really expect that every sermon will be might-
ily used by God?" responded Spurgeon.

"Well, of course not." said the young man.

"That sir, is the problem."

What are your expectations of God? When you pray, do
you believe God will answer? The bleeding woman got what
she expected. It is not the size of your faith that makes the difference, it is the size of your God. Jesus Christ can be trusted
with the largest of problems. Today as you pray be confident
that Christ will answer.

True faith is never found alone; it is always accompanied by expectation. The person who believes the promises of God expects to see them fulfilled. Where there is no expectation there is no faith.

—A. W. Tozer

Day 41
THE FRUIT OF THE GOSPEL

All over the world this gospel is bearing fruit and growing, just as it has been doing among you since the day you heard it and understood God's grace in all its truth.
Colossians 1:6

In *Point Man* magazine Steve Farrar tells this story: "When George McCluskey married and started a family, he decided to invest one hour a day in prayer, because he wanted his kids to follow Christ. After a time, he expanded his prayers to include his grandchildren and great-grandchildren. Every day between 11 A.M. and noon, he prayed for the next three generations. As the years went by, his two daughters committed their lives to Christ and married men who went into full-time ministry. The two couples produced four girls and a boy. Each of the girls married a minister, and the boy became a pastor.

"George's first two great-grandchildren were boys. Upon graduation from high school, the two cousins chose the same college and became roommates. During their sophomore year, one boy decided to go into ministry. James, the other cousin didn't. He undoubtedly felt some pressure to continue the family legacy, but he chose to pursue his interest in psychology.

"James earned his doctorate and eventually wrote books for parents that became bestsellers. Today many people are blessed by the ministry of George McCluskey's great-grandson, Dr. James Dobson, founder of Focus on the Family."

Now is a great time to start praying for your family. Christ is faithful and will honor your prayers. The fruit produced can last generations.

> The whole story (of the soil) thus becomes a parable about a learner's responsibility and about the importance of learning with one's whole will and obedience, and not merely with one's head.
> —C. F. D. Moule

Day 42
POSSESSED BY POSSESSIONS

For the love of money is a root of all kinds of evil.
Some people, eager for money, have wandered from the faith
and pierced themselves with many griefs.
1 Timothy 6:10

Alexander the Great was king of Macedonia and conqueror of the Persian Empire. He is considered a military genius. Young Alexander learned rhetoric, literature, and science from Aristotle. When Alexander was twenty his father was assassinated. He quickly disposed of the conspirators and set out to complete his father's plans of conquering the Persians. The Persians had invaded Greece 150 years earlier and Alexander set out for revenge.

In the spring of 334 B.C. Alexander's army encountered the Persians led by King Darius III. His forces easily defeated the forty thousand mercenaries who fought for the Persians. The Mace-donians plundered their captives and continued to advance into Persia. The main force of the Persian army lay ahead. Some have estimated that the Persian regular army was between 250,000 and 500,000 men. Seeing that his soldiers were carrying too much plunder, and knowing that a fierce battle was just ahead, Alexander ordered all of the spoil to be placed in a heap. He then burned the heap to lighten the men's load and to refocus their efforts. Alexander then courageously led his cavalry to a smashing victory over the Persians near the Aegean coast.

Do you remember when you could move all your earthly possessions in the back of your car? Does it now take a couple of moving vans? Possessions are fine as long as they don't possess you. Ask Christ what is weighing you down. Take the necessary steps to lighten your load.

> Avarice is often created by prosperity and the consequent possession of money. It is also often powerfully present in the lives of those who are devoid of wealth.
> —G. Campbell Morgan

Day 43
MERCY SEASONS JUSTICE

And the Lord's servant must not quarrel; instead,
he must be kind to everyone, able to teach, not resentful.
2 Timothy 2:24

In Shakespeare's *The Merchant of Venice,* Antonio, the merchant, borrows the sum of three thousand ducats (twenty-five thousand dollars) from the moneylender Shylock. If Antonio cannot repay this debt he is required to repay Shylock with a pound of flesh. Antonio loses the money in a business venture and Shylock brings him to court in order to extract his pound of flesh.

Portia was Antonio's attorney. This intelligent, beautiful, and gentle woman tries to reason with Shylock to be merciful. Shylock responds, "On what compulsion must I? tell me that."

Portia replies, "The quality of mercy is not strained; It

droppeth as the gentle rain from heaven upon the place beneath: it is twice blest; It blesseth him that gives and him that takes: It is mightiest in the mightiest, it becomes the throned monarch better than his crown, his scepter shows the force of temporal power, The attribute to awe and majesty, Wherein does sit the dread and fear of kings; But mercy is above the scepter sway, It is enthroned in the heart of kings, it is an attribute to God himself; And earthly power does then show likest God's when mercy seasons justice."

In a world that shouts for fairness and justice, a Christian should speak with kindness and mercy. When mercy seasons justice Christ is glorified. Are you more concerned with seeking justice than granting mercy? Today in prayer ask the Lord Jesus how you can be less quarrelsome and more merciful.

Kind words are never wasted. Like scattered seeds,
they spring up in unexpected places.
—Charles Spurgeon

Day 44

FROM HEAVEN ABOVE CAME ALL

But you are a chosen people, a royal priesthood, a holy nation,
a people belonging to God, that you may declare the praises
of him who called you out of darkness into his wonderful light.
Once you were not a people, but now you are the people
of God; once you had not received mercy,
but now you have received mercy.
1 Peter 2:9–10

In 1732 Franz Joseph Haydn was born into a working-class Austrian family. When he was eight Haydn was recruited by the St. Stephen's Cathedral in Vienna to sing in their choir. While in Vienna he studied violin, voice, and musical composition. He became friends with Wolfgang Amadeus Mozart and George Frideric Handel. Upon hearing Handel's "Israel in Egypt" Haydn was inspired to write the oratorio "The Creation."

Haydn wrote, "I never was so devout as during that time I was working on 'The Creation'; every day I was on my knees and asked God to give me strength to enable me to pursue the work to its completion." Critics say that "The Creation" is a masterwork in the highest sense. Nothing could be added, nothing should be changed.

In Vienna, in 1808, there was a performance of "The Creation" with Haydn in attendance. The old composer, in a wheelchair, was brought into the hall. The was electrified with his presence. When the musicians burst forth with full power into the passage, "And there was light," a crescendo of applause broke out. The composer struggled to his feet. Mustering all his strength, Haydn raised his trembling arms upward crying, "No, no! Not from me, but from thence—from heaven above came all!"

Praise Jesus Christ, that He is the light of the world. All praise to Him for His mercy. Today in prayer praise the Lord for His love towards you.

> In Jesus is the light of the knowledge of God. When a
> man comes to know Jesus, he comes to know goodness.
> —William Barclay

Day 45
WHEN A SPIDER'S WEB IS A WALL

*If this is so, then the Lord knows how to
rescue godly men from trials and to hold the unrighteous
for the day of judgment, while continuing their punishment.
This is especially true of those who follow the corrupt desire
of the sinful nature and despise authority.
Bold and arrogant, these men are not
afraid to slander celestial beings.*
2 Peter 2:9–10

In A.D. 250 near Naples, Italy, a man named Felix of Nola became a believer in Jesus Christ. He made his living by farming his family's land and gave away all excess food to those who had need. That year the Roman Emperor Decius began persecuting Christians. Felix's land was confiscated and he was imprisoned. There he endured scourging and other punishments. One night he made his escape. But his captors set out to hunt him down.

Felix came upon a dilapidated building and hid himself in a hole in the wall. He had scarcely entered the hole when a spider began to spin a web over the opening. The pursuers saw the spider's lacy veil blocking the entrance and they didn't bother to look inside. They figured that no one could have entered the hole without disturbing that delicate curtain of silk. Later Felix hid in a dry well for six months until the persecutions of Christians ended with the death of Decius. He lived to an advanced age and his charity and faith were an inspiration to the early church. Felix of Nola later summed up his experience in the wall with these words, "Where God is, a spider's web is a wall; where he is not, a wall is but a spider's web."

If you want to hide from danger the safest place is found in Jesus Christ. Today thank Christ that He is your protector and defender.

Safety does not depend on our conception of the absence of danger. Safety is found in God's presence, in the center of his perfect will.

—T. J. Bach

Day 46
A MONUMENT TO NOTHING

Watch out that you do not lose what you have worked for,
but that you may be rewarded fully.
Anyone who runs ahead and does not
continue in the teaching of Christ does not have God;
whoever continues in the teaching
has both the Father and the Son.
2 John 8–9

In the center of Edinburgh, Scotland is Calton Hill, 350 feet above sea level. From it are seen many rows of Georgian rooftops, the turrets of the Palace of Holyrood House, and the narrow inlet of the sea known as the Firth of Forth.

In 1816, William Playfair designed the National Monument to sit on Calton Hill for a tribute to the soldiers who had fought in the Napoleonic Wars. The National Monument was to be made out of marble and designed to the exact dimensions as the Parthenon in Athens, Greece. In 1822 funds ran out for the project and through the years the marble started to crumble. Today the war memorial looks as if it went through a war itself. The "city's crown jewel" became the "city's disgrace." It was a project never meant for Edinburgh.

People try to build their own monuments; carve out their own destiny. But Christ wants us to draw near to Him. He desires us to continue in the teaching found in the Bible. Take a few moments and ask Christ, "Am I running ahead of You in my life?" If you are, return to God's Word.

The end of knowledge is to know God, and out of
that knowledge to love him and imitate him.
—John Milton

Day 47
YOU ARE ALL ONE IN CHRIST

There is neither Jew nor Greek, slave nor free,
male nor female, for you are all one in Christ Jesus.
Galatians 3:28

When Franz Josef, emperor of the Austro-Hungarian
empire, died in 1916 at the age of eighty-six a procession of
dignitaries escorted his coffin down the stairs of the Capuchin
Monastery in Vienna. At the bottom of the steps was a great
iron door leading to the Hapsburg family crypt. Behind the
door stood the Cardinal-Archbishop of Vienna.

Following the prescribed ceremony established centuries
before, the officer in charge stood at the door and cried, "Open!"

The Cardinal responded, "Who goes there?"

"We bear the remains of his Imperial and Apostolic
Majesty, Franz Josef I, by the grace of God, Emperor of Austria,
King of Hungary, Defender of the Faith, Prince of Bohemia-
Moravia, Grand Duke of Lombardy, Venezia, Styrigia. . ." and
continued to list the emperor's thirty-seven titles.

The Cardinal replied, "We know him not. Who goes
there?" The officer spoke again, this time using a shorter and
less ostentatious title reserved for times of expediency.

"We know him not. Who goes there?"

The officer tried a third time. "We bear the body of Franz
Josef, our brother, a sinner like us all!"

At that, the doors swung open, and the body of Franz
Josef was admitted to its resting place.

Through death Christ destroyed the barriers that separate
believers and unified us in one family. Do you allow age,

appearance, intelligence, political persuasion, economic status, race, or theological perspective to separate you from other Christians? Today ask Jesus for the insight to see beyond such barriers to the unity of the body of Christ.

> The unity of believers with each other and with God will testify to the world the fact that the Father has sent the Son.
>
> —Millard J. Erickson

Day 48
SIN AND CHRIST'S CROSS

May I never boast except in the cross of our Lord Jesus Christ,
through which the world has been crucified to me,
and I to the world.
Galatians 6:14

In John Bunyan's allegorical *The Pilgrim's Progress,* the main character, Christian, at long last arrives at the Cross: "Now I saw in my dream, that the highway up which Christian was to go, was fenced on either side with a wall, and that wall was called Salvation. Up this way, therefore, did burdened Christian run, but not without great difficulty, because of the load on his back.

"He ran thus till he came at a place somewhat ascending; and upon that place stood a cross, and a little below, in the bottom, a sepulcher. So I saw in my dream, that just as Christian came up to the cross, his burden loosed from off his shoulders, and fell from off his back, and began to tumble, and so continued to do till it came to the mouth of the sepulcher, where it fell in, and I saw it no more.

"Then was Christian glad and lightsome, and said with a merry heart, 'He hath given me rest by his sorrow, and life by his death.'"

At the cross of Christ we lose our burden of sin and receive forgiveness from God. Do you rejoice that you have been crucified with Christ? Today give thanks to Christ that you are saved by His death and are no longer a slave to sin.

He that has no cross deserves no crowns.
—Francis Quarles

Day 49
TRY THANKSGIVING

You are my God, and I will give you thanks;
you are my God, and I will exalt you.
Psalm 118:28

Henry W. Frost was a missionary to China. While at a missionary conference Frost discovered that: "Nothing so pleases God in connection with our prayer as praise. . .and nothing so blesses the man who prays as the praise which he offers. I got a great blessing once in China in this connection. I had received sad news from home and deep shadows had covered my soul. I prayed but the darkness did not vanish. I summoned myself to endure but the darkness only deepened. Then I went to an inland station and saw on the wall of the mission home these words: 'Try Thanksgiving.' I did, and in a moment every shadow was gone, not to return. Yes, the psalmist was right. 'It is a good thing to give thanks unto the Lord.' "

Frost was so overjoyed by this discovery that he wrote his own poem entitled "Praising." Here are the last few lines:

Oh, then, add your note, rejoicing, to the praise,
Thanks to God for all things voicing, through the days;
Till the earthly singing's done, till the heavenly is begun,
Till the anthem, round Christ's feet, swells complete!

Millions of people on this earth have gods made of stone or wood or paper. Offering thanks to such gods is useless. Today in prayer give thanks that your Savior is the true God and worthy of all praise.

We do thank God from the depths of our hearts for allowing us to be tried by himself. The result will be to his glory.

—Henry W. Frost

Day 50
THE GOOD MEASURE

Give, and it will be given to you.
A good measure, pressed down, shaken together
and running over, will be poured into your lap.
For with the measure you use,
it will be measured to you.
Luke 6:38

President Herbert Hoover attended Stanford University when it first opened its doors in 1891. Hoover and other students were in charge of bringing guest lecturers to the campus. He invited the famed Polish pianist Ignacy Paderewski to play at the university. Paderewski agreed to come at the cost of two thousand dollars.

When it came time for the concert Hoover and the other students had only sold $1,600 worth of tickets. The students offered to work off the four hundred dollar debt. Paderewski would hear nothing of it. He told them to settle expenses then take twenty percent for themselves. Any remaining money would help with Paderewski's own expenses.

Hoover did pay the debt however. In 1919 he was president of the United States. Paderewski was Premier of Poland.

Poland was in a national emergency with thousands suffering from malnutrition. Hoover authorized the American Food Mission to bring food, clothing, and medical supplies into the country. This saved Poland from disaster.

Years later Paderewski repaid Hoover by performing at the White House.

We receive by the same standard that we give. How is your measure? Does it need lengthening? Today give thanks that Christ will always outgive you no matter how much you give to others.

God judges what we give by what we keep.
—George Müller

Day 51
THE HOUND OF HEAVEN

For the Son of Man came to seek and to save what was lost.
Luke 19:10

Francis Thompson was a nineteenth century English poet. He intended to become a priest, then turned to medicine but failed to graduate. He was living in poverty and addicted to opium when he sent some poems to Wilfrid and Alice Meynell's magazine, *Merry England*. The couple took the impoverished poet into their home, helped him publish his poems, and cared for him until his death at age forty-eight.

Thompson's most celebrated poem, "The Hound of Heaven," portrays God as a bloodhound—used for centuries by the English to pursue people on the run. The poem begins:

I fled Him, down the nights and down the days;
I fled Him, down the arches of the years;

I fled Him, down the labyrinthine ways
Of my own mind; and in the mist of tears
I hid from Him, and under running laughter.
Up vistaed hopes, I sped;
and shot, precipitated,
Adown titanic glooms of chasméd fears,
From those strong feet that followed, followed after. . .

Do you remember how lost you were before Jesus found you? Today in prayer thank the Lord for pursuing and saving you.

To say I was searching for God was like saying that a mouse was searching for a cat.

—C. S. Lewis

Day 52
THE RESCUER

What a wretched man I am! Who will rescue me from this body
of death? Thanks be to God—through Jesus Christ our Lord!
So then, I myself in my mind am a slave to God's law,
but in the sinful nature a slave to the law of sin.
Romans 7:24–25

Jerry McAuley was born in 1839 in County Kerry, Ireland. At thirteen years old McAuley was sent to America to live with his sister in New York City. He was soon involved with a gang on Water Street. They robbed boats by night and sold the goods by day. "I rose through all the grades of vice and crime," he testified, "till I became a terror and nuisance in the Fourth Ward." At nineteen Jerry was arrested, convicted, and sentenced to fifteen years in Sing Sing Prison.

After five years in prison McAuley picked up a Bible. As

he read he was fixed upon the truth. He read the book through a second time and gave his life to Jesus Christ. This changed Jerry McAuley. He witnessed of his faith while in prison and was paroled seven years early.

McAuley returned to Water Street and opened the first street mission in the United States. Alcoholics, tramps, everyone who needed Christ's love were welcomed at the Water Street Mission. Jerry McAuley was forty-five years old when he went home to be with the Lord. Half of his life he was trapped in sin but the remainder of his life he was free in Christ.

Three sins a day is not bad by human standards. But if you live to be seventy this adds up to 76,650 sins. Thanks be to God that He rescues you from yourself. Today in prayer confess your sins to Christ—thank Him for forgiveness.

> I confess my own unrighteousness; I confess my weakness unto thee, O Lord.
>
> —Thomas à Kempis

Day 53
THE COMFORTER

Praise be to the God and Father of our Lord Jesus Christ,
the Father of compassion and the God of all comfort,
who comforts us in all our troubles, so that we can
comfort those in any trouble with the comfort
we ourselves have received from God.
2 Corinthians 1:3–4

In the early 1990's, JoAnn Buckler-Dollins experienced a season of crisis, trauma, and grief. Her husband suffered and died of an undiagnosed illness; she nearly died from a toxic infection; and her daughter narrowly escaped death in a serious automobile accident. JoAnn was in the pits of deep despair. But

God comforted JoAnn. She found healing in the Bible's promises, the Spirit's presence, and Christian counseling.

As God healed her, JoAnn shared her experiences of God's comfort with friends and associates who had also experienced loss. She eventually organized a ministry called GROWTH (Grief Recovery through Ongoing Work Toward Healing). She helps grieving adults to find hope and healing through weekly Christ-centered support groups and periodic educational workshops.

JoAnn began her ministry in her church but her circle of influence soon expanded throughout her community. She helps other churches establish their own grief recovery support groups, provides leadership training, organizes educational workshops, and instructs family counselors on the grief recovery process. She also speaks to groups and provides resources and networking in her community.

JoAnn says: "To serve the Lord through helping others is my greatest quest in life."

God comforts us not to make us comfortable but to make us comforters. Has God ever strengthened, encouraged, or given you hope to deal with your troubles? Today ask the Lord to show you how you can pass on His comfort to others.

Only a life lived for others is the life worthwhile.
—Albert Einstein

Day 54
UNCLE TOM TELLS THE GOSPEL

*But Stephen, full of the Holy Spirit, looked up to heaven and
saw the glory of God, and Jesus standing at the right hand
of God. "Look," he said, "I see heaven open and the Son
of Man standing at the right hand of God."*
Acts 7:55–56

In the novel *Uncle Tom's Cabin* Harriet Beecher
Stowe tells of Tom, sold from his good master in Kentucky to
live in Mississippi under the wrathful hand of Simon Legree.

One day two slaves escape. Legree dispatches two other
slaves, Quimbo and Sambo, to torture Tom for information.
"Tom heard the message with a forewarning heart. . . .But
he felt strong in God to meet death, rather than betray the
helpless. . . . looking up, [Tom] said, 'Into thy hands I com-
mend my spirit! Thou hast redeemed me, oh Lord God of
truth!' " As Tom is dragged off to Legree a higher voice says,
"Fear not them that kill the body, and, after that, have no
more that they can do."

Legree questions Tom of the fugitives' whereabouts. Tom
refuses to answer; but says "Mas'r, if you was sick, or in trouble, or dying, and I could save ye, I'd give ye my heart's blood;
and, if taking every drop of blood in this poor old body would
save your precious soul, I'd give 'em freely, as the Lord gave his
for me. . . . O, Mas'r! .. Do the worst you can, my trouble'll
be over soon; but if you don't repent, yours won't never end."

Legree is stunned but beats Tom to within a whisper of
life. Then Quimbo and Sambo ask the wounded man, "O,
Tom! do tell us who is Jesus, anyhow?" Tom leads the two men
to salvation.

Sometimes our greatest testimony comes in adversity.
Give thanks that Christ is standing victoriously at the right
hand of the Father.

Those who are full of the Holy Spirit are always looking steadfastly upwards. They look not at the things
which are seen, but at those which are not seen. To
them heaven stands always open.

—F. B. Meyer

Day 55
BOAST IN THE LORD

It is because of him that you are in Christ Jesus, who has
become for us wisdom from God—that is, our righteousness,
holiness and redemption. Therefore, as it is written:
"Let him who boasts boast in the Lord."
1 Corinthians 1:30–31

Thomas Beecher was one of the children of the famed
clergyman Lyman Beecher. His older sister was Harriet
Beecher Stowe, the author of *Uncle Tom's Cabin* and a leading
abolitionist. His older brother was Henry Ward Beecher, one
of the most dynamic pastors in nineteenth century America.

Thomas was chaplain of the New York Volunteers during
the Civil War and then settled in Elmira, New York, to be minister of the Independent Congregational Church. There
Beecher built a church gymnasium, library, theater, and danc-
ing room, all unheard of at the time. His methods were uncon-
ventional but his message was the lordship of Jesus Christ.

Once Thomas was guest preacher at Henry Ward's Plymouth Church in Brooklyn, New York. When Thomas stepped
to his brother's pulpit some disappointed people started
toward the exits. Calmly he raised his hand and said, "All those
who came here this morning to worship Henry Ward Beecher
may withdraw from the church; all who came to worship God
may remain."

67

Are you prone to boast of something other than Christ and His love for you? Today in prayer give thanks to the Lord that He is gracious. Only because of His grace do you have life in Christ.

We are not in the world bearing witness to Christ.
We are in Christ bearing witness to the world.
—G. Allen Fleece

Day 56

YOU CANNOT OUTGIVE GOD

If we have sown spiritual seed among you, is it too much if we reap a material harvest from you? If others have this right of support from you, shouldn't we have it all the more?
But we did not use this right. On the contrary, we put up with anything rather than hinder the gospel of Christ.
1 Corinthians 9:11–12

Henry P. Crowell was a brilliant student who knew the Lord. But at age seventeen he was diagnosed with tuberculosis. Accepted at Yale University, Crowell put off college on his doctor's orders. During this time he heard D. L. Moody preach. Moody challenged his hearers to follow him to Great Britain to win ten thousand souls to Christ. Henry's health prevented him from traveling but he wrote: ". . .by the grace of God I would be God's man! To be sure I would never preach like Moody. But I could make money and help support the labors of men like Moody." He prayed, "Oh God, if you will allow me to make money to be used in Your service I will keep my name out of it so You will have the glory."

Thus started a lifetime of tithing. Crowell first gave ten percent of his earnings. He experienced business setbacks but kept giving ten percent. But he realized that just as the tenth he gave belonged to God, so did the nine-tenths which he kept. In 1881 he bought a struggling company in Ravenna, Ohio, called Quaker Mill. Within ten years Quaker Oats was a household name in America.

Late in life Crowell said: "For over forty years I have given sixty to seventy percent of my income to God. But I've never gotten ahead of God! He has always been ahead of me!"

You cannot outgive God. Are you supporting your minister, pastor, church, and missionaries? Today give thanks to Christ that you can support the work of God.

> God has given us two hands—one to receive and the other to give to others. We are not cisterns made for hoarding; we are channels made for sharing. If we fail to fulfill this divine duty and privilege we have missed the meaning of Christianity.
>
> —Billy Graham

Day 57
THE STRENGTH OF DEPENDENCE

Give us today our daily bread.
Matthew 6:11

Pandita Ramabai was a Hindu widow who became a Christian at the turn of the twentieth century. She established a missionary school for High Caste widows in India and was also a Bible translator. Pandita describes her mission's daily dependence on the Lord; "Two of our large wells were quite dried up, and very little water was left in our other two wells. Many of our friends were praying that God would give us water—and so He did. More than nineteen hundred people, besides over one hundred cattle and buildings that are fast going up, required a great deal of water. Each of the two wells had all its contents used up every day; every evening one could see the bottom of the wells, and would wonder where the water would come from for tomorrow! But there came a fresh supply in the morning in each well, and it lasted all day."

Christ wants us to be dependent on Him, not to keep us weak, but to make us strong in Him. Charles Swindoll calls this "living on the ragged edge." It is a trust that God will provide if I come to Him in prayer. If you find yourself trusting in the things God has provided you instead of the Provider Himself, it may be time to loosen your grasp on those things. In prayer come to Christ with open hands dependent on Him to provide your needs.

> It is a tragedy when a man has no invisible means of support.
>
> —T. J. Bach

Day 58
CALVARY'S LOVE

For we are God's workmanship, created in Christ Jesus to do good works, which God prepared in advance for us to do.
Ephesians 2:10

Amy Carmichael left her native Ireland for Dohnavur, India where she lived fifty-six years ministering to women and children. She spent much of her energy rescuing children whose parents sold them as Hindu temple prostitutes. She cared for the sick and through her prayers a hospital was built in Dohnavur. She built foster homes for orphan children and at the time of her death in 1951 there were some nine hundred children living in mission homes throughout the city.

In 1931 Amy suffered an accident which left her as an invalid. Undaunted, she ministered through prayer, wrote thirteen books, kept in correspondence with friends and fellow workers, and wrote songs and poems.

Carmichael was a tireless servant of Jesus Christ. Here she explains her approach to service: "If in dealing with one who does not respond, I weary of the strain, and slip from under the burden, then I know nothing of Calvary Love. If I have not the patience of my Savior with souls who grow slowly; if I know little of travail till Christ be fully formed in them, then I know nothing of Calvary Love. If I avoid being 'ploughed under' with all that such plowing entails of rough handling, isolation, uncongenial situations, strange tests, then I know nothing of Calvary Love."

We know Calvary's love when we follow Christ. That means putting aside our own dreams, desires, and comforts. Today in prayer ask Christ to teach you Calvary's love.

> Lord, do Thou turn me all into love, and all my love into obedience, and let my obedience be without interruption.
>
> —Jeremy Taylor

Day 59
LOVE IS THE BEST WAY

In fact, everyone who wants to live a godly life in Christ Jesus will be persecuted.
2 Timothy 3:12

Richard Wurmbrand was an atheist Romanian Jew with tuberculosis. When he was convalescing in a sanitarium a kindly carpenter gave him a Bible. Wurmbrand became a Christian. When the English mission church in Bucharest was abandoned because of the invasion of the Nazis, Wurmbrand stepped in as the pastor. He continued as pastor after the war

71

when the Communists controlled Romania. On Sunday, February 29, 1948, Richard Wurmbrand was seized by the secret police. He spent fourteen years in prison; three years in solitary confinement thirty feet underground.

During his imprisonment Wurmbrand was tortured extensively. Yet he continued to share his faith in Christ and led some of his guards to Christ. Wurmbrand testified, "Alone in my cell, cold, hungry, and in rags, I danced for joy every night." During his imprisonment, he asked a fellow prisoner, "Have you any resentment against me that I brought you to Christ?" The man responded, "I have no words to express my thankfulness that you brought me to the wonderful Savior. I would never have it another way."

Wurmbrand was released from prison in 1956. When asked, "What have you learned from your suffering?" He answered, "First, that there is a God; second, Christ is our Savior; third, there is eternal life; and fourth, love is the best way."

Today in prayer remember the Lord is a faithful God, Christ is our Savior, there is eternal life, and that love is the best way. Our hearts dance with joy by faith in Jesus Christ.

> For five years we never went outside our doors without a volley of curses from our neighbors.
>
> —C. T. Studd

Day 60

BELIEVE AND YOU WILL BE SAVED

"Sirs, what must I do to be saved?" They replied, "Believe in the Lord Jesus, and you will be saved—you and your household."
Acts 16:30–31

Cornelius Smith was a gypsy tinker who lived with his family in a tent in Essex, northeast of London. At night he played the violin in pubs while his children danced and collected money. Cornelius was often in and out of jail for a list of minor offenses. One day a prison chaplain told him the good news about Jesus Christ and Smith trusted the Lord.

The youngest of his children was Rodney who dedicated his life to Christ at age fifteen. Rodney "Gipsy" Smith went on to be one of the most popular evangelists in Great Britain and the United States. For almost seventy years thousands came to know the Lord through his preaching.

One of Rodney's favorite texts was from Acts 16 and he reminded his listeners that if they truly received Christ, their conduct would be transformed. He referred to this change of behavior as "stripe washing" because of what the Philippian jailer did for Paul and Silas after he was converted. But salvation itself is found in trusting in Jesus Christ. Gipsy not only knew that personally and preached it, but saw it lived out in his own father's decision for Christ.

The gift of salvation is free. It was paid for at the highest cost imaginable—the death of the Son of God. Now all we have to do is believe in Him. If someone asked you today, "What must I do to be saved?" how would you reply? Today in prayer give thanks that salvation is yours by trusting in Christ.

Give him absolute control; never take a step without his guidance—this is the secret of grace and joy.
—John Wilbur Chapman

Day 61
INNOCENT AS CHARGED

If. . .I am guilty of doing anything deserving death,
I do not refuse to die.
But if the charges brought against me by these Jews are not true,
no one has the right to hand me over to them.
I appeal to Caesar!
Acts 25:11

In 1780 General Benedict Arnold turned against the American Revolution and attempted to give the British the plans to the fortress at West Point, New York. To do this he contacted John Andre for help. Andre was the Adjutant General of the British Army in North America—the top aide of the leading British General. In an intriguing twist of history, the traitor Arnold made it safely to the British lines and Andre was caught. The Americans were enraged that Arnold had betrayed the Revolution. Their response was to hang Andre as a spy. No one fully believed him to be a spy: He was wearing British uniform when arrested and had only paved the way for Arnold's escape.

At Andre's tribunal the eyewitness Benjamin Tallmadge wrote: "I never saw a man's whose fate I foresaw who I sincerely pitied. He is a young man of great accomplishment. . .He will undoubtedly suffer death. . .and though he knows his fate, seems to be as cheerful as if he was going to an assembly." John Andre had become a Christian days before his death and wrote the poem, "My Hiding Place" as a testimony of his peace in the Lord.

When we have made peace with Christ, we can have a clean conscience and stand before any court. Do you find yourself not fearing God yet fearing human judgment? Today in prayer give thanks that you can come to Christ to receive the forgiveness and strength that will stand up in any court.

Ere long a heavenly voice I heard, And mercy's angel soon appeared; He led me at a placid pace, To Jesus, as a hiding place.

—John Andre

Day 62

WISDOM, KNOWLEDGE, AND HAPPINESS

A man can do nothing better than to eat and drink and find satisfaction in his work. This too, I see, is from the hand of God, for without him, who can eat or find enjoyment?
To the man who pleases him, God gives wisdom, knowledge and happiness, but to the sinner he gives the task of gathering and storing up wealth to hand it over to the one who pleases God. This too is meaningless, a chasing after the wind.
Ecclesiastes 2:24–26

Adam Clark spent forty years writing his commentary on the Scriptures. Noah Webster labored thirty-six years and crossed the Atlantic Ocean twice to gather material needed to make his dictionary absolutely accurate. Sir Walter Scott put in fifteen-hour days and so wrote a book every two months. John Milton rose at four o'clock every morning in order to have sufficient hours to compose and rewrite the poetry which stands among the best in the world. Catherine Booth helped found the Salvation Army, was an influential preacher, and raised eight godly children. John Wesley traveled over 250,000 miles on horseback and preached an average of three sermons a day for fifty-four years. Fanny Crosby was blind yet was a prolific hymn writer and published over two thousand hymns.

Robert Louis Stevenson seems to have been speaking of such people when he wrote: "The things nearest are best— breath in your nostrils, light in your eyes, flowers at your feet, duties at your hand, the path of right just before you. Then do not grasp at the stars, but do life's plain, common work as it comes, certain that daily duties and daily bread are the sweetest things of life."

When we are satisfied with the work the Lord has placed immediately before us, we receive in addition to satisfaction, wisdom, knowledge, and happiness. Today in prayer, give thanks to Christ for the work He has given you to do.

> There is only one way to improve one's work—love it.
>
> —Phillips Brooks

Day 63
REMEMBER THE CREATOR

However many years a man may live,
let him enjoy them all.
But let him remember the days of darkness,
for they will be many.
Ecclesiastes 11:8

In 1783 Charles Simeon came to Cambridge, England, as the Vicar of Holy Trinity Church. At twenty-three years old he consistently preached an uncompromising message of the gospel of grace in Christ. His message was so dynamic that eventually his congregation did not attend his meetings. They locked their pews so no one else could attend either. Church officers locked Simeon out of the church on Sunday mornings. During these difficult days university students threw bricks through the church's windows; Simeon preached on the streets and people ignored him.

But Simeon persevered and ministered for forty years. His unswerving message was "Jesus Christ, crucified for sinners." One of the most famous of his followers was Henry Martyn who became a missionary to India. Some believe that Simeon was the most evangelical clergyman in the Church of England at that time.

While Simeon lay on his deathbed he smiled and asked those in his room, "What do you think especially gives me comfort as I face death?" All were silent. "It is the creation! I ask myself, 'Did the Lord create the world or did I?' He did! Now if He made the world and all the rolling spheres of the universe, He certainly can take care of me. Into Jesus' hands I can safely commit my spirit!"

If you remember the Creator your perspective on life is changed. Do you have a tough time enjoying life? Today in prayer give thanks that the Creator of the universe holds your life in His hand.

May you live all the days of your life.
—Jonathan Swift

Day 64
HELP WANTED

When he came near the den, he called to Daniel in an anguished voice, "Daniel, servant of the living God, has your God, whom you serve continually, been able to rescue you from the lions?"
Daniel 6:20

In 1907 Sir Ernest Shackleton led an expedition to Antarctica and came within ninety-seven miles of the South Pole. In 1914, when Shackleton tried again, he placed an advertisement in a London newspaper. It read: "Men wanted for hazardous journey. Small wages, bitter cold, long months of complete darkness, constant danger. Safe return doubtful." There was such an overwhelming response to the advertisement that Shackleton exclaimed, "It seemed as though all the men in Great Britain were determined to accompany us."

What if God were to take out an advertisement in the newspaper? Here is how it may read:

Help Wanted—Men and women to follow and serve the Lord Jesus Christ. Openings worldwide. Below is a sample of some of the positions open, please take note of the reference when applying:

Pastors and Teachers—To prepare God's people for works of service (Ephesians 4:12).

Administrators—Able to plan and organize (1 Corinthians 12:28).

Elders—Encourages others by sound doctrine (Titus 1:9).

Waiting On Tables—Responsible for the distribution of food (Acts 6:1–3).

Rewards are eternal. Must be available to serve immediately.

Daniel was known for his service to the Lord. Are you serving Christ today? Ask the Lord that your service may be for His glory.

If you wish to be a leader you will be frustrated, for very few people wish to be led. If you aim to be a servant you will never be frustrated.

—Frank F. Warren

Day 65

THE GRANDEUR OF HEROD; THE GLORY OF GOD

But you, Bethlehem Ephrathah,
though you are small among the clans of Judah,
out of you will come for me one who will be ruler over Israel,
whose origins are from of old, from ancient times.
Micah 5:2

In the Judean hills nine miles south of Jerusalem lies a large hill that has been truncated by thousands of workmen. This was once the Herodium, both a fortress and palace built by King Herod. Designed to overlook the entire area, this lavish statement of Herod's power rose 2,460 feet above sea level. Its only means of access was a series of two hundred steep steps. The Herodium was considered as impenetrable as Masada.

This fortress was also a luxurious palace with a large reception hall, Roman baths and pools, frescoed walls, and massive columns. It had a villa which was accessible only by boat in the middle of a man-made pond. Its beautiful landscaping and buildings covered forty-five acres and was roughly the same size as India's Taj Mahal.

In the shadow of the Herodium, three and a half miles distant, lay a small village, the home of shepherds. This was Bethlehem where God chose to be born into humanity. There was no grandeur there. Glory was born in a lowly place. Thank Christ today that He cares for the humble people in the lowly places.

It was Bethlehem, David's city, that the Jews expected David's greater Son to be born; it was there that they expected God's Anointed One to come into the world. And it was so.

—William Barclay

Day 66
IMPOSSIBILITY BECOMES POSSIBILITY

Jesus looked at them and said, "With man this is impossible,
but not with God; all things are possible with God."
Mark 10:27

At age thirty Debbie Francis was diagnosed with Hodgkin's disease. At that time she was pregnant with her second child. The doctors advised her to terminate the pregnancy and to begin chemotherapy immediately. She refused, knowing that even though she was putting her own life at risk it was worth it for her child. In December, 1995, Debbie gave birth to her child. A month later she began chemotherapy.

In May, 1996, Debbie completed her last treatment for Hodgkin's disease. Her immune system was weakened and Debbie contracted pneumonia. For weeks she clung to life as her family and friends prayed. Debbie's weight and pulse dropped. The doctors isolated her and allowed only the closest of family members to visit. Physicians said that less than five percent of patients with similar conditions had survived.

Though heavily sedated and unable to speak Debbie could move her fingers. A friend recognized these movements as International Sign Language and gave her husband and parents a chart so they could interpret Debbie's signing. This communication brought hope to Debbie. Through the weeks, the Lord restored Debbie's health and today she is home with her family.

Jesus Christ displays His power in our weakness. If you find yourself in an impossible situation—Jesus Christ is still the King. Ask Christ to make the impossible possible so that He may be glorified.

> Only an all-powerful God can do the impossible with the impossible.

—Eleanor L. Doan

Day 67
FREEDOM AND TRUST

In the same way, their wives are to be women worthy
of respect, not malicious talkers but temperate
and trustworthy in everything.
1 Timothy 3:11

To attend the University of Virginia a student must agree to abide by its honor system. The honor system was created on July 4, 1842, by a professor seeking to dispel any tension between the faculty and students. Students are required to write this pledge: "On my honor as a student, I have neither given nor received aid on this examination (or assignment)." The honor system is student-run. Violations go through an investigative process. If there is enough evidence a student comes to trial before an honor committee and if found guilty could be dismissed from the university. To outside critics this may sound oppressive but those who have attended the University of Virginia have found freedom in trust. This honor system extends beyond the university to the city of Charlottesville and to Albemarle County, Virginia—wherever a student represents the University of Virginia.

Christians represent Jesus Christ. Though we are freed from our sins by God, any untrustworthy act on our part damages the reputation of Christ. Today resolve that, with Christ's help, you will be trustworthy.

God, give us men! A time like this demands strong minds, great hearts, true faith, and ready hands; Men whom the lust of office does not kill; Men whom the spoils of office can not buy; Men who possess opinions and a will; Men who have honor; Men who will not lie.

—Josiah Gilbert Holland

Day 68
WE ARE ALL EQUAL HERE

I charge you, in the sight of God and Christ Jesus and the
elect angels, to keep these instructions without partiality,
and to do nothing out of favoritism.
1 Timothy 5:21

Arthur Wesley was a shy, withdrawn boy whose Irish mother described him as "food for powder and nothing more." He was considered the dullard of the family. So Arthur was sent to a military school in France. He was commissioned an officer in the British army at age eighteen and rose through the ranks. In the Peninsular War, Wesley gained notoriety by helping the Portuguese drive the French back into Spain.

In 1815 Arthur Wesley, now known as the Duke of Wellington, distinguished himself by defeating Napoleon on the battlefield at Waterloo. Celebrated as Europe's liberator, the duke said, "The hand of Almighty God has been upon me this day. I hope to God that I have fought my last battle." Wellington served as Prime Minister of Great Britain from 1828–1832.

In his later years, as the duke received communion at his parish church, a poor old man knelt beside him. An usher motioned to the man to move away from the duke. Wellington reached out and clasped the man's hand and whispered, "Do not move, we are all equal here."

Black, white, rich, poor, old, young—we are all equal in the eyes of Christ. Do not let any worldly prejudices seep into your life. Favoritism is ugly. In prayer ask Christ to point out areas of your life where you show favoritism. Ask Him to take this away and make all people equal in your heart.

> The parable of the good Samaritan demonstrated
> that there are no limits to neighbor love.
> —James W. Thompson

Day 69
A PASSION REPLACED

People will be lovers of themselves, lovers of money, boastful,
proud, abusive, disobedient to their parents, ungrateful,
unholy, without love, unforgiving, slanderous, without self-control,
brutal, not lovers of the good, treacherous, rash, conceited,
lovers of pleasure rather than lovers of God—having a form of
godliness but denying its power. Have nothing to do with them.
2 Timothy 3:2–5

In 1612 Shah Jahan, prince of India, married Mumtaz Mahal. Theirs was a deep romantic love. They were inseparable. She was his confidant, his counselor, and inspired him to acts of charity and benevolence. She bore fourteen children and died while giving birth. Overcome by grief, Shah Jahan sought to memorialize his wife and set out to build the most beautiful temple possible. This memorial is the Taj Mahal.

It took twenty-two years to build the Taj Mahal. Marble is used throughout. Jade, sapphires, pearl, and other precious stones decorate the walls of the mausoleum. In the center of the Taj lies Mahal's sepulcher.

As the building of the temple progressed Shah Jahan's grief began to disappear. The process of building was his new passion. One day while walking through the construction site he bumped against an old wooden box. Shah Jahan brushed the dust off his leg and ordered a worker to throw the box out. Jahan didn't know he had ordered the disposal of his beloved wife's coffin, forgotten amidst the construction of her memorial.

Godliness without Jesus Christ is no godliness at all. As we grow in Christ we must remain in Him. Take time to ask the Lord Jesus, "Are You still the passion of my life?"

> Godliness is the knowledge of God in the mind; the grace of God in the soul; the love of God in the heart; the obedience to God in the life.
> —James D. Burns

Day 70
IGNORANCE AND THE GRAND DESIGN

During the night the mystery was revealed to Daniel in a
vision. Then Daniel praised the God of heaven and said:
"Praise be to the name of God for ever and ever;
wisdom and power are his."
Daniel 2:19–20

The last major work of Michelangelo Buonarotti was the architectural design of the Vatican's St. Peter's Basilica. Michelangelo was born into Florentine aristocracy and was temperamentally resistant when faced with any type of human coercion. He is quoted as saying, "I cannot live under pressures from patrons, let alone paint."

When Michelangelo worked on St. Peter's he was criticized by some of the workers. They didn't like what was being built and told him so. The great artist responded, "Even if I were able to make my plans and ideas clear to you—which I am not—I am not obliged to do so. I must ask you to do your best to help me and when the work is complete the conception will be better understood." Those who found fault with Michelangelo's work did so out of ignorance. They could not understand the mind of the artist and so could not see his grand design.

When we go through difficult times we may wonder, "What is the Lord doing?" Take heart, the Master Architect knows perfectly well what He is doing. He is creating something more beautiful than you can ever imagine. What is mysterious to you is in plain view to Jesus Christ. What part of Christ's plan is a mystery to you? Today take that concern to Him, yet resolve to cooperate in God's work upon you.

Men may acquire knowledge, but wisdom is a gift direct from God.

—Bob Jones, Sr.

Day 71
THE SHIPWRECKED CONQUERORS

*It would have been better for them not to have known the way
of righteousness, than to have known it and then to turn their
backs on the sacred command that was passed on to them.
Of them the proverbs are true: "A dog returns to its vomit," and,
"A sow that is washed goes back to her wallowing in the mud."*
2 Peter 2:21–22

In the summer of 55 B.C., Julius Caesar, one of the greatest military conquerors in history, set caution aside and set out to conquer Britain. But the British were waiting for him. As Caesar's transports sailed along the coast of Britain, British soldiers on foot and horseback paralleled the fleet. The army was denied an easy landing. So Caesar ordered his ships to dash toward the shore and beach themselves. For the first ashore there was no turning back. They were unable to return to the continent because their ships were wrecked. There was nothing left for them to do but to advance and fight. At first the Roman legions were confused and terrified but a beachhead was established. The Romans then sent their main landing force to reinforce the troops ashore and Caesar scored another victory.

Sometimes when Christians encounter spiritual warfare they want to retreat to their former life. But this cannot be an option. Are you tempted to give up Christ and leave the faith? In prayer ask Christ to take over your battles. Resolve that victory is yours in Christ. Stand firm and do not turn back.

A man should never forget the responsibility which knowledge brings.

—William Barclay

Day 72
SAFETY IN THE SIMPLE TRUTH

It gave me great joy to have some brothers come and
tell about your faithfulness to the truth and
how you continue to walk in the truth.
3 John 3

Hugh Latimer was educated at Cambridge University and licensed by the university to preach anywhere in Great Britain. In 1535 he became bishop of Worcester and was one of Henry VIII's senior advisors.

Once Latimer gave a sermon in the court of Henry VIII. The king was displeased at the message. He ordered Latimer to preach again the following Sunday and to apologize for the words he had previously preached. Henry had already disposed of several wives so to have a preacher killed would be nothing to him.

The next Sunday Latimer began his sermon: "Hugh Latimer, do you know before whom you are speaking this day? To the mighty monarch, King Henry VIII, who can take away your life. Consider well whose Word you are sent to deliver—that of the great and mighty God who is everywhere present! He holds all the ways and is able to cast your soul into Hell! Therefore, take care that you deliver your message faithfully." He then repeated with more vigor the same sermon that he had preached one week earlier. Everyone expected Henry to condemn Latimer to death. The king rose and said, "I bless God that I have such an honest servant!"

Christ said, "I am the way and the truth and the life." Follow Christ, tell the truth and trust the Lord with the outcome. As Hugh Latimer found out: If you tell the truth and remain humble both God and man are pleased.

> In any emergency in life there is nothing so strong
> and safe as the simple truth.
>
> —Charles Dickens

Day 73
THE MARRIAGE OF JOHN WESLEY

Each one should remain in the situation
which he was in when God called him.
1 Corinthians 7:20

John Wesley was the most prominent evangelist of the eighteenth century. He made his mark both in Great Britain and the United States and was the driving force in the establishment of the Methodist church.

Wesley was forty-eight when he married Mary Vazeille. He had never been married before and Mary was the widow of a prominent London merchant. She had known John and his brother Charles for about two years. Charles was "thunderstruck" when he heard of his brother's intentions to marry her. Mary was known as a vulgar woman prone to hysteria.

Soon the problems others saw became apparent in the marriage. John traveled a great deal and Mary neither enjoyed traveling nor staying alone. John was set in his ways and showed little interest in domestic concerns. Mary did not possess a drive to serve the Lord. When John wrote consoling letters to widows Mary's jealousy flared. She wrote scandalous letters to newspapers lying about John's character. She had episodes of violence and finally left John after twenty years of marriage. Mary died alone and John wasn't informed of her death until three days after the funeral.

Everyone desires a happy marriage. But the Lord first calls us to do his will. Do you want to be married or wish to be single? Today in prayer thank the Lord for your marital status. This is God's will for you today so that you can live this day for His glory.

Don't marry someone you can live with, marry someone you cannot live without.

—Josh McDowell

THE RIGHTEOUSNESS OF GOD BY FAITH

I will give thanks to the LORD because of his righteousness
and will sing praise to the name of the LORD Most High.
Psalm 7:17

Martin Luther hated the idea of "the righteousness of God." In his mind the term meant "God is righteous and he punishes the unrighteous sinner." But Luther studied the Word of God and the Spirit of God worked. Luther writes: "I began to understand that the righteousness of God is that through which the righteous live by a gift of God, namely through faith. Here I felt as if I were entirely born again and had entered paradise itself through gates that had been flung open. . .and I extolled the sweetest word with a love as great as the loathing with which I had hated the term, 'the righteousness of God.' "

In 1522 Luther completed his German translation of the New Testament. Then he turned his efforts to music for worship. He said, "I wish to compose sacred hymns so that the Word of God may dwell among the people also by means of song." Among other hymns Luther wrote "A Mighty Fortress Is Our God." In 1526 he produced an order of worship which included hymns and congregational responses—an innovation at the time. This worship was Luther's thankful expression that the righteousness of God had brought him life through faith in Christ.

The righteousness of God is a gift we receive by faith in Christ. What a marvelous gift! The Lord has freely given you this gift of righteousness! Today give thanks and praise to Christ for His righteousness!

Gratitude is not the memory, but the homage of the heart rendered to God for his goodness.

—N. P. Willis

Day 75
RECEIVE GOD'S WORD

At midnight I rise to give you thanks for your righteous laws.
Psalm 119:62

*J*ohn Calvin of Geneva, Switzerland, was one of the most important theologians in history. His multivolume work *Institutes of the Christian Religion* is the main doctrine for polity in reformed churches.

Calvin strongly believed in the authority of Scripture. He said, "Let us not take it into our heads either to seek out God anywhere else than in the sacred Word, or to think anything about him that is not prompted by his Word, or to speak anything that is not taken from that Word."

He said: "By [the Word of God] they confidently dare all things, compel all the strength, glory, and sublimity of the world to submit to its majesty and to obey it, rule over all things from the highest to the lowest, build up the house of Christ, overturn the kingdom of Satan, feed the sheep, destroy the wolves, exhort and instruct the teachable, rebuke, reprove, and refute the rebellious and stubborn, loose, bind, and finally, hurl thunderbolts—but doing all things in the Word of God."

Before reading the Bible, John Calvin often prayed: "O Lord, heavenly Father, in whom is the fullness of light and wisdom, enlighten our minds by your Holy Spirit, and give us grace to receive your Word with reverence and humility, without which no one can understand your truth. For Christ's sake, Amen."

Where would we be if God had not given us His Word? And without it how would we know God's Son? Today give thanks to God for the Bible.

> The greatest of his mercies is his Word, which excites faith, and teaches us to recognize God in his ways and works.

> —Carl Moll

Day 76
A FRESH START

Therefore, I tell you, her many sins have been forgiven—for she loved much. But he who has been forgiven little loves little.
Luke 7:47

Harry Monroe was in a Detroit courtroom. The charge was counterfeiting. He was guilty. But he was also remorseful and told the judge that, if given a chance, he would turn his life around. The judge told the young man, "I trust God and I trust you to carry on."

Harry left Detroit. In Chicago he went into a bar, ordered a drink, and was lifting the glass to his lips when he realized, "If I drink this I'm right back where I was."

Out on the busy sidewalk he heard music. It was coming from the Pacific Garden Mission. Harry went in, sat down, and for the first time heard the gospel. But when asked to believe he responded, "You stick to your business and I'll stick to mine."

But the preacher was patient and led Harry to the Savior. Harry couldn't sleep that night. He had a new life in Christ! The following Sunday he shared his testimony at the mission. For the next thirty-five years Harry Monroe ministered with a grateful heart at the mission and in 1892 became its superintendent.

Do you appreciate the forgiveness you have received from Christ? Today in prayer tell God how much you love Him and how much you are thankful for the fresh start He has given you.

> But still it is proper that our love should be increased by a consideration of his goodness; and they who feel —as Christians do—that they are the chief of sinners, will feel under infinite obligation to love God and their Redeemer, and that no expression of attachment to him can be beyond what is due.
>
> —Albert Barnes

Day 77
PEACE IN PENN'S WOODLANDS

This is the victory that has overcome the world, even our faith.
1 John 5:4

William Penn was the son of a famous British Admiral in the seventeenth century. He became a Christian in the Quaker church at age twenty-two. Following his father's death Penn was bequeathed a large area of land in North America which became known as Pennsylvania—Penn's woodlands. Penn was determined to govern Pennsylvania according to God's commandments.

The Indians of Pennsylvania hated the white man's settlements. Yet Penn sought a peace that would last. At the great elm at Shakamaxon Penn met with the local tribes. There they made the only treaty between Europeans and Native Americans that did not end in bloodshed. Penn's love in Christ for humanity was so compelling that both sides kept the peace.

In his sermon "A Call to Christendom" Penn said, "For in Christ Jesus, the light of the world, are hid all the treasures of wisdom and knowledge; redemption and glory. They are hid from the worldly Christian, from all who are captivated by the lusts of the world. For whoever sees them must come to Christ Jesus, the true light of their consciences, bring their deeds to him, love him and obey him."

Today in prayer ask the Lord to strengthen your faith so that the world may know the victory of love.

It is a great deal easier to do that which God gives us to do, no matter how hard it is, than to face the responsibilities of not doing it.

—Dr. J. R. Miller

Day 78
NICHOLAS HERMAN'S WAY OF WORSHIP

Worship the LORD in the splendor of his holiness;
tremble before him, all the earth.
Psalm 96:9

Nicholas Herman spent eighteen years in the French Army before he decided to give his life to the Lord. He became a cook in a monastery, took the name Brother Lawrence, and remained there for thirty years. He is remembered for a series of letters collected after his death and published under the title *The Practice of the Presence of God.* Below he shares how he worshipped the Lord in his everyday life:

". . .after having given myself wholly to God. . .I renounced, for the love of Him, everything that was not He; and I began to live as if there was none but He and I in the world. . . I worshipped Him the oftenest that I could, keeping my mind in His holy Presence, and recalling it as often as I found it wandered from Him. I found no small pain in this exercise, and yet I continued it, notwithstanding all the difficulties that occurred, without troubling or disquieting myself when my mind had wandered involuntarily. I made this my business, as much all the day long as at the appointed times of prayer; for at all times, every hour, every minute, even in the height of my business, I drove away from my mind everything that was capable of interrupting my thought of God."

We can worship God in our day-to-day life. Today in prayer consider how you can worship Christ in the way of Brother Lawrence.

To worship is to quicken the conscience, by the holiness of God, to feed the mind with the truth of God, to purge the imagination by the beauty of God, to open the heart to the love of God, to devote the will to the purpose of God.

—William Temple

Day 79
THE AZTEC'S UNKNOWN GOD

In the past, he let all nations go their own way.
Yet he has not left himself without testimony:
He has shown kindness by giving you rain
from heaven and crops in their seasons;
he provides you with plenty of food
and fills your hearts with joy.
Acts 14:16–17

*B*efore Spain conquered Mexico the Aztec civilization was one of the most advanced in the New World. The Aztecs were skilled craftsmen, constructed large and ornate pyramids, had an intricate calendar system, and used hieroglyphic writing. But for all of their technological advancements the Aztecs were immersed in polytheistic worship and human sacrifice. They have been called the "Assyrians of North America"—their society rested on the dual concepts of war and love of beauty.

The height of the Aztec Empire occurred during the reign of King Netzahualcoyotl who ruled from 1431–1472. He was a warrior and a statesman-philosopher. When he pondered the worship of the Aztec gods he said, "Verily, the gods that I am adoring, what are they but idols of stone without speech or feeling? They could not have made the beauty of the heaven, the sun, the moon, the stars, which light the earth, with its countless streams, its foundations and waters. There must be some God, invisible and unknown, who is the universal Creator." The Aztecs had a name for this supreme unknown god: Ipalnemohuani, Giver of Life.

In every human heart is the knowledge that there is something or someone greater than themselves. We know that this is Jesus Christ. He has made Himself known so that all humanity may have eternal life. Today in prayer thank Christ that you can share His love with those who do not yet know of it.

Sometimes a nation abolishes God, but fortunately God is more tolerant.

—Herbert V. Prochnow

Day 80
GET UP AND AT IT

Then Philip ran up to the chariot and heard the man reading Isaiah the prophet. "Do you understand what you are reading?" Philip asked.
Acts 8:30–31

Henry John Heinz was an industrious teenager who turned a business of selling horseradish grown in his mother's garden into the largest pickle and condiment manufacturing company in the world. H. J. Heinz built his company to be a people-oriented place. It is said that no fairer, franker man in business affairs ever lived. He helped promote the Pure Food and Drug Act in the U.S., which greatly enhanced the quality of processed foods. His epigram was that every successful business must be "run from the heart." His other memorable saying was: "Make all you can honestly, save all you can prudently, and give all you can wisely."

One day at an evangelistic service the speaker challenged Heinz saying, "You are a believer but with all your energy why aren't you up and at it for the Lord?" The young businessman went home in anger. That night he couldn't sleep. At four o'clock in the morning he prayed that God would use him to lead others to Christ. Soon afterwards at a meeting of bank presidents Heinz turned to the man next to him and told him of his joy in knowing Jesus. His friend looked at him in surprise and said, "Because I knew you were a Christian, I've wondered many times why you never spoke to me about salvation." That man became the first of 267 people H. J. Heinz eventually led to Jesus Christ.

People's hearts are ready to hear the good news about Jesus Christ if we only would share His joy with them. Today give thanks that the Lord is your hope and ask for an opportunity to share Him with others.

> There is an urgent need in the church today for more Christians who will speak for Christ and thus daily witness for him.
>
> —Lyman Beecher

Day 81
THE LORD AND I DID IT BETWEEN US

None of the rulers of this age understood it, for if they had,
they would not have crucified the Lord of glory.
However, as it is written: "No eye has seen, no ear has heard,
no mind has conceived what God has prepared for those who
love him"—but God has revealed it to us by his Spirit.
The Spirit searches all things, even the deep things of God.
1 Corinthians 2:8–10

At age twenty-three Joseph Scriven had just graduated from Trinity College in Dublin and was engaged to be married. But on the night before his wedding his fiancée accidentally drowned. Shattered, Scriven left Ireland and immigrated to Port Hope, Ontario, Canada. For twelve years he grieved over his fiancée. Then one night in 1855 Scriven poured out his heart to the Lord. He prayed that Christ would relieve his grief and promised to serve Him faithfully. The Holy Spirit inspired Scriven to write the poem "Pray Without Ceasing." Today it is known as the hymn "What A Friend We Have In Jesus."

Joseph Scriven lived out his life in Port Hope dedicated to the service of the community. As a lay-preacher he habitually preached on the love of Jesus Christ. Thirty-one years after he wrote his poem a friend discovered it and asked Scriven if he could send it to a religious journal. Ira Sankey, a gospel singer, saw the poem and set it to a melody composed by C. C. Converse. In Scriven's later years he was asked how he wrote "What A Friend We Have In Jesus." He replied, "The Lord and I did it between us."

When tough times come people ask, "Why me?" Without prayer we are unable to comprehend what the Lord has prepared. Are you going through difficult times? Today be thankful that God knows the agonies of life and can make something magnificent out of your life.

> What a Friend we have in Jesus, all our sins and griefs
> to bear! What a privilege to carry everything to God
> in prayer! O what peace we often forfeit, O what
> needless pain we bear, all because we do not carry
> everything to God in prayer!
>
> —Joseph Scriven

Day 82
DON'T PRAY LIKE HUCKLEBERRY FINN

When you ask, you do not receive, because you ask with wrong motives, that you may spend what you get on your pleasures.
James 4:3

Mark Twain writes in the *Adventures of Huckleberry Finn*: "Then Miss Watson she took me in the closet and prayed, but nothing come of it. She told me to pray every day, and whatever I asked for I would get it. But it warn't so. I tried it. Once I got a fish-line, but no hooks. It warn't any good to me without hooks. I tried for the hooks three or four times, but somehow I couldn't make it work. By-and-by, one day, I asked Miss Watson to try for me, but she said I was a fool. She never told me why, and I couldn't make it out no way. I set down, one time, back in the woods, and had a long think about it. I says to myself, if a body can get anything they pray for, why don't Deacon Winn get back the money he lost on pork? Why can't the widow get back her snuff-box that was stole? Why can't Miss Watson fat up? No, says I to myself, there ain't nothing in it."

Many people sincerely ask God for something and when they don't receive it, give up on prayer. But prayer is meant to bring us closer in our relationship with Jesus Christ. It is meant to bring Him glory. Praying for yourself and for needs is not wrong if the motive is to bring glory to God. If your requests bring glory to Jesus Christ, you are on solid ground.

> The fundamental law in prayer is this: Prayer is given and ordained for the purpose of glorifying God. Prayer is the appointed way of giving God an opportunity to exercise His supernatural powers of salvation. And in so doing He desires to make use of us.
> —E. M. Bounds

Day 83
STAYING POWER IN THE SPIRITUAL RACE

Do you not know that in a race all the runners run, but only one gets the prize? Run in such a way as to get the prize. Everyone who competes in the games goes into strict training. They do it to get a crown that will not last; but we do it to get a crown that will last forever.
1 Corinthians 9:24–25

Michelle Akers has been called the greatest woman soccer player to ever play the game. A member of the U.S.

Women's National Soccer Team since 1985, she scored an incredible ten goals in six tournament games in 1991. But in late 1993 she collapsed on the field at an Olympic Sports Festival and was diagnosed with Chronic Fatigue Syndrome (CFS). She was reduced from a world-class athlete to an invalid. Simply doing her laundry could knock her out for days or weeks.

Michelle became a Christian in high school but in September, 1994, she rededicated her life to Jesus Christ. She was encouraged by Joshua 1:9: "Have I not commanded you? Be strong and of good courage; do not be afraid, nor be dismayed; for the Lord your God is with you wherever you go" (NKJV). Michelle recentered her life on Christ and disciplined herself to come back as a soccer player. Even with CFS she depended on Christ to provide the strength, courage, and peace to overcome her problems. In 1996 she played in the Olympics in Atlanta and led her team to the gold medal.

Training in godliness does not require physical stamina. As you follow and serve your Lord you grow stronger in Him. In the end you receive an everlasting crown. Today take time to talk with the Lord about this prize. Look to Him as you run life's race.

> It is necessary, however, to exercise self-control in all things if staying-power is to be maintained so that the spiritual race is run consistently to the end of the course and the coveted prize won.
>
> —F. F. Bruce

Day 84
PEACE IN PRAYER

I sought the LORD, and he answered me;
he delivered me from all my fears.
Psalm 34:4

In her autobiography Fanny Crosby describes a night that she spent at her grandmother's house as a little girl: "When I went to see her she always gave me the room that I liked best; and I shall never forget one night that I spent there. . . . The night was beautiful. I crept toward the window; and through the branches of a giant oak that stood just outside, the soft moonlight fell upon my head like the benediction of an angel while I knelt there and repeated over and over these simple words, 'Dear Lord, please show me how I can learn like other children.'

"At this moment the weight of anxiety that burdened my heart was changed to the sweet consciousness that my prayer would be answered in due time. If I had been restless and impatient before, from that time forth I was still eager, but confident that God would point a way for me to gain the education which I craved. . . . I was not content always to live in ignorance; and, in the course of time, in a way of which I had no previous intimation, my wish was to be granted in fullest measure."

Peace does not come from internal visualization or an attempt to control our surroundings. Peace comes from seeking Jesus Christ. He delivers us from our fears and anxieties. In prayer today turn over all of your fears and anxieties to the Prince of Peace.

Let nothing disturb you; let nothing dismay you; all things pass: God never changes, Patience attains all it strives for. He who has God finds he lacks nothing: God alone suffices.

—Teresa of Avila

Day 85
OUR CITIZENSHIP IN HEAVEN

Consequently, you are no longer foreigners and aliens, but fellow
citizens with God's people and members of God's household,
built on the foundation of the apostles and prophets,
with Christ Jesus himself as the chief cornerstone.
Ephesians 2:19–20

To become a citizen of the United States a person must go through a lengthy process. If approved, this is their oath of allegiance to the United States:

I hereby declare, on oath, that I absolutely and entirely renounce and abjure all allegiance and fidelity to any foreign prince, potentate, state or sovereignty, of whom or which I have heretofore been a subject or citizen; that I will support and defend the Constitution and laws of the United States of America against all enemies, foreign and domestic; that I will bear true faith and allegiance to the same; that I will bear arms on behalf of the United States when required by the law; that I will perform noncombatant service in the armed forces of the United States when required by the law; that I will perform work of national importance under civilian direction when required by the law; and that I take this obligation freely without any mental reservation or purpose of evasion; so help me God.

Our citizenship in heaven is based on our faith in Jesus Christ. In Him we become fellow citizens and members of the household of faith. Today praise Christ that He has made you a citizen of heaven and in Him you can place the full weight of your trust.

The true Christian is the true citizen, lofty of purpose, resolute in endeavor, ready for a hero's deeds, but never looking down on his task because it is cast in the day of small things; scornful of baseness, awake to his own duties as well as to his rights, following the higher law with reverence, and in this world doing all that in his power lies, so that when death comes he may feel that mankind is in some degree better because he lived.

—Theodore Roosevelt

Day 86
HONOR YOUR PARENTS

"Honor your father and mother"—which is the first commandment with a promise—"that it may go well with you and that you may enjoy long life on the earth."
Ephesians 6:2–3

Here is the tale of "The Old Man and His Grandson" from *Grimm's Fairy Tales*:

There was once a very old man whose eyes had become dim. When he sat at table he could hardly hold the spoon and spilt the broth upon the tablecloth or let it run out of his mouth. His son and his son's wife were disgusted at this so they made the old grandfather sit in the corner behind the stove and they gave him his food in an earthenware bowl. And he used to look towards the table with his eyes full of tears.

Once his trembling hands could not hold the bowl and it fell to the ground and broke. The young wife scolded him. Then they bought him a wooden bowl.

They were sitting thus when the grandson of four years old began to gather together bits of wood upon the floor. "What are you doing there?" asked the father. "I am making a little trough," answered the child, "for father and mother to eat out of when I am big."

The man and his wife began to cry. Then they took the old grandfather to the table and henceforth always let him eat with them and likewise said nothing if he did spill a little of anything.

In what ways do you show respect to your parents? Today in prayer thank the Lord for the father and mother who gave you life.

> Honoring your parents is an attitude accompanied by actions that say to your parents: "You are worthy. You have value. You are the person God's sovereignty placed in my life. You may have failed me, hurt me, and disappointed me at times, but I am taking off my judicial robe and releasing you from the courtroom of my mind. I choose to look at you with compassion— as people with needs, concerns, and scars of your own."
>
> —Dennis Rainey

Day 87
GOD WALKS WITH US

We live by faith, not by sight.
2 Corinthians 5:7

Ludwig Nommensen was a Danish missionary to the Batak people on the island of Sumatra in Southeast Asia. There a village chief gave him two years to learn the customs of the people and convince them that he had a message worth hearing. At the end of this period the tribal leader said to Nommensen, "We know what is right for we too have laws that say we must not steal or take our neighbors' wives or tell lies."

"That's true," the missionary answered quietly, "but my Master supplies the power needed to keep these laws." The chief was startled. "Can you really teach my people to live better?" he inquired.

"No, I can't, but if they receive Jesus Christ, God will give them the strength to do what's right."

Nommensen was permitted to remain another six months. He preached the gospel and taught the villagers of the Holy Spirit's work in believer's lives. At the end of this period the Batak chief said, "You may stay longer. Your religion is better than ours for your God walks with men and gives them strength to do the good things He requires."

Since we have believed, Jesus Christ lives in us to empower us to live a life that is pleasing to God. Today in prayer thank Christ that you can live by faith.

> Faith is taking God at His word. Faith is not belief without evidence. It is belief on the very best of evidence—the word of Him "that cannot lie."
> —R. A. Torrey

Day 88
THANKS FOR OTHER CHRISTIANS

How can we thank God enough for you in return for all the joy we have in the presence of our God because of you? Night and day we pray most earnestly that we may see you again and supply what is lacking in your faith.
1 Thessalonians 3:9–10

Charles Haddon Spurgeon was a gifted preacher in Great Britain during the latter part of the nineteenth century. He served the huge Metropolitan Tabernacle in London and helped found a pastor's college and an orphanage, both of which are still in existence today.

One night during the last few years of Spurgeon's ministry he shared the pulpit with Mark G. Pearce, a young, gifted preacher, author, and artist. During a break in the service, Pearce said to Spurgeon, "When I was a young fellow, I used to sit over there and hear you expound the Scriptures. You'll never know how much good you did for me. I was so inspired, I could go for weeks just feeding on what you told us and heeding your wise admonitions."

Charles Spurgeon was overwhelmed with joy and gratitude. With tears welling in his eyes he said, "God bless you, brother. I never knew I had helped you that much."

Sharing our lives with other Christians and helping them grow in their own faith is an important aspect of being a Christian. In prayer today thank the Lord for the Christians in your life. This week as you talk to other believers let them know how you appreciate them and how they have strengthened your faith in Jesus Christ.

> The grace of God leads to thanksgiving, an activity which results in the increase of God's glory as more and more people recognize his goodness.
> —I. Howard Marshall

Day 89

DEATH RESULTS IN LIFE

We are hard pressed on every side, but not crushed;
perplexed, but not in despair; persecuted, but not abandoned;
struck down, but not destroyed.
We always carry around in our body the death of Jesus,
so that the life of Jesus may also be revealed in our body.
2 Corinthians 4:8–10

The explorers in the New World reported that the tribes of the Amazon jungle used a poison on their arrows that incapacitated their victims within a minute. Certain death followed. This deadly plant extract is called curare. Dr. Benjamin Brodie experimented on curare and discovered that even though paralysis quickly set in, the heart did not stop. The victim lacked muscle power to breathe but could escape death by artificial respiration until the drug wore off.

Physicians found that curare is not a poison but rather an important medicine. It can relax muscles so curare can be used as an anesthetic. In 1942 Doctors Harold Griffith and Enid Johnson reported that curare "may prove to be a drug which will occasionally be of great value, and will give us the means of providing the surgeon rapidly with excellent relaxation at critical times." Today curare derivative known as tubocurarine is used as a skeletal muscle relaxant.

The Cross brings certain death to those who believe in Jesus Christ. But then the Holy Spirit breathes eternal life into them. Today in prayer tell God that you want to know Him as the life-giving Spirit.

> When God would educate a man, He compels him to learn bitter lessons. He sends him to school to the necessities rather than to the graces, that, by knowing all suffering, he may know also the eternal consolation.
> —Celia Burleigh

Day 90
THE BASIS FOR ACTION

Noah did everything just as God commanded him.
Genesis 6:22

In August 1942, General Bernard Law Montgomery was given command of the British Eighth Army in North Africa. Prior to Montgomery, the army had not had a military victory during the war. His predecessor was General Gott, a man who had a listening ear and provided sympathy, advice, and encouragement to his men. Lord Carver later said that Gott "imagined all too keenly what casualties meant in terms of human suffering. Perhaps he was too great of a man to be a really great soldier." Montgomery was not callused to his men, but he was determined to win the war. He was focused on victory in North Africa. He knew in order to defeat his foe he would have to maintain discipline.

Only four weeks after taking command, Montgomery drove back German General Erwin Rommel at the Battle of Alam Halfa. Eight weeks later he won a stunning victory at the Battle of El Alamein. When asked how he was able to turn around the fortunes of the British Army, he said: "Orders no longer formed the basis of discussion, but for action. Previously orders had generally been queried by subordinates right down the line. I was determined to stop this state of affairs at once."

Building an ark when it isn't raining may sound like a bad idea. But Noah did everything just as God commanded him. To Noah, God's Word was not basis of discussion, but a call to action. Are you following the commands God has given to you? Today in prayer thank Christ for His love and follow Him wherever He leads.

Obedience is the fruit of faith; patience the bloom on the fruit.

—Christina Rossetti

Day 91
OF BUTTERFLIES AND BEES

*Now the Bereans were of more noble character than the
Thessalonians, for they received the message with great
eagerness and examined the Scriptures every day
to see if what Paul said was true.*
Acts 17:11–12

How Christians take in the Word of God differs as much as the contrast between how butterflies and bees take in nourishment. A butterfly darts here and there going after only high-energy pollen and sipping from flowers that have little nectar. It only takes enough pollen and nectar to feed itself. Throughout its solitary life, a butterfly will travel thousands of miles, but in the end it never sees the reproduction of its own kind.

The bee on the other hand will burrow down to the bottom of a flower's cup to drag out as much pollen and nectar as possible. It collects as much pollen on its hind legs and nectar in its body as possible before returning to its hive. Once in the hive it communicates with other bees through a dance so they too can find good nourishment. The bee then shares the pollen and nectar with the young and with those that cannot leave the hive. The production of honey is the result of stored flower nectar from the worker bees. This stored food source sustains the entire hive during difficult times.

How do you read the Bible? Do you flit from one subject to another like a butterfly? Or do you dig in with great eagerness and deeply examine the Scriptures? Today in prayer give thanks to Christ for the spiritual nourishment found in the Word.

Christian nobility of soul exhibits two features: readiness to receive truth and eagerness to examine the evidence.

—Johann Peter Lange

Day 92
REMORSE VS. REPENTANCE

First to those in Damascus, then to those in Jerusalem
and in all Judea, and to the Gentiles also, I preached
that they should repent and turn to God and prove
their repentance by their deeds.
Acts 26:20

The Parthenon was the chief temple built by the Greeks to honor their goddess Athena. Completed in 432 B.C. on the hill of the Acropolis in Athens, the marble edifice is 101 feet by 228 feet and is recognized as one of the most beautiful examples of classical Greek architecture. Though its exterior remains pretty much intact, its interior has been gutted through centuries of looting. Over the colonnades, high relief scenes of mythical battles were once seen. In the interior of the building there used to be ninety-two wall panels depicting the mythical birth and triumphs of the goddess Athena.

At the gateway of the temple there was an altar. Called the Altar of Tears, this was not a place to offer sacrifices or offerings. It was a quiet, simple spot where worshipers could go to weep and relieve their hurt and guilt. Though their emotions were temporarily assuaged through remorse, the altar of tears could not provide forgiveness through repentance.

John the Baptist preached repentance. So did Jesus Christ, Peter, Paul, and the other apostles. Repentance is more than remorse, it is a conscious decision for change. Do you feel a need to repent of anything, great or small? Today come to God and repent of your sin by faith in Jesus Christ. God waits for you with open arms.

Repentance is not something God demands of you before he will take you back, it is simply a description of what going back is like.

—C. S. Lewis

Day 93
BE THANKFUL FOR EVERYTHING

*For everything God created is good, and nothing
is to be rejected if it is received with thanksgiving.*
1 Timothy 4:4

*I*magine that starting tomorrow the only things that remain in your life are the things for which you thank God:

The alarm didn't go off! Where did the alarm clock go? Oh, I forgot to thank God for it. Well, I'll have to be late for work. Work? Did I thank God for my job? Oh well, I guess I won't have to worry about being late for work, I don't have a job anymore. But I did thank God for my meals. At least I won't go hungry. What's this in the mail? An eviction notice! Oh no! I forgot to thank God for my home! And the telephone has been quiet all morning. Oops, no telephone. Well, I'll use a pay phone. Where's my car? What happened to my pocket change? Who was I going to call anyway? Oh, I've never thanked the Lord for my friends. Well, at least I have my health. Have I ever thanked the Lord for my health? . . .

There are so many things in this life for which we fail to thank the Lord. Your talents, your family and friends, the beauty of creation, all of these and much more are gifts from your heavenly Father. Today ask God to give you a thankful heart and acknowledge your dependence on His good gifts.

I thank Thee, my Creator and Lord, that Thou hast given me this joy in Thy creation, this delight in the works of Thy hands.

—Johann Kepler

Day 94
PRAISE THE LORD JESUS CHRIST!

Yours, O LORD, is the greatness and the power and the glory
and the majesty and the splendor, for everything in heaven
and earth is yours. Yours, O LORD, is the kingdom;
you are exalted as head over all.
1 Chronicles 29:11

Brother Lawrence was a cook in a monastery just outside of Paris during the seventeenth century. For thirty years, he toiled in obscurity. He never wrote a book, never preached a sermon. Yet Brother Lawrence wrote letters which were assembled into a book called *The Practice of the Presence of God* that has influenced people for generations.

Lawrence's days were filled with baking, cooking, cleaning dishes, mopping, and scrubbing. Yet he kept all of this in perspective and continually praised the Lord while he worked. He took mental breaks to briefly focus on Christ and praise Him. Though Lawrence was essentially a servant, few have expressed intimacy with God as did he. Lawrence knew the peace and joy of praising the Lord everywhere—in a kitchen or a cathedral, God is there! Despite the hubbub and noise all around he cultivated a permanent attitude of prayer and praise.

Praise the Lord Jesus Christ!

Praise ye the Lord, the Almighty, the King of creation! O my soul, praise Him, for He is thy health and salvation! All ye who hear, Now to His temple draw near; Join me in glad adoration!

—Joachim Neander

MAKE THE MOST OF TIME

*There is a time for everything, and a season for every activity
under heaven: a time to be born and a time to die, a time to
plant and a time to uproot, a time to kill and a time to heal, a
time to tear down and a time to build, a time to weep and a
time to laugh, a time to mourn and a time to dance, a time to
scatter stones and a time to gather them, a time to embrace and
a time to refrain, a time to search and a time to give up, a time
to keep and a time to throw away, a time to tear and a time to
mend, a time to be silent and a time to speak, a time to love
and a time to hate, a time for war and a time for peace.*
Ecclesiastes 3:1–8

The extinct Mayan culture was obsessed with time.
They studied the movement of the planets and charted the
stars. They devised intricate calendars which are as accurate as
our modern calendar. Plantings, harvests, and sacrifices were
strictly based on this calendar.

The ninth Caesar of Rome, Vitellius (A.D. 69), offered a
sum equivalent to $250 million to the priests in the empire if
they could recover one minute of lost time. The best they
could do was turn their clocks back.

We are no different than these ancients. In our time-
conscious world we want to make every minute count. The
best way to do this is to invest our lives in things that have last-
ing value. Do you spend enough time in the Word of God and
with other people? Today in prayer give thanks that the Lord
has given you the time for your life. Ask that you may use that
time to bring Him glory.

> We never shall have any more time. We have, and we
> have always had, all the time there is.
> —Arnold Bennett

ON TOP OF THE WORLD

So I say to you: Ask and it will be given to you; seek and
you will find; knock and the door will be opened to you.
For everyone who asks receives; he who seeks finds;
and to him who knocks, the door will be opened.
Luke 11:9–10

Robert E. Peary desired to be the first man to stand at the North Pole. For seven years, beginning in 1891, Peary learned how to travel and survive in the Arctic. He lived among the Eskimos who taught him how to live off the land, how to travel by dogsled, and how to navigate in the Arctic regions. In 1897 the American Geographic Society awarded Peary the Cullom Gold Medal for his mapping work of Greenland. But the quest to be the first man at the North Pole still burned within him.

On April 12, 1897, Peary received orders from the Secretary of the Navy ordering him to California. But Peary asked the prominent Republican Charles Moore for a favor: A leave from the Navy for five years in order to continue polar exploration. Moore secured the leave from President McKinley within forty-eight hours.

For the next five years Peary pressed close but could not get nearer than four hundred miles from the pole. In 1902 he wrote, "The game is off. My dream of sixteen years is ended. I have made a good fight, but I cannot accomplish the impossible."

Then the newly elected President Teddy Roosevelt threw his full weight behind the Peary expeditions. He approved of the enterprise because of national pride. With new vigor Peary searched for ways to close that four hundred miles. Finally on April 6, 1909, twenty-three years after his first expedition, Richard Peary hoisted the American flag over the North Pole. He was on top of the world.

Asking, seeking, knocking—all continuous actions. Christ

encourages us to continue praying to do His will. Are you discouraged when prayer is not answered right away? Today in prayer thank Jesus for the perseverance to follow Him.

> What should we do except go confidently to God,
> "who gives to all liberally," and opening his hand fills
> all things living.
>
> —Bernard of Clairvaux

Day 97
PUT IT IN WRITING

In the first year of Belshazzar king of Babylon, Daniel had a dream, and visions passed through his mind as he was lying on his bed. He wrote down the substance of his dream.
Daniel 7:1

In 1752, prior to the French and Indian War, when George Washington was a twenty-year-old military officer, he wrote down several of his prayers:

"Almighty God, and most merciful father. . .I yield thee humble and hearty thanks that thou hast preserved me from the dangers of the night past, and brought me to the light of this day, and the comforts thereof, a day which is consecrated to thine own service and for thine own honor. Let my heart, therefore Gracious God, be so affected with the glory and majesty of it, that I may not do mine own works, but wait on thee, and discharge weighty duties thou requirest of me. . .pardon, I beseech thee, my sins, remove them from my presence, as far as the east is from the west, and accept of me for the merits of thy son Jesus Christ, that when I come into thy temple, and compass thine altar, my prayer may come before thee as incense; and as thou wouldst hear me calling upon thee in prayers, so give me grace to hear thee calling on me in thy word, that it may be wisdom, righteousness, reconciliation, and peace to the saving of my soul in the day of the Lord Jesus. . . . Amen."

Writing provides insight on our own spiritual growth and helps us to remember! Today in prayer, praise the Lord that He is faithful and write down how He has shown His faithfulness to you so you will remember His love.

> Let me remember, O Lord, the time will come when the trumpet will sound, and the dead shall rise and stand before the judgment seat.
>
> —George Washington

Day 98
THE ADVANCE MAN

A voice of one calling: "In the desert prepare the way for the LORD; make straight in the wilderness a highway for our God."
Isaiah 40:3

The person who prepares for the arrival of an important person is known as the advance man. He or she arranges publicity, protocol, speaking schedules and all the details for this person. Some advance men are entrusted with small but important details, while others influence policy and make supporting speeches.

The title "advance man" was coined in 1897 when Congressman H. R. Gibson of Tennessee called President McKinley "that great priest and apostle of protection, and that great advance agent of prosperity." In this case the important "person" is prosperity and the advance man is McKinley. There is an old saying that advance men teach their young protégés. "If you arrive with the candidate, you are not advancing."

John the Baptist arrived in advance of Jesus Christ and the kingdom of God calling people to repentance. When Jesus arrived John had to decrease in stature. Today we stand before the second coming of Christ. We are His advance men. We are to prepare the way for His second coming. Do you ever tell others the good news that Christ is coming again? Do you need to brush up on how to share the gospel? If so, ask your minister or pastor where you can learn the basics of sharing the "good news" that Christ is coming again. In prayer ask the Lord for the boldness to tell others of His return.

> The great cry of every heart is that God will help us to be ready for whatever he has for us.
> —Bob Pierce

Day 99
HE GAVE HIMSELF FOR OUR SINS

Grace and peace to you from God our Father and the Lord Jesus Christ, who gave himself for our sins to rescue us from the present evil age, according to the will of our God and Father.
Galatians 1:3–4

Rembrandt Harmenszoon van Rijn (1606–1669) left no diaries or documents describing his life. It is known that at age thirteen he decided to paint rather than follow his father's footsteps as a miller. Rembrandt studied under Jacob Isaacsz van Swanenburch and became an immediate favorite in Holland as a portrait painter. He produced approximately six hundred paintings, three hundred etchings and fourteen hundred drawings. One third of these have a Biblical theme: *Abraham and Isaac, The Blinding of Samson, The Feast of Belshazzar, The Raising of Lazarus, Descent from the Cross,* etc.

In *The Raising of the Cross* the viewer's eyes are drawn to the Savior as He is nailed to the cross. The cross is in the process of being raised by a group of men. Next the eye focuses on the magistrate in the background—detached, supervising the work. Finally they rest upon a young man at Christ's feet clutching the cross as it is being raised. His face is that of Rembrandt the artist. This signifies that the artist acknowledged his part in crucifying the Lord but also held onto the cross for his own salvation.

The crucifixion of Christ is not an abstract event. It really happened. Christ willingly gave Himself for our sins to rescue us from sin and restore our relationship with God. How do you look upon the cross? Today give thanks that Christ rescued you and you are saved by grace.

> Because my transgressions are multiplied and my own efforts at self-justification more a hindrance than a furtherance, therefore Christ the Son of God gave Himself unto death for my sins, "To believe this is to have eternal life."
>
> —Martin Luther

Day 100
THE MATCHLESS ONE

The Spirit clearly says that in later times some will abandon the faith and follow deceiving spirits and things taught by demons.
1 Timothy 4:1

How many different religions are there in the world? Not even the experts know. *The Encyclopedia of Religion* (New York: Macmillan, 1987) lists forty religions or groups of religions. But in each group, such as African Traditional Religions, there are hundreds of smaller religions. *The 1997 World Almanac* lists such broad categories as quasi religions, pseudoreligions, parareligions, mystic systems, and brotherhoods of numerous varieties. These are the known established religions.

One relatively new religion is Penguinism, founded in Finland, which believes the higher power is a mighty penguin! This is known as animism—the worship of animals and the natural world. So there could be millions of religions if people worshiped their favorite animal, insect, plant, or rock.

Then there are the atheists, the agnostics, the humanists, the freethinkers, and the secularists. There are limitless ways of personal spirituality.

But we trust a Person with a proven track record. Jesus Christ is matchless. His teaching, His conduct, His miracles, and His resurrection elevate Christ above all. Only one Person can fill the void in the human heart—only One is worthy of worship—Jesus Christ. This week keep Christ first in all that you do. And when you meet nonbelievers, remember that they need Him too! Keep them in your prayers. Be willing to share the good news of the gospel.

> To the unbeliever all religions are alike, just like all
> colors are alike in the dark.
>
> —William Taylor

Day 101
TEACH YOUR CHILDREN WELL

I have been reminded of your sincere faith, which first lived in your grandmother Lois and in your mother Eunice and, I am persuaded, now lives in you also.
2 Timothy 1:5

William McKinley was president of the United States from 1897 until his assassination in office on September 6, 1901. One of his last requests was to hear his mother's favorite hymn "Nearer, My God, to Thee."

McKinley often spoke out about his faith in Jesus Christ. In an address when he was governor of Ohio he said, "The time has gone by when a young man or woman in the United States has to apologize for being a follower of Christ." In his

117

first presidential inaugural address he invoked "the guidance of God Almighty." Many who knew McKinley described him as a man of intelligence, exemplary character, and likable personality. How did McKinley become such a man?

McKinley credited his mother's faith in Jesus Christ. He regularly attended church, was superintendent of Sunday school, and taught Sunday school classes. But it was at home where he learned to trust in Christ. Throughout his life McKinley either wrote or telegraphed his mother, Nancy, every day. When she lay on her deathbed he immediately took a train from Washington D.C. to be with her in Canton, Ohio.

Some of the best lessons of life are caught and not taught. Nancy McKinley's faith in Jesus Christ was deep and her son saw its value. Today in prayer give thanks to Christ for the role models in your life. Ask Jesus to deepen your faith in Him so others may be encouraged by your life.

The best academy, a mother's knee.
—James Russell Lowell

Day 102
DON'T LOOK AT
THE OUTWARD APPEARANCE

But the LORD said to Samuel, "Do not consider
his appearance or his height, for I have rejected him.
The LORD does not look at the things man looks at.
Man looks at the outward appearance,
but the LORD looks at the heart."
1 Samuel 16:7

In early 1997, the Seattle board of tourism began using a beautiful photo to promote its travel guide. The photo, a spectacular shot of the Seattle skyline, was taken from the stern of a ferry. The Space Needle is in the foreground with

Mount Rainier majestically standing in the background under a clear, blue sky. Under the photo is the slogan, "The place you've been trying to get to." There is only one problem. It is a doctored photo, an impossible scene. Artists used a computer to create a beautiful, but untrue picture.

If the photograph were accurate, the ferry actually would be sailing several hundred feet above Seattle's Ballard neighborhood—this would require extraordinarily high tides. In fact, Seattle's Queen Anne Hill and its expensive homes would disappear underwater. The ferry would have to dock at the Space Needle, one half mile inland and several hundred feet above sea level. Yet an ad agency representative describes the photo as the "quintessential view of Seattle." People love the photo and requests for the free travel guides have more than doubled.

Do you find yourself looking too much at a person's appearance and not their heart? Today in prayer ask the Lord to give you wisdom to look beyond outward appearances and to see the heart.

> The eye that searches and knows us penetrates to the heart—it is there only that God finds genuine elements of worship.
>
> —W.G. Blaikie

Day 103
THE THIRD STRAND

Your beauty should not come from outward adornment, such as braided hair and the wearing of gold jewelry and fine clothes. Instead, it should be that of your inner self, the unfading beauty of a gentle and quiet spirit, which is of great worth in God's sight.
1 Peter 3:3–4

The braiding of hair is found in almost every culture in recorded history. The Talmud mentions that Jewish women in Biblical times often wore their hair long and braided. They placed simple combs and hairpins in their hair. The ladies of the Roman aristocracy exhibited the extreme in hair fashion. They would sit for hours while servants plaited and curled their tresses into artistic shapes. False hair was pinned into the existing hair and gold pins, ivory and tortoiseshell combs, jewel-studded headbands, and nets of gold thread held it all together.

In *Leadership Magazine* Catheryn Paxton illustrates that the simple braid can demonstrate the importance of God's place in the marital relationship. She wrote, "A braid appears to contain only two strands of hair. But it is impossible to create a braid with only two strands. If the two could be put together at all, they would quickly unravel. Herein lies the mystery: What looks like two strands but requires a third. The third strand, though not immediately evident, keeps the braid tightly woven. In a Christian marriage, God's presence, like the third strand in a braid, holds the husband and wife together."

Grooming is important. But cultivating a quiet, gentle spirit that honors the Lord is of far more consequence. Are you spending more time in front of the mirror than you are alone with Christ? Today spend time with the God who loves you above all fashion.

> A tasteful and magnificent dress lends added dignity to the wearer: but effeminate and luxurious apparel fails to adorn the body, and only reveals the sordidness of the mind.
>
> —Quintilian

THE DOOMSDAY CLOCK

First of all, you must understand that in the last days scoffers
will come, scoffing and following their own evil desires.
2 Peter 3:3

The Doomsday Clock was developed in 1947 by the Bulletin of Atomic Scientists. It graphically depicts the threat of nuclear annihilation. Then it was set at seven minutes to midnight. In 1953 the minute hand was moved to two minutes to midnight. This followed successful hydrogen bomb tests by the United States and the Soviet Union. In 1963 the clock was moved back to twelve minutes to midnight—the superpowers had signed the Partial Test Ban Treaty.

In 1968 France and China acquired nuclear weapons—the Doomsday Clock was set to seven minutes before midnight. In 1972 the clock was moved back to twelve minutes before midnight following the signing of the first Strategic Arms Limitation Treaty. In 1984 it was reset to three minutes before midnight—the arms race was accelerating. In 1988 the clock was again moved back to six minutes before midnight with the treaty to eliminate intermediate-range nuclear forces and the collapse of Communism. In 1991 the time was seventeen minutes to midnight—the superpowers had signed the Strategic Arms Reduction Treaty.

Today the clock is at eight minutes before midnight due to China's military buildup and inadequate security for weapons-grade nuclear material. Some people scoff and say, "Midnight never came and it never will come."

There will come a time when everyone will stand before the Lord. Do you know someone who scoffs at God's judgment? Today pray for that person. Ask Jesus to give you the opportunity to share the love of God.

Since the apostles have predicted this time, the church should not be surprised or discouraged but prepare itself for action.

—Edwin A. Blum

Day 105
MASS COMMUNICATION

I wrote to the church, but Diotrephes, who loves to be first, will have nothing to do with us. So if I come, I will call attention to what he is doing, gossiping maliciously about us. Not satisfied with that, he refuses to welcome the brothers. He also stops those who want to do so and puts them out of the church.

3 John 9–10

Dr. Hadley Cantril was a professor of psychology at Princeton University. Once he analyzed the radio broadcast "The War of the Worlds." Why did it cause such panic in 1938? He is also the author of *Patterns of Human Concerns.* This book discusses how men and women react to thirty different human concerns.

One day Dr. Cantril conducted an experiment on some of his students. He wanted to find out how quickly gossip spread. He selected six of his students and individually told each of them, in the strictest confidence, the false rumor that the Duke and Duchess of Windsor were planning to drop in on a university dance. Within a week most of the six thousand members of the Princeton student body had heard the rumor and town officials telephoned the school to ask why they hadn't been informed of the royal visit. This pleasant rumor spread quickly. But Dr. Cantril observed that slanderous gossip traveled much faster.

Gossip is a fashionable sin. Are you a gossip? Before you speak of someone else, pray: "Lord, would I say this to You and

to the person who is the subject of this rumor?" You may want
to keep your thoughts to yourself.

> Never believe anything bad about anybody unless
> you feel that it is absolutely necessary—and that God
> is listening while you tell it.
>
> —Henry Van Dyke

Day 106
THE TRUE INHERITANCE

*Because you are sons, God sent the Spirit of his Son into our
hearts, the Spirit who calls out, "Abba, Father." So you are
no longer a slave, but a son; and since you are a son,
God has made you also an heir.*
Galatians 4:6–7

On October 7, 1871, the Great Chicago Fire burned
twenty-nine hours and destroyed seventy-three miles of streets.
There were three hundred people killed, over 100,000 people
made homeless, and $192 million in property destroyed. Thirty
percent of all buildings in Chicago were destroyed including
eight public schools, forty churches, the railroad depot, and all
the retail stores.

After the fire a man said to D. L. Moody, "I hear you lost
everything in the fire."

"Well, you understand wrong; I didn't," Moody replied.

"How much do you have left?"

"I can't tell you; I have a good deal more left than I lost."

The man continued, "You can't tell how much you have?"

Moody replied, "No."

"I didn't know that you were ever that rich. What do you
mean?"

"I mean just what I say. I got my old Bible out of the fire;

that is about the only thing. One promise came to me. . .'He that overcometh shall inherit all things; and I will be his God and he shall be my son.' You ask me how much I am worth. I don't know. You may go and find out how much the Vanderbilts are worth, and the Astors, and Rothchilds, but you can't find out how much a child of God is worth. Why? Because he is a joint-heir with Jesus Christ."

Do you value your spiritual inheritance above everything here on earth? Give thanks that fire cannot take away your inheritance in Christ.

> God has no poor children. If we overcome we shall inherit all things.
>
> —D. L. Moody

Day 107
SACRED FIRE

I will praise you, O LORD, with all my heart;
I will tell of all your wonders. I will be glad and rejoice in you;
I will sing praise to your name, O Most High.
Psalm 9:1–2

ollowing the French Revolution in 1789 a variety of leaders and coalition governments tried unsuccessfully to lead France. On November 10, 1799, Napoleon Bonaparte, a young military hero, emerged as the country's leader.

Napoleon commanded fierce loyalty among his soldiers because he understood his men: "The French soldier is the most difficult to lead. He is not a machine to set in motion but a reasoning being you must govern. When he approves of the operations and respects his commanders there is nothing he cannot do." Napoleon wanted to instill in his soldiers "feu sacre"— sacred fire. He wanted his men to serve beyond the call of duty.

He wanted them to fight beyond their means and win or die trying. Often a mortally wounded French soldier would give a final salute, "Vive l'Emprereur!" Long live the Emperor!

Once, the story goes, a French soldier was wounded in the chest. As a surgeon was attempting to remove the bullet the man whispered, "If you go much deeper, Doctor, you'll come to the Emperor!"

Our devotion should be given to the One who died for us—Jesus Christ. Allow a sacred fire to burn in your heart for Him. Thank Christ and rejoice in His love with your whole heart.

> Thou has given so much to me. Give one thing more—a grateful heart.
>
> —George Herbert

Day 108
HOW CAN ONE KEEP WARM ALONE?

Two are better than one, because they have a good return for their work: If one falls down, his friend can help him up. But pity the man who falls and has no one to help him up! Also, if two lie down together, they will keep warm. But how can one keep warm alone? Though one may be overpowered, two can defend themselves. A cord of three strands is not quickly broken.
Ecclesiastes 4:9–12

On April 18, 1521, Martin Luther was called before Emperor Charles V of Rome at the Diet of Worms, Germany, to answer the question "Will you recant your writings that are critical of papal teaching?" Luther made his historic reply, "Here I stand. I can do no other. God help me! Amen." With this answer Luther was a condemned man. Charles V ordered that Luther be given a twenty-one day safe-conduct back to

Wittenberg. Luther was forbidden to ever preach or write again.

On April 26 Luther left Worms and proceeded to Wittenberg. On the evening of May 3, outside of Mohra, Germany, Luther's carriage was stopped by five masked horsemen. In silence they threw a knight's cloak over his shoulders, placed him on an extra horse, and in a few moments all of them had disappeared into the forest, covering their tracks as they rode.

Luther's captors took a circuitous route to the castle at Wartburg where his friend Frederick the Elector gave him sanctuary from certain martyrdom. Luther later referred to Wartburg as "my Patmos." There he enjoyed the ten most productive months of his life translating the Bible into German.

Are you a Lone Ranger in the faith? God has placed people around you so all will grow in the faith and love of Jesus Christ. Today in prayer give thanks for the people God has brought into your life. Pray that together you will enjoy mutual encouragement.

> Friendship makes prosperity brighter, while it lightens adversity by sharing its griefs and anxieties.
> —Marcus Tullius Cicero

Day 109
GOD IS WITH US

Open for me the gates of righteousness; I will enter and give thanks to the LORD. This is the gate of the LORD through which the righteous may enter. I will give you thanks, for you answered me; you have become my salvation.
Psalm 118:19–21

One night while John Wesley was speaking with a porter he discovered that the fellow had only one coat and didn't even have a bed. Yet he was an unusually joyful man, filled with gratitude to God. Wesley thoughtlessly joked about the man's misfortunes saying, "And what else do you thank God for?" The porter smiled and, "I thank Him that He has given me my life and being, a heart to love Him, and above all a constant desire to serve Him!" This answer moved John Wesley to examine the attitude of his own heart.

Eventually John Wesley valued "a clean heart, a single eye, a soul full of God!" And when he lay on his deathbed, his last words were, "The best of all is God is with us."

The Gentleman's Magazine, a publication that was not particularly kind to him in life, honored John Wesley with these words, "Though his taste was classic, and his manners elegant, he sacrificed that society in which he was particularly calculated to shine; gave up those preferments which his abilities must have obtained, and devoted a long life in practicing and enforcing the plainest duties. Instead of being 'an ornament to literature,' he was a blessing to his fellow creatures; instead of being 'the genius of the age,' he was the servant of God!"

Thank Jesus Christ that He is your salvation. Thank Him that He has given you a heart to love Him. Today remember, "The best of all is God is with us."

God is as present as the air.

—Michael Hollings

Day 110
THAT DAY WILL CLOSE LIKE A TRAP

Be careful, or your hearts will be weighed down with dissipation, drunkenness and the anxieties of life, and that day will close on you unexpectedly like a trap.
Luke 21:34

The city of Pompeii, founded circa 800 B.C., was a bustling city. In A.D. 79 Mount Vesuvius erupted and buried the city. Its approximately twenty thousand inhabitants had ample warning that the volcano would erupt and so there were only two thousand people left in the city when the disaster struck. The lava and ash that engulfed the city left casts of people in their final moments of life.

What were some of these people doing? One man was found clutching a beautiful bronze statue. Some children were killed in their playroom. One woman's petrified body was clutching jewels. A housekeeper was found holding two keys and two vessels of silver. A rich man and his wife were dragging valuable possessions when they were overtaken. A family was eating dinner. It seems that every one of the two thousand victims had this in common: They could have left the city earlier.

Is something preventing you from following Christ? Be careful of your heart. Pray that it will not be weighed down with dissipation, drunkenness, and the anxieties of life. Seek the Lord so that day will not close on you unexpectedly like a trap.

> Whatever weakens your reason, impairs the tenderness of your conscience, obscures your sense of God, or takes off the relish of spiritual things—whatever increases your authority of your body over your mind—that thing to you is sin.
>
> —John Wesley

DO NOT TRUST APPEARANCES

"Lord," Ananias answered, "I have heard many reports about
this man and all the harm he has done to your saints in
Jerusalem. And he has come here with authority from
the chief priests to arrest all who call on your name."
Acts 9:13–14

D.L. Moody left Northfield, Massachusetts, for Boston when he was seventeen. There he gave his life to Jesus Christ. He moved to Chicago and found success selling shoes. There Moody worked in the inner city evangelizing children through the YMCA. In 1860 he quit the shoe business to devote his life full-time to ministry.

A Chicago businessman recalls his first impression of Moody: "The first time I ever saw him was in a little shanty that had been abandoned by a saloonkeeper. He had managed to get possession of the place in order to hold a meeting that night. . . . When I came in, the first thing I saw was a heavy-set man standing up holding a small black boy in his arms. By the light of a few tallow candles he was trying to read to him the story of the prodigal son. . . . I thought, 'If the Lord can ever use such an instrument as that for his honor and glory, it will certainly astonish me!'

"After the meeting was over, Moody said to me. 'Mr. Reynolds, I have only one talent; I have no education, but I love the Lord Jesus Christ. I want to do something for him. Pray for me.'" Moody eventually preached to over 100 million people. At least one million of these made decisions for Jesus Christ.

Do you tend to judge others by their appearance? In prayer tell God that you are willing to be like Ananias and pray for others despite appearances.

There is no trusting appearances.

—Richard B. Sheridan

Day 112
EQUAL JUDGMENT

*You, therefore, have no excuse, you who pass judgment on
someone else, for at whatever point you judge the other, you
are condemning yourself, because you who pass judgment do
the same things. Now we know that God's judgment against
those who do such things is based on truth. So when you,
a mere man, pass judgment on them and yet do the same things,
do you think you will escape God's judgment?*
Romans 2:1–3

Ypres, Belgium, was the scene of three battles during
World War I. Severe fighting between the Allied forces who
held the city and the Germans who sought to capture it
resulted in over 250,000 casualties. In April, 1915, the second battle of Ypres was a stalemate. But the German army
had just developed a secret weapon and was eager to employ
it against their enemy.

At 5:00 P.M. on April 22 a fierce bombardment ripped
into the Allied lines releasing chlorine gas. French, Canadian,
and Algerian troops choked, vomited, and ran in terror with
the release of the gas. A breach of some four miles quickly
opened in the Allied lines. The Germans, surprised at the success of the gas attack, quickly advanced into the void. But the
German troops who led the charge into the breach were not
trained in gas warfare. They did not even possess gas masks.
They ran into their own chlorine gas and suffered the same
debilitating effects. The allies regrouped under British General
Smith-Dorrien. They placed wet handkerchiefs over their
mouths and noses and successfully repelled the German attack.

The same rules apply to all. But thanks be to God who
saves us through Jesus Christ. Do you pass judgment on others for something you also do? Today thank Christ that you
escaped His judgment because you accepted His mercy.

We should observe, therefore, how much self-love can blind people into making false judgments. The Jews judged correctly concerning the Gentiles; but when it concerned themselves, although they were equal in guilt, they would not admit that they were equally the subjects of condemnation.

—Robert Haldane

Day 113
THE GREATNESS OF PRAYER

Call to me and I will answer you and tell you great and unsearchable things you do not know.
Jeremiah 33:3

In 1490 Albrecht Dürer and Franz Knigstein were friends and struggling artists. Both were poor and worked to support themselves while they studied art. Work took much of their time. Advancement was slow. Finally they agreed to draw lots—one of them would work to support both of them while the other studied art. Albrecht won and went on to study while Franz worked to support them.

After Albrecht had finished his studies and had attained success he returned to his friend to keep his end of the bargain. But the years of hard labor had taken their toll on Franz's hands. They had become stiff and twisted from manual labor. Franz was no longer able to hold a brush.

One day Albrecht came upon Franz praying. With knees bent and gnarled hands folded Franz was asking for his friend's success. Albrecht was so moved by the scene that he sketched Franz's folded hands.

Five hundred years later Albrecht Dürer's work is featured in art museums of the world. No piece of his artwork is more loved than "The Praying Hands."

The efforts of greatness are fleeting. The Lord wants us to

seek Him with our whole heart. Jesus Christ wants to do great and immeasurable things in our lives. We may not be like Albrecht Dürer in art. But we can be like Franz Knigstein in prayer. Call upon Christ to do great and wonderful things through your petitions.

No man is greater than his prayer life.
—Leonard Ravenhill

Day 114
AN INTRODUCTION TO THE FATHER

In him and through faith in him we may approach God
with freedom and confidence. I ask you, therefore,
not to be discouraged because of my sufferings
for you, which are your glory.
Ephesians 3:12–13

Tad Lincoln was his father's best friend. "Tad," short for tadpole, was Abraham Lincoln's constant companion and was the only family member officially photographed with the president. Often the youngster would play in his father's office until he fell asleep. Lincoln would scoop him up in his arms and carry him to bed. Tad was called mischievous, open, loving, and loud. Lincoln would play tops with his young son, bounce him on his knee, and developed a secret "knock code" where Tad would identify himself at a closed door. It was Tad Lincoln who got his father to officially draft a "Presidential pardon" for the Thanksgiving turkey, a tradition which has carried on to this day.

One day a Kentucky delegation was waiting to see Lincoln. Tad approached them and asked, "Do you want to see Old Abe?" They laughed and replied, "Well, yes." Tad walked into his father's office and said "Papa, may I introduce some friends to you?" Lincoln answered, "Yes, Son." Tad then brought in the men who had been waiting. He formally introduced the gentlemen though they already were known by the president. Lincoln placed his son on his knee and gave him a kiss.

We have access to the Father because of His love for the Son. Jesus Christ has introduced us to the Father. Are you tentative in coming to the Lord in prayer? Today give thanks to Jesus that He has made it possible for you to confidently come to the Father.

> Give me a heart too brave to ask thee anything.
> —John Galsworthy

Day 115
BUILD ME CHILDREN

Fathers, do not exasperate your children; instead,
bring them up in the training and instruction of the Lord.
Ephesians 6:4

When he was fifty-seven years old General Douglas MacArthur had his first and only son. This boy brought out the gentleness in the general. Here is a prayer entitled "A Father's Prayer" which MacArthur wrote for his son:

Build me a son, O God, who will be strong enough to know when he is weak and brave enough to face himself when he is afraid; one who will be proud and unbending in honest defeat, but humble and gentle in victory. Build me a son whose wishes will not replace his actions—a son who will know thee, and that to know himself is the foundation stone of knowledge. . . .

Build me a son whose heart will be clear, whose goal will be high; a son who will master himself before he seeks to master others; one who will learn to laugh, yet never forget how to weep; one who will reach into the future, yet never forget the past, and after all these things are his, this I pray, enough sense of humor that he may always be serious yet never take himself too seriously. Give him humility so that he may always remember the simplicity of true greatness, the open mind of true wisdom, the meekness of true strength; then I, his father, will dare to whisper, "I have not lived in vain."

Are the young children in your life learning about the love of Jesus Christ? Today ask Christ for wisdom to train a child in the knowledge of God.

Christian nurture must begin with earliest childhood, with the beginning of the child's life.
—M. B. Riddle

Day 116
THE NEW CREATION

Therefore, if anyone is in Christ, he is a new creation;
the old has gone, the new has come!
2 Corinthians 5:17

George Bernard Shaw wrote a wonderful comedy called "Pygmalion" which is the basis for the musical favorite "My Fair Lady." It tells of Professor Henry Higgins who boasts that he can change the speech and manners of a Cockney flower girl into those of a duchess. This flower girl, Eliza Doolittle, becomes Higgins "human guinea pig." He takes her into his household to learn proper English. For her part Eliza wants to escape her poor background and hopes to work in a middle-class flower shop.

For weeks Eliza has difficulty learning a new accent. She is subjected to endless diction drills. With her we have all learned to say, "The rain in Spain falls mainly on the plain." Gradually Eliza's diction and manners are refined. Through her own will and Higgins' persistent teaching Eliza undergoes a beautiful change. She moves gracefully at a garden party and is presented as a lady at a formal reception. Her voice, her walk, her manners have all been transformed from a woman of the street to that of a lady of society. Eliza has not only developed an outward grace but also an inner beauty which is seen in her mature outlook on life.

When we accept Christ we become new creatures. Put aside your old ways of life. Today thank the Lord that He is transforming you into His image.

> When we are born again the Holy Spirit begins to work in us and there will come a time when there is not a bit of the old order left.
>
> —Oswald Sanders

Day 117
BOLL WEEVILS AND PROSPERITY

And we know that in all things God works for the good of those who love him, who have been called according to his purpose.
Romans 8:28

In 1915 a boll weevil infestation descended upon the cotton crops of the South. Crop damage exceeded $1 million that year. The farmers of Enterprise, Alabama, were as hard hit as any by the blight.

Meanwhile, George Washington Carver had been experimenting with peanuts. He knew their value. "Burn your cotton, plow under your fields and plant peanuts," he advised. Carver had this confidence because he had prayed to God: "Please, Mr. Creator, will you tell me why the peanut was made?" Carver then learned how to break the peanut down into starches, fats, sugars, and amino acids and how to make face powders, printer's ink, butter, shampoo, creosote, vinegar, soaps, and wood stains out of peanuts. Carver developed over 100 cooking recipes for peanuts.

The value of peanuts skyrocketed. Peanut farming proved to be twice as profitable as cotton farming without the risk of boll weevils. In 1919 the people of Enterprise erected a memorial in the center of the town's main street—a carved stone in the likeness of the boll weevil. The inscription reads, "Profound appreciation to the boll weevil and what it has done as a herald of prosperity."

The Lord often allows trials to unsettle our lives. Sometimes it takes a difficult time to redirect our lives to His purpose. Are you going through a difficult period in your life? Today thank Christ that not everything is good but can be used for good when placed in His hands.

> Everything is needful that he sends. Nothing is needful that he withholds.
>
> —John Newton

Day 118
THE EFFECTIVE INVITATION

He said to them: "It is not for you to know the times or dates the Father has set by his own authority. But you will receive power when the Holy Spirit comes on you; and you will be my witnesses in Jerusalem, and in all Judea and Samaria, and to the ends of the earth.
Acts 1:7–8

Alexander Whyte was the pastor at Free St. George's in Edinburgh, Scotland, from 1870 until 1916. He had a deep appreciation of God's grace to save sinners and this was reflected in his passionate preaching.

During Whyte's ministry a salesman by the name of Rigby traveled to Edinburgh regularly just to hear him preach.

Rigby often invited his business associates to accompany him to the services. One Sunday morning he asked a fellow to go to church with him. Reluctantly the man agreed. When this man heard Whyte's message he was so struck that he returned with Rigby to the evening service. That night he trusted Jesus Christ as his Savior.

The next morning Rigby walked past the home of Pastor Whyte and stopped to tell him how his message had affected his friend's life. When Whyte learned that his visitor's name was Rigby, he exclaimed, "You're the man I've wanted to see for years!" Quickly, Whyte went to his study and returned with a bundle of letters. He read Rigby some excerpts from the letters, all of them telling of changed lives. They were all men Rigby had brought to hear the gospel at Free St. George's Church.

We all can be friends to those who do not know the Savior. Like Rigby we can invite them to church. Today in prayer thank the Lord for this effective way to witness for Him.

Witnessing is the unfulfilled part of man's devotion.
—Mark Lee

Day 119
CHRISTIAN GROWTH

Brothers, I could not address you as spiritual but as worldly—mere infants in Christ. I gave you milk, not solid food, for you were not yet ready for it. Indeed, you are still not ready.
1 Corinthians 3:1–2

Justin Martyr, a second-century Palestinian, sampled the philosophies of Aristotle, Pythagoras, Plato, and others and concluded that they were empty. But he was impressed by Christians' devotion to God. An older believer explained to Justin that Jesus Christ is the fulfillment of Old Testament

137

prophesy and Justin gave his life to Christ.

Justin called Christianity the only true philosophy. To him faith in Jesus Christ and reason were inseparable. He saw his life and the lives of those around him change and so wrote: "We, who formerly delighted in fornication, now strive for purity. We who used magical arts, have dedicated ourselves to the good and eternal God. We who loved the acquisition of wealth more than all else, now bring what we have into a common stock and give to every one in need. We who hated and destroyed one another and on account of their different manners would not receive into our houses men of a different tribe now, since the coming of Christ, live familiarly with them. We pray for our enemies; we endeavor to persuade those who hate us unjustly to live conformably to the beautiful precepts of Christ, to the end that they may become partakers with us of the same joyful hope of a reward from God, the ruler of all."

Christians grow and change by taking in the Word and saying, "Yes," to Christ. Give thanks for the changes Christ has made in your life and ask Him to continue molding you into His image.

> The spiritual person is able to see the difference between what is of God and what is of man, what is of flesh and what is of the Spirit.
>
> —H. A. Ironside

HISTORIC ACTS

*Many have undertaken to draw up an account of the things
that have been fulfilled among us, just as they were handed
down to us by those who from the first were eyewitnesses and
servants of the word. Therefore, since I myself have carefully
investigated everything from the beginning, it seemed
good also to me to write an orderly account for you,
most excellent Theophilus.*
Luke 1:1–3

The great archaeologist Sir William Ramsay was educated at Aberdeen and Oxford and spent long vacations in Asia
Minor. He was trained in the German historical school of the
mid-nineteenth century and taught that the Book of Acts was
not historically accurate. He was firmly convinced of this and
set out to prove it.

But Ramsay researched the archaeological sites reported
in the Book of Acts. Eventually the evidence he uncovered
compelled him to reverse his beliefs. Ramsay's writings are in
agreement with the historical accuracy as reported in Luke's
gospel and the Book of Acts.

Ramsay said, "Luke is a historian of the first rank; not
merely are his statements of fact trustworthy; he is possessed of
the true historic sense; he fixes his mind on the idea and plan
that rules in the evolution of history, and proportions the scale
of his treatment to the importance of each incident. He seizes
the important and critical events and shows their true nature
at greater length, while he touches lightly or omits entirely
much that was valueless for his purpose. In short, this author
should be placed along with the very greatest of historians."

Luke and the other biblical authors were not trying to
write best-sellers. They were reporting the truth about Jesus
Christ. If a skeptic like Sir Ramsay was convinced of the accuracy of Luke's writing, shouldn't you likewise embrace the Bible?

Today in prayer thank Christ that you can depend on His word.

> How firm a foundation, ye saints of the Lord, is laid
> for your faith in his excellent Word! What more can
> he say than to you he hath said—to you, who for
> refuge to Jesus have fled?
>
> —K in *Rippon's Selection of Hymns,* 1787

Day 121
WORTH THE PAIN

That is why I am suffering as I am. Yet I am not ashamed,
because I know whom I have believed, and am convinced that
he is able to guard what I have entrusted to him for that day.
2 Timothy 1:12

One night when the medical student Roger Bannister was studying anatomy he wondered whether he could run a mile in under four minutes. It had never been done before.

Bannister, an Olympic sprinter, knew how much training this endeavor would require. And he had to keep up his medical studies. For months he trained for hours every day, followed a strict diet, and studied eight to ten hours a day.

Two pacesetters were running with him when Bannister took off at the gun. It was May, 1954, and he was running for the record. Bannister hit the first lap in 57.5 seconds and pushed hard to maintain pace on a slow track. He finished the second lap in 1:58.2. At the end of the third lap, Bannister's time was 3:00.5.

His body was screaming with pain and his step was beginning to falter. Bannister describes what happened during that last lap: "I said to myself, 'If you run until you collapse on that track, you're going to make this four-minute mile. If your knees hit the track, you're going to give everything you have, you're going to do it; you know you can. For eight months

140

you've trained. You can do it.' "

Bannister fought pain, sprinted down the backstretch, crossed the finish line, and fell into the arms of his friends. Time: 3:59.4.

Put your life into the hands of the living God who loves you more than you can imagine. Any pain you endure for His name will be erased by His joy.

> I know not how the Spirit moves, convincing men of
> sin, revealing Jesus through the Word, creating faith
> in him.
>   But "I know who I have believed, and am per-
> suaded that he is able to keep that which I've com-
> mitted unto him against that day."
> —Daniel W. Whittle

Day 122
WHAT IS WHITER THAN SNOW?

Again Jesus said, "Simon son of John, do you truly love me?"
He answered, "Yes, Lord, you know that I love you."
Jesus said, "Take care of my sheep."
John 21:16

Queen Victoria dedicated her life to Christ at a young age and tried to lead Great Britain in a godly manner. Such was not the case of her oldest son Edward, Prince of Wales. As Lady Warwick said, "The Prince was so tireless in pursuit of pleasure that he and his friends turned night into day." Edward was known as a habitual gambler at both horses and cards. He had numerous love affairs and fathered at least one child out of wedlock. Though Queen Victoria once said that "England has become great and happy by knowledge of the true God through Jesus Christ," Edward apparently did not share his mother's high calling to responsible leadership.

Once Edward went to visit a country nobleman. His host's young daughter climbed up on his knee and quickly charmed the prince. After a few moments she inquired, "Do you like to make guesses?" "Yes," the prince replied with a smile. "Please, sir, can you tell me what is whiter than snow?" Unprepared for such a strange remark, the royal visitor looked confused and finally gave up. The young child with a sweet rebuke in her eyes, said, "Oh, Prince, I'm sorry, but every soul washed in Jesus' blood should know that he's been made whiter than snow!"

Leadership not only requires a commitment to the Savior but a realization that those being led are precious in God's sight. Today give thanks that you are Christ's, made whiter than snow with His blood.

> The ministry of the gospel is the poorest of trades and the noblest of callings.
>
> —Theodore Cuyler

Day 123
OUT OF SIGHT AND IN YOUR PRAYERS

I urge, then, first of all, that requests, prayers, intercession and thanksgiving be made for everyone—for kings and all those in authority, that we may live peaceful and quiet lives in all godliness and holiness. This is good, and pleases God our Savior, who wants all men to be saved and to come to a knowledge of the truth.
1 Timothy 2:1–4

In 1876, the Scottish missionary Mary Slessor was sent to a part of West Africa where no colonial power was in control. She ministered in an area where witchcraft and barbarous customs of human sacrifice were common. Her life was in constant danger and she was once asked what prayer meant to her. "My life is one long, daily, hourly record of answered prayer for physical health. . .for guidance given marvelously, for errors and dangers averted, for enmity to the gospel subdued, for food provided at the exact hour needed, for everything that goes to make up life and my poor service. I can testify with a full and often wonder-stricken awe that I believe God answers prayer. I know God answers prayer. If you are ever inclined to pray for a missionary, do it at once, wherever you are. Perhaps she may be in great peril at the moment. Once I had to deal with a crowd of warlike men in the compound, and I got the strength to face them because I felt that someone was praying for me just then."

In our fast-paced world we often take the attitude, out of sight, out of mind. But the Lord wants you to remember not only those who are in your immediate lives, but also the leaders of your government, missionaries abroad, and leaders in your church. In your prayers today remember at least one person who is far away.

> Remember that God is our only trust. To Him, I commend you. . . . My son, neglect not the duty of secret prayer.
> —Mary Washington in a parting letter to her son,
> George Washington

THE WORD'S WISDOM AND THE SPIRIT'S TACT

When Arioch, the commander of the king's guard, had gone out to put to death the wise men of Babylon, Daniel spoke to him with wisdom and tact. He asked the king's officer, "Why did the king issue such a harsh decree?" Arioch then explained the matter to Daniel. At this, Daniel went in to the king and asked for time, so that he might interpret the dream for him.

Daniel 2:14–16

Alexander Whyte ministered to the Lord in Scotland. His habit was to ask the Lord each morning to give him a specific Scripture verse for the day that would be useful as he talked to people about Christ. One morning the Holy Spirit impressed upon his heart the words of Micah 7:18, "He delighteth in mercy" (KJV). He went into many homes sharing that helpful message.

Late in the afternoon Whyte stopped at the office of a promi-nent attorney in Edinburgh who was also a Christian. After Whyte had talked with him for a while the man brushed his pen and paper to one side. Looking into Whyte's face he said, "Have you any word for an old sinner like me?" Whyte was surprised, but after a moment's pause the Holy Spirit reminded him of his text for the day. "He delighteth in mercy," the minister replied and saying little else, left the office. The next morning at breakfast a note was delivered from the lawyer with this testimony: "Thank God for that word of Scripture you gave me yesterday; it was just what I needed. I will never doubt him again!"

Christ has given us His Word for good judgment and the Holy Spirit to express His Word. Do you rely on both the Word of God and the Holy Spirit? Today ask the Lord to give you a special Scripture to share with others and remember to ask for the grace to express it in the Holy Spirit.

Tact is the knack of making a point without making
an enemy.

—Howard W. Newton

Day 125
A KING'S AWE

*In my vision at night I looked, and there before me was one
like a son of man, coming with the clouds of heaven. . . .
He was given authority, glory and sovereign power;
all peoples, nations and men of every language worshiped him.
His dominion is an everlasting dominion that will not pass away,
and his kingdom is one that will never be destroyed.*
Daniel 7:13–15

King George II of Great Britain ruled from 1727 to
1760 and was the last king of England to appear on a battlefield
when the British fought the French in the War of Austrian
Succession. During his reign he survived an armed rebellion,
two threats of invasion, and three parliamentary crises. Though
he was not well-loved throughout Britain, he did command
everyone's respect.

One of the patrons of King George's court was George
Frideric Handel, regarded as Britain's finest composer. In 1741,
the king commissioned him to write the "Messiah." In three
weeks Handel wrote this great composition. At its premiere performance in Dublin, Ireland, over seven hundred people packed
into the hall. King George, one of the most powerful men in the
world, was in the audience. The king was deeply moved by the
words of Scripture sung in the "Messiah." At the "Hallelujah
Chorus" he could not restrain himself any longer. King George
stood up and with him stood everyone in the hall in reverence
to the King of Kings, Jesus Christ.

If someone famous walked into your room right now you
probably would be surprised and awed. And yet the King of

Kings has His eyes on you this moment. Today in prayer praise Jesus Christ that He has an imperishable Kingdom and that everyone will stand in awe of Him one day.

King of Kings and Lord of Lords, Hallelujah! Hallelujah!
—George Frideric Handel

Day 126
LISTEN TO THE WORD

He humbled you, causing you to hunger and then feeding you with manna, which neither you nor your fathers had known, to teach you that man does not live on bread alone but on every word that comes from the mouth of the LORD.
Deuteronomy 8:3

Isobel Kuhn was a missionary in China. Her mission was located on the east bank of the Salween River. During the early days of World War II the Japanese were advancing throughout China. The Japanese guns could be heard throughout the day from Kuhn's mission house and their fires seen in the night. A young man knocked on the mission's door. "Teacher," he said, "the Japanese are coming. Mama says you are to go to the House of Grace."

Instead of bolting in fear, Isobel suggested reading Scripture. An associate read Psalm 91. When he came to the words, "Thou shalt not be afraid of. . .the terror by night," Isobel interrupted. "That's enough, Charlie," she said, "Good night." The whole village was in turmoil at the sound of gunfire. But Isobel heard God's voice and went to sleep. In the morning she learned that someone from the east bank of the river had stolen the ferryboat. The natural result was gunfire.

In the midst of gunfire and alarm Isobel Kuhn's confidence was in the Lord and the Word. He developed in her a boldness to push through frightening situations despite her fears.

Often in prayer we treat God as if He were a telephone answering machine. We expect to do all the talking. As you pray today take time to listen and hear what God has to say in the Word.

> Reading God's word regularly, and praying habitually in the secret place of the most high puts one where he is absolutely safe from the attacks of the enemy of souls and guarantees him salvation and final victory, through the overcoming power of the lamb.
> —E. M. Bounds

Day 127
LOVE THE NEIGHBOR NEXT DOOR

"The most important [commandment]," answered Jesus,
"is this: 'Hear, O Israel, the Lord our God, the Lord is one.
Love the Lord your God with all your heart and with all your
soul and with all your mind and with all your strength.'
The second is this: 'Love your neighbor as yourself.'
There is no commandment greater than these."
Matthew 12:29–31

In the late 1950's, David Wilkerson ministered to gang members in Brooklyn, New York; in an area replete with drug addicts and prostitutes. Wilkerson saw little results at first. One of the most feared gang leaders was Nicky Cruz. This man was so bad that he had once knifed his own brother. Resistant and bitter to Wilkerson, Nicky once pulled a switchblade on the urban missionary and said, "I'm gonna cut you, preacherman!" With much more than just quick wit, Wilkerson replied, "Nicky, you can cut me into a thousand pieces and each one of them will say 'I love you!' "

Nicky Cruz was disarmed. He had never encountered someone who could love him. Cruz eventually gave his life to Jesus Christ. He then led his entire gang to Christ and they surrendered their weapons to police. Nicky Cruz today continues to lead men and women out of gangs and to the Lord Jesus Christ.

The Lord doesn't want your things, He wants you. He wants your heart, soul, mind, and strength focused on Him. David Wilkerson could never have gone to Brooklyn to minister unless He loved Christ with a passion. Today focus on loving Jesus Christ. Then loving your neighbor won't seem quite so difficult.

To love the whole world for me is no chore; my only real problem's my neighbor next door.
—C. W. Vanderbergh

Day 128
TRAIN FOR ETERNITY

Have nothing to do with godless myths and old wives' tales; rather, train yourself to be godly. For physical training is of some value, but godliness has value for all things, holding promise for both the present life and the life to come.
1 Timothy 4:7–8

The movie *Chariots of Fire* revolves around the real lives of two athletes who competed in the 1924 Summer Olympics in Paris. Eric Liddell and Harold Abrahams were sprinters. To Abrahams, running and winning were necessities of life. They were his ticket to a better life. He later became an attorney, radio broadcaster, and sports administrator, and served as chairman of the British Amateur Athletics Board from 1968 to 1975. He wrote extensively about sports, in particular the Olympics.

Liddell trained hard for the Olympics but the Lord was his priority. During the Paris Olympics Liddell caused a stir when he refused to run the 100-meter race on Sunday. Instead he chose to run the 400-meter race on a weekday. He won the gold. Eric Liddell went to China as a missionary after the 1924 Olympics. When asked later if he missed competitive running, especially in the 1928 Olympics he replied, "Of course it is natural for a chap to think over all that sometimes, but I'm glad I'm at the work I'm engaged in now. A fellow's life counts for far more at this than the other. Not a corruptible crown, but an incorruptible, you know."

Will the fruits of your labor last for eternity? Training and discipline are good. They are even better if your aim is godliness. Today ask the Lord how you can train for the incorruptible crown.

> This crown, which believers shall wear, is laid up for them; they have it not at present, for here they are but heirs; they have it not in possession, and yet it is sure.
> —Matthew Henry

Day 129
DON'T RUSH TO JUDGE

Therefore judge nothing before the appointed time; wait till the Lord comes. He will bring to light what is hidden in darkness and will expose the motives of men's hearts. At that time each will receive his praise from God.
1 Corinthians 4:5

On May 9, 1957, 1st Lt. David Steeves left San Francisco on a routine flight to Selma, Alabama. His T-33 jet trainer never arrived. An intense search was mounted in the Colorado Rocky Mountains where Steeves' plane was last spotted. The day before Mother's Day the Air Force declared Steeves dead and informed his mother.

On July 1 David Steeves emerged from the Sierra Mountains. He reported that his jet had blown up while in flight and he had parachuted to safety. With severely sprained ankles and without food Steeves crawled for fifteen days until he stumbled onto a deserted ranger's cabin. There he convalesced. Steeves then walked forty miles out of the wilderness.

Soon rumors raged about the missing jet. Steeves had either sold it to Mexico or given it to the Russians. Without explanation the *Saturday Evening Post* backed out on a ten thousand dollar offer for Steeves' story. Steeves' personal life was destroyed but the Air Force cleared him of wrongdoing.

Steeves spent much of the rest of his life searching the area of the crash. He never found the T-33 before he died in 1965.

In 1977 Boy Scouts hiking in Kings Canyon National Park came across wreckage. The Air Force confirmed it was Steeves' T-33. It had exploded in flight.

Where facts are absent, rumor often substitutes. Do you judge others before the facts are in? Today give thanks to Christ that one day His light will reveal the motives of everyone's heart.

If you judge people you have no time to love them.
—Mother Teresa

Day 130
HOLD DOWN THE HOME FRONT

"For this reason a man will leave his father and mother
and be united to his wife, and the two will become one flesh."
This is a profound mystery—but I am talking about Christ
and the church. However, each one of you also must love his
wife as he loves himself, and the wife must respect her husband.
Ephesians 5:31–33

Douglas MacArthur II, nephew of the famous World War II general, served in the State Department as a principal planner for overseas trips when John Foster Dulles was Secretary of State. One evening these two were working late prior to an overseas trip. MacArthur was putting the finishing touches on briefing books and arranging final details for the trip. Just after eight o'clock MacArthur left Dulles' office. Then Dulles' telephone rang and Dulles picked up his extension at the same time his secretary did. On the line was MacArthur's wife Warvie, known as a woman who wasn't afraid to speak her mind. She proceeded to give Dulles' secretary an earful. She was furious about her husband's long hours. She was trying to track him down and decided to give the first person who answered a telephone her opinion of the intolerable working conditions at the State Department: "I'll tell you where MacArthur is. MacArthur is where MacArthur always is, weekdays, Saturdays, Sundays, and nights—in that office!"

Dulles quietly put down his telephone and called MacArthur. He gave him this terse order: "Boy, I insist that you leave your office right away. Your home front is crumbling!"

The home is where the greatest intimacy and the greatest problems can occur. That is why we must keep it a priority in our life with Jesus Christ. Are you neglecting the home front? Today give thanks to Christ for your family and ask Him how to strengthen it for His glory.

In the family you've got the greatest intimacy, the greatest potential for fulfillment. Christ wants us to make the family a model of what He's able to do in human experience. The family is responsible for reaching out to society, getting outside itself and offering Christ to others.

—Howard Hendricks

Day 131
THE PARABLE OF THE HARP

Finally, all of you, live in harmony with one another; be sympathetic, love as brothers, be compassionate and humble.
1 Peter 3:8

Here is a contemporary parable: A king in an ancient palace hired a famous musician to build a beautiful harp. Members of the king's household would gather in the evenings to listen to the enchanting music of this harp. After the king died, his son, the prince, brought his family to live in the castle and hired a musician to play the harp. But the harp was out of tune. No one could be found with the skill to tune it. So the prince had the beautiful harp covered and declared it a useless ruin.

One night an old man came to the castle seeking shelter. The prince took the stranger in. During the evening meal the old man looked at the harp and asked why it had been covered. The prince explained that the harp had lost its tune and no one could tune it. "May I try?" the visitor asked. The prince agreed. Soon the sound of enchanting music filled the room again. The prince asked the stranger, "How could you tune the harp when no one else could?" The old man smiled and said, "I am the one who made this harp."

You are like that beautiful harp—but you were created by

God. Sometimes the world can knock you out of tune. Only Jesus Christ can make us again as God designed us. Today in prayer, ask Christ to retune your life so you can show His love to others.

> Unity will only come when Christians are humble and bold enough to lay hold on the unity already given in Christ and to take it more seriously than their own self importance and sin.
> —C. E. B. Cranfield

Day 132
THE LORD IS NOT SLOW, JUST PATIENT

But do not forget this one thing, dear friends: With the Lord a day is like a thousand years, and a thousand years are like a day. The Lord is not slow in keeping his promise, as some understand slowness. He is patient with you, not wanting anyone to perish, but everyone to come to repentance.
2 Peter 3:8–9

In 1853 a mission society discussed closing a station in Ongole, India, because only ten people had been won to Christ in fifteen years. Ongole is in the union state of Andhra Pradesh, the fifth largest state in India, located in the southeast part of the country. Over 167 languages are spoken in that area. Only two men petitioned for the continued support of this work. They argued that these believers must not be abandoned. Someone called them the "Lone Star" church of India.

Samuel F. Smith, author of the song "My Country 'Tis of Thee," was a member of that mission board. When considering this situation Smith wrote: "Shine on, Lone Star, in grief and tears, and sad reverses oft baptized; shine on amid thy founders' fears; lone stars in heaven are not despised."

He read this poem to his colleagues and as a result they unanimously voted to continue the work. Because of this decision God worked and hundreds of people in India became Christians. Thirty years later the Ongole church had grown to 15,000 members. Today three and a half percent of the population of Ongole is Christian. The Lord has rewarded the efforts of all who have patiently labored in this region.

In a hurry-up world the Lord is patiently working out His plan. Do you ever feel like the Lord has quit working? Today give thanks for God's patience and rejoice that Christ is working and waiting for everyone to come to repentance.

> There is no succession of time with God; no past, no future. He dwells in the eternal present, as I am.
> —F. B. Meyer

Day 133
LIVINGSTONE AND STANLEY

Dear friend, do not imitate what is evil but what is good.
Anyone who does what is good is from God.
Anyone who does what is evil has not seen God.
Demetrius is well spoken of by everyone—
and even by the truth itself. We also speak well of him,
and you know that our testimony is true.
3 John 11–12

Henry M. Stanley was a reporter employed by the *New York Herald*. His task was to find Dr. David Livingstone, a well-known missionary to Africa, an accomplished explorer, and the first European to see Victoria Falls. After his wife's death Livingstone threw himself into his life's work in the interior of Africa. Last seen in 1865, he was presumed dead.

In 1871 Stanley finally found Livingstone on the shores

of Lake Tanganyika in today's Tanzania. For months Stanley followed Livingstone and tried to persuade the fifty-eight-year-old missionary to return to England.

During this time Stanley wrote: "Had my soul been brass, and my heart of tin, the powers of my head surely compelled me to recognize, with due honor, the Spirit of goodness which manifested itself in him. Had there been anything of the Pharisee or the hypocrite in him, or had I but traced a grain of meanness or guile in him, I had surely turned away a skeptic. But my everyday study of him, during health and sickness, deepened my reverence and increased my esteem. He was, in short, consistently noble, upright, pious, and manly all the days of my companionship with him."

David Livingstone followed Jesus Christ. Over 100 years after his death Livingstone's reputation is that of a man who loved both God and humanity. He would go anywhere to share the good news about Jesus Christ. Who are your role models? Are they men and women who place Christ first? Today in prayer ask the Lord to send to you a person who can be such an example to you.

It is well said, "Everyone is born an original and dies a copy."

—*Decision Magazine*

Day 134
CHRISTIAN FREEDOM

It is for freedom that Christ has set us free. Stand firm, then, and do not let yourselves be burdened again by a yoke of slavery.
Galatians 5:1

Henrietta Mears is called the mother of Sunday school. Born in Fargo, North Dakota, in 1890, Mears surrendered her life to Christ at the age of seven. After graduating at the top of her class from the University of Minnesota in 1913 she taught chemistry at a nearby high school.

After teaching in public high schools for fourteen years Mears joined the staff of First Presbyterian Church in Hollywood, California, as director of Christian education. Through revolutionary teaching methods and curriculum the Sunday school attendance jumped from four hundred to more than six thousand. With Cyrus Nelson, Mears founded Gospel Light Publications in 1933 to distribute her curriculum worldwide. In 1939 she founded Forest Home Conference Center in southern California —a place for church youth to enjoy "happy memories and high points of decision."

Henrietta Mears knew the secret of true freedom. She wanted her students to know it too. "A bird is free in the air," she told them. "Place a bird in the water and he has lost his liberty. A fish is free in the water but leave him on the sand and he perishes. He is out of his realm. . . . The Christian is free when he does the will of God and is obedient to God's command. This is as natural a realm for God's child as the water is for the fish."

Do you use your freedom to live for God or for yourself? Today thank Jesus Christ for the freedom He purchased for you with His precious blood.

> Most successful football players are free to perform at their best only when they know what the expectations are, where the limits stand. I see this as a biblical principle that also applies to life, a principle our society as a whole has forgotten; you can't enjoy true freedom without limits.
>
> —Tom Landry

Day 135
THE CONSCIENCE INFORMS
AGAINST ITSELF

Let us draw near to God with a sincere heart in full assurance
of faith, having our hearts sprinkled to cleanse us from a guilty
conscience and having our bodies washed with pure water.
Hebrews 10:22

This is the story of Ibycus and the cranes:

Ibycus was a pious Greek poet on his way to the chariot races and musical competitions held in Corinth. He was alone but for a flock of cranes overhead taking the same course in their migration to a southern climate. "Good luck to you, my friends, I take your company for a good omen," called Ibycus.

He entered a narrow pass in the road—two robbers accosted him. Realizing that his death was close at hand, he called, "Cranes, take up my cause since no voice but yours answers to my cry." So saying, he died.

The crowd at the coliseum was buzzing with talk of the recent murder. A chorus sang tribute to Ibycus "Happy is the man who keeps his heart pure from guilt and crime! But woe to him who has done the secret murder." Just then the flock of cranes flew over and a cry burst forth from an uppermost bench: "Look! Look! My friend, there are the cranes of Ibycus!"

"Of Ibycus! Did he say?" the crowd wondered. "The murderer has informed against himself. Seize the man who uttered that cry and the other to whom he spoke!" Pale with terror the murderers went before the judge, confessed their crime, and suffered punishment.

God has cleansed us from guilt through Jesus Christ. Are you feeling guilty of any sin? Today in prayer confess your sins. God desires you to have a clean conscience.

> No flattery can heal a bad conscience, so no slander
> can hurt a good one.
>
> —Thomas Watson

Day 136
WE DIED TO SIN

What shall we say, then? Shall we go on sinning so that grace
may increase? By no means! We died to sin;
how can we live in it any longer?
Romans 6:1–2

The Siberian Grigory Novykh was a charismatic young man. A mystic and occult figure, his name in Russian was Rasputin—Debauched One.

Rasputin attracted followers by demonstrating prophetic powers and a gift of healing. He comforted the Russian czar's hemophiliac son and thus established close ties to the Russian throne. His followers saw him as a living saint.

Rasputin believed that the best way to be close to God was through repentance and the best way to feel repentance was to engage in outlandish sins. So he took many mistresses, frequented brothels, and deadened the passions of his flesh through alcohol. When his lusts were temporarily satisfied Rasputin assumed the piety of a monk. He totally lacked discipline and was unable to read, write, or even utter a coherent prayer.

Nikolai Arsenev wrote: "What [Rasputin] preached was excess, and an orgiastic philosophy, a mixture of paganism and the most sacred Christian mysteries, an ecstasy, a deliberate frenzy, both sensual and at the same time religious, or at least quasi-religious."

The Lord offers salvation by grace. But He desires to walk with us so that we can experience the joy of grace. Some

Christians feel that the Lord loves them only after they repent. Today ask Christ that you might love grace and hate sin.

> The guilt of sin remains on that man in whom the love of sin remains.
>
> —Charles Spurgeon

Day 137
SUFFERING AND REWARD

Then he said to them all: "If anyone would come after me, he must deny himself and take up his cross daily and follow me."
Luke 9:23–24

Giuseppe Garibaldi was an Italian patriot who helped unify Italy. Twice he was a leader for Italian unification and twice he had to flee in exile. During the first exile Garibaldi learned guerrilla warfare in the jungles of South America. A reporter who interviewed him during this period was surprised how poorly Garibaldi lived. He only had one candle in a makeshift hut and he could easily carry all of his possessions. Following his second exile in 1859 Garibaldi returned to Italy and raised a private army to fight against Austria. It was called the Redshirt Army and numbered over one thousand volunteers. Using guerrilla tactics they defeated the larger Austrian army. One day while Garibaldi was recruiting volunteers for the war he approached a group of young men who were standing on a street corner. He asked them if they would like to enlist in his cause. "What do you offer?" they asked.

"Offer?" replied Garibaldi. "I offer you hardship, hunger, rags, thirst, sleepless nights, long marches, privations innumerable, and finally victory in the noblest cause that ever confronted you!" Many men followed Garibaldi. They not only repulsed the Austrian invasion but also formed the first central government in Italy since Roman times.

Christ offers us the cross. But in the end we will be with Him in glory. Is the thought of picking up a cross unappealing? Today in prayer thank Christ that He rewards those who follow Him.

> What we give up for Christ we gain. What we keep
> back for ourselves is our real loss.
>
> —J. Hudson Taylor

Day 138
HE SERVED SINNERS

But you are not to be like that. Instead, the greatest among
you should be like the youngest, and the one who rules like
the one who serves. For who is greater, the one who is at the
table or the one who serves? Is it not the one who is at the table?
But I am among you as one who serves.
Luke 22:26–27

Booker T. Washington was born a slave in Franklin, Virginia, in 1856. After emancipation he paid his way through the Hampton Normal and Agricultural Institute in Virginia by working as a janitor. He went on to become president of the Tuskegee Institute in Alabama and one of the most respected black men in turn-of-the-century America.

One winter day while visiting New York, Washington was struggling to get to Grand Central Railway Station. The winter wind blew fiercely and the rain blinded him as he lugged his suitcases toward the terminal. He had to pause often and rest to regain his strength before trudging on.

He was at the point of collapse when a man appeared by his side, took the suitcases, and said, "We're going the same way. You look as if you could use some help." When they reached the shelter of the station Washington asked, "Please, sir, what is your name?" The man replied, "The name, my friend, is Roosevelt. Teddy Roosevelt." Roosevelt was then governor of New York, formerly the leader of the Rough Riders of Spanish-American War fame. A friendship began that day when a governor carried the bags of a weary traveler.

Is there anyone you can encourage along life's way? Are there people you can't help because you feel they are beneath you? Today thank Christ that He served sinners and gave His life for sin.

It is ours to say what David's followers said to their master: "We are your servants, ready to do whatever my Lord the King commands."

—W. H. Griffith Thomas

Day 139
THE STEPS OF FAITH

Why not? Because they pursued it not by faith but as if it were by works. They stumbled over the "stumbling stone."
Romans 9:32

Phillips Brooks graduated from Harvard University at nineteen years of age. He had a slight speech impediment and the school's president said that he could be successful in almost anything except as a preacher. But the Lord is strong when we are weak. Brooks went on to become one of the most eloquent ministers in America. He said:

"There is no sun that lights me, but I know upon the other side there is light; and as I go I stumble over ugly roots that trip me up. . . . The obstacles are the incidents. But now I am up to the top! There billows the sun before me and I am illumined by his glory.

"Now, that is just the way with Christians. It is not the experience of sin, it is not the conviction and wretchedness of sin that is the object of the Christian life. The soul humbled under its sins has only just reached the threshold of the new Christian experience. I beg you to understand this, my dear friends. . .because this is what gives a glorious and triumphant tone to Christian experience. It is the recognition of the life of Jesus Christ as the pattern of the life into which we have to be shaped by our continued obedience to him."

If we must stumble over something then let it be a non-essential object of life. Let's always focus on Christ. Today in prayer thank Christ that we can place our faith in Him.

> The steps of faith fall on the seeming void and find rock beneath.
>
> —John Greenleaf Whittier

Day 140
THE WORK OF PRAYER

They all joined together constantly in prayer, along with the women and Mary the mother of Jesus, and with his brothers.
Acts 1:14

Andrew Murray was born in Cape Town, South Africa, in 1828. His father was a Scottish Presbyterian who served a Dutch Reformed Church. His mother was of French Huguenot and Lutheran extraction. This diverse background made Murray an ecumenical preacher who focused on Jesus Christ. Ordained at age twenty Murray served numerous churches throughout South Africa. He promoted missions within South Africa and to the Transvaal and Malawi tribes. He is best known as a writer—*Abide in Christ, With Christ in the School of Prayer*, and *Waiting on God* are all classic works instructing Christians how to deepen their prayer life.

A woman once came to Murray with a problem: She couldn't pray. He said, "Why, then, do you not try this? As you go to your inner chamber, however cold and dark your heart may be, do not try in your own might to force yourself into the right attitude. Bow before Him and tell Him that He sees in what a sad state you are, and that your only hope is in Him. Trust Him, with a childlike trust, to have mercy upon you, and wait upon Him. You have nothing—He has everything." The woman followed His advice and discovered that her trust in Christ's love helped her pray even when prayer did not come easily.

We can let the Lord do the work of prayer through us. Bend your knee, trust in Him, and wait upon Him. Give thanks to Christ that you can come to him always.

> May he give us a large and strong heart to believe
> what mighty influence our prayers can exert.
> —Andrew Murray

Day 141
HOW TO HAVE NO FRIENDS

When he came to Jerusalem, he tried to join the disciples, but they were all afraid of him, not believing that he really was a disciple. But Barnabas took him and brought him to the apostles. He told them how Saul on his journey had seen the Lord and that the Lord had spoken to him, and how in Damascus he had preached fearlessly in the name of Jesus.
Acts 9:26–27

Charles M. Schwab was an innovative entrepreneur who helped spark the growth of the steel industry in the United States. He was an unschooled, untrained laborer but by age nineteen became an assistant manager of the Edgar Thomson Steel Works in Braddock, Pennsylvania. He effectively improved labor and community relations and boosted steel productivity through technological advancements. By age thirty-five Schwab was president of the Carnegie Steel Company.

In his seventies Schwab was a victim of a nuisance lawsuit. He could have settled for a fraction of the amount named but refused to do so. He let the case run its course, won it easily, and before leaving spoke to the court:

"I'd like to say, here, in a court of law, and speaking as an old man, that nine-tenths of my troubles are traceable to my being kind to others. Look, you young people; if you want to steer away from trouble, be hard-boiled. Be quick with a good loud no to anyone and everyone. If you follow this rule, you'll be seldom molested as you tread life's pathway. Except," the industrial giant paused, a broad smile lit his kindly features, "except you'll have no friends, you'll be lonely and you won't have any fun!"

Jesus befriended the unpopular and the unlovely. Do you shy away from certain types of people? Today in prayer ask Christ to bring someone into your life to whom you can show Christian love.

The true friend is one who is faithful in adversity and who abides with us in the darkness of night.
—Clarence E. Macartney

Day 142
THE NAMES OF GOD

All the prophets testify about him that everyone who believes in him receives forgiveness of sins through his name.
Acts 10:43

William Shakespeare wrote in *Romeo and Juliet:* "What's in a name? That which we call a rose by any other name would smell as sweet." Although the name by which a place or thing is called may be insignificant, a person's name is significant because it is a vital part of his or her identity. In ancient times, a person's name represented his character or described his nature.

God reveals Himself through His many names and titles. Like sparkling diamonds the names of God reveal the many facets of His nature, character, and activities to help us better understand Him.

To Moses, God revealed His eternal, unchanging nature through the name "I Am that I Am." The name Jesus means "Jehovah saves." This indicates His special role as Savior. The name Immanuel reminds us that God is with us. King David experienced the Lord as Shepherd and the prodigal son of the parable experienced God as Father. The Anglo-Saxons reflected the goodness of the Lord in their name for Him. They called Him God, a shortened version of the word good. H. L. Willmington, in his *Book of Bible Lists,* catalogs 117 scriptural names for Jesus.

God has forgiven our sins through the precious name of Jesus Christ. Today in prayer consider the names of the Triune God. Give thanks for all they mean in your experiences of Him.

> If we believe in Him we shall all be justified by Him as our righteousness.
>
> —Matthew Henry

Day 143
CARE FOR THE GOOD OF OTHERS

"Everything is permissible"—but not everything is beneficial.
"Everything is permissible"—but not everything is constructive.
Nobody should seek his own good, but the good of others.
1 Corinthians 10:23–24

Booker T. Washington was born a slave in Virginia. From work in salt mills and coal mines he rose to become one of the leading educators at the turn of the century. He founded the Tuskegee Institute in 1881, a center of learning and agricultural training. He was a confidant and advisor to Andrew Carnegie, John D. Rockefeller and President Theodore Roosevelt. Booker T. Washington taught about the dignity, necessity, and beauty of work.

When he was still a young slave boy in Virginia he wore a tow shirt. Such a shirt was made from refuse flax—extremely coarse and stiff. The fibrous flax made cloth an instrument of torture with a thousand little pinpoints pricking the flesh. After a tow shirt was worn for six weeks it became comfortably broken in. Little Booker was in misery wearing his first shirt. His body was continually being scratched. Then, Booker later wrote, "My brother John, who is several years older than I am, performed one of the most generous acts that I ever heard of one slave relative doing for another. On several occasions when I was being forced to wear a new flax shirt, he generously agreed to wear it for several days, until it was broken-in." John did this silently, under no other compulsion than the love for his brother.

Christ endured the pain of the cross on our behalf. Likewise we should seek the good of others. Today in prayer give thanks for Christ's example of love and ask to know how to seek good for others.

> You are placed amidst the delightful liberties and resources of your Father's home, without grudging and without doubt. But you are placed there not simply to enjoy, but to use; not only to be free, but to have the privilege of contributing to the freedom of others around you.
>
> —H. C. G. Moule

Day 144
TRUST IN CHRIST

In God, whose word I praise, in God I trust; I will
not be afraid. What can mortal man do to me?
Psalm 56:4

John Wesley started his ministry when he was twenty-five years old. For the next ten years his was not a very fruitful ministry. Even though he had intellectual conviction, Wesley had not made a personal commitment to Jesus Christ. The Spirit of God started his work on May 24, 1738, while Wesley was in London visiting St. Paul's Cathedral. He was restless and listened carefully to the anthem that was sung. In his journal he wrote about the words in the hymn: "The phrase, 'trust in the Lord' (repeated constantly throughout) seized me. Trust, trust, trust; I would; I must; I could think of nothing else." That evening at a prayer meeting at Aldersgate Street, the words from Martin Luther's preface to the Book of Romans touched John Wesley and he gave his life to Jesus Christ.

Years later, he wrote the following prayer which helps the believer to both give thanks to Christ and to ask the Lord for trust in His Word:

"I advise everyone before he reads the Scriptures to use this or the like prayer: 'Blessed Lord, who hast caused all holy scriptures to be written for our learning, grant that we may in such wise hear them, read, mark, learn, and inwardly digest them, that by patience and comfort of thy holy word, we may embrace and ever hold fast the blessed hope of everlasting life, which thou hast given us in our Savior Jesus Christ.' "

Trust in Christ. You can only follow Him when you walk in the Spirit and are guided by His Word. Do you find it difficult to trust fully in Christ for all aspects of your life? Today in prayer make John Wesley's prayer your prayer. Ask Christ that His Word may fully penetrate your life so you can trust in Him.

"Trust in the Lord." There is something touching about the simplicity of this statement.

—H. C. Leupold

Day 145
THE HANDLE ON YOUR HEART

I pray that out of his glorious riches he may strengthen you
with power through his Spirit in your inner being,
so that Christ may dwell in your hearts through faith.
And I pray that you, being rooted and established in love,
may have power, together with all the saints,
to grasp how wide and long and high
and deep is the love of Christ, and to know this
love that surpasses knowledge—that you may be filled
to the measure of all the fullness of God.
Ephesians 3:16–19

The English painter William Holman Hunt was born in London in 1827 and entered the schools of the Royal Academy in 1844. In 1848 he was a principal founder of the Pre-Raphaelite Brotherhood which protested low standards in British art. These artists turned from the Royal Academy's style of painting and pledged themselves to paint accurately and faithfully from nature in precise detail. Hunt visited the Holy Land three times to study the historical and natural settings and lighting for his religious paintings.

Hunt's best-known religious painting is *The Light of the World* (1853). In it Christ, dressed in royal robes, is shown in a garden at midnight, holding a lantern in his left hand, and knocking on a heavily paneled door with his right. This painting is rich in spiritual symbolism because it originated from Hunt's own experience of conversion.

When the painting was unveiled a critic remarked to the

painter, "Mr. Hunt, the work is unfinished. There is no handle on the door." Hunt answered, "That is the door to the human heart. It can be opened only from the inside."

Christ does not force Himself upon you. He waits outside the door of your heart. Have you opened your heart to Christ? Today fellowship with Him—help Christ make His home in your heart.

> In botany, he who knows mere names but has never
> seen a flower is as reliable as he who can expound on
> the finer points of theology, but has never known the
> love of Christ in his heart.
>
> —Charles Spurgeon

Day 146
THE WAR ZONE

Therefore put on the full armor of God, so that when the
day of evil comes, you may be able to stand your ground,
and after you have done everything, to stand. Stand firm then,
with the belt of truth buckled around your waist,
with the breastplate of righteousness in place.
Ephesians 6:13–14

Estean Lenyoun grew up in San Diego's inner city, a tough kid involved in gangs and drugs. Fortunately, he earned an athletic scholarship and left his neighborhood for college. He became a successful community developer and a millionaire at twenty-four, but he lost it all when money became his god. In 1991 he committed his life to Christ and returned to the inner city to use his gifts for God's kingdom.

Estean and others purchased an apartment complex near where he was raised. The neighborhood was a boiling pot of gangs, drug deals, and drive-by shootings. "It was spiritual warfare," Estean said, "the kind that requires wearing God's armor twenty-four hours a day to survive."

They began to clear out the drugs and clean up the property. They established rules that supported their no drugs, no gangs, no violence, no compromise standard and reported all lawbreakers to the police. They stood firm in the face of physical violence, threats, drive-by shootings, and vindictive people. Caring Christians helped them refurbish the apartments, build playgrounds, and replace the dump with a park.

Today the gated community is a place of refuge and hope for three hundred people who are growing, working, and living a better life. The team attributes their success to prayer, God's armor, the police, and Christians.

Are you covered with God's armor of truth, righteousness, peace, faith, salvation, and the Word? Today in prayer thank God for this armor.

> The armor in detail, as set forth here, is provided that the child of God should be "able to stand" against the wiles of the devil.
>
> —Jessie Penn-Lewis

Day 147
TODAY IS SALVATION'S DAY

For he says, "In the time of my favor I heard you,
and in the day of salvation I helped you." I tell you,
now is the time of God's favor, now is the day of salvation.
2 Corinthians 6:2

James Chalmers was a Scottish missionary to New Guinea. While he was on furlough from the mission field a woman came to him and said, "Brother Chalmers, I've prayed and pleaded with my daughter but I can't get her to accept Christ." He replied, "Let me talk with her."

Chalmers met with the young woman and learned that

she had been under conviction of sin for many weeks but had put off making a decision. The missionary asked, "Suppose I tell your mother you don't want her to talk to you about your salvation for a whole year. Would that suit you?" The woman answered, "I don't really like that idea. It might not be safe. I could die before then."

"Yes, that's true," replied the missionary. "Suppose we make it six months." That didn't satisfy her either. "What about telling her not to talk to you or pray for your salvation for three months?" The girl was silent but the Holy Spirit was working in her heart. Suddenly she saw how foolish she was to put off Christ and cried out, "I don't think it's safe to put it off at all!" She then knelt there and asked Christ into her heart.

Tomorrow may never come for those who do not know Jesus Christ. Do you know someone who needs Christ's salvation? Ask the Lord to make today the day of salvation for someone you know.

> The elect are the "whosoever wills"; the non-elect are the "whosoever won'ts."
>
> —D. L. Moody

Day 148
WHAT TO DO WHEN YOU ARE AT A STANDSTILL

I thank and praise you, O God of my fathers:
You have given me wisdom and power,
you have made known to me what we asked of you,
you have made known to us the dream of the king.
Daniel 2:23

$\mathcal{S}$amuel Morse has been called "the American Leonardo da Vinci" because of his ability as both an artist and an inventor. Morse was the son of a distinguished clergyman and was a graduate of Yale University. In 1843 he won Congressional support to build a forty-one-mile telegraph line from Washington D.C. to Baltimore. After months of stringing electrical wire Morse sent the first long-distance telegraph message. "What hath God wrought!" was his historic message.

Years later, when he was professor at New York University, Morse was asked, "When you were making your experiments at the university, did you ever come to a standstill, not knowing what to do next?" Replied Morse: "I'll tell you frankly—I prayed . . .and God gave me the wisdom that I needed. That's why I never felt I deserved the honors that came to me. . . because of the invention associated with my name. I had made a valuable application of the use of electrical power, but it was all through God's help. It wasn't because I was superior to other scientists. When the Lord wanted to bestow this gift on mankind, he had to use someone. I'm grateful he chose to reveal it to me."

Jesus Christ will give you wisdom if you pray for it. Today thank Christ that he is the answer to your questions.

> A thankful heart is not only the greatest virtue, but the parent of all other virtues.
> —Marcus Tullius Cicero

Day 149
THE SATISFACTION OF WORK

That everyone may eat and drink, and find
satisfaction in all his toil—this is the gift of God.
Ecclesiastes 3:13

Leo Tolstoy was born into the privileged class in Russia. In 1873, four years after completing his classic novel *War and Peace,* two of his children died. In his midforties, with health, wealth, fame, and a happy marriage, Tolstoy did not enjoy peace. He wrote, "A strange condition of mental torpor began to grow upon me. . . . The same questions continually presented themselves to me: 'Why?' and 'What afterward?'. . . My life had come to a sudden stop. I could breathe, eat, drink, sleep, indeed I couldn't help doing so. But there was no real life in me. . . . Life had no meaning for me." During this time Tolstoy gave his life to Jesus Christ.

In 1880 Tolstoy devoted himself to a life of physical labor. He rose at dawn and worked in the fields and gave what he earned to the poor. In his later years Tolstoy enjoyed a closeness to the Lord he had never enjoyed before. On August 27, 1895 he wrote the following about editing his diaries ." . .let my diaries stay as they are. At least they will show that despite all the triviality and worthlessness of my youth, I was still not abandoned by God, and, if only in my old age, began to understand him a little and love him."

To do the work that the Lord has set before you gives satisfaction. Are you restless about your life? Today in prayer ask Christ to show you the important things of life.

God's gifts put man's best dreams to shame.
—Elizabeth Barrett Browning

Day 150
JUST DO IT!

Do not merely listen to the word, and so deceive yourselves.
Do what it says.
James 1:22

*M*ike Singletary was one of football's greatest linebackers. Once while watching a highlight film prior to a championship game other players were dozing. But Mike was so excited that he knocked over a table, shouting "Let's play now! Let's play now!" His infectious enthusiasm spilled over to his teammates and into the following day's game.

During his pro football career Mike got serious about his walk with Jesus Christ. "It was in 1985, the first year of my marriage to Kim, that I discovered I couldn't be the great husband, man of his word, and man of God that I wanted to be unless I chose to serve God wholeheartedly. I suddenly realized I couldn't do it on my own." Mike turned to the Bible as the playbook for his life. He let God coach him instead of calling his own game. "I realized I was going to have to deal with some hurt for awhile but the most important thing was I learned to live life the way God meant it to be lived. And the Bible is so important because it is the book of life. . . . It has all the answers in there that anybody could ever possibly want to know."

Even a tough Hall of Fame middle linebacker admits that the correction of God's Word can be difficult. Today in prayer ask the Lord to instruct you from the Bible and then just do it!

> And I can also heartily testify that the safe guidebook
> by which one may be led to Chirst is the Bible, the
> Word of God, which is inspired by the Holy Ghost.
> —George Williams

Day 151
THE REWARD FOR PERSISTENCE

God "will give to each person according to what he has done."
To those who by persistence in doing good seek glory, honor
and immortality, he will give eternal life.
Romans 2:6–7

Early in the twentieth century Rodney "Gipsy" Smith was one of the most popular preachers in the U.S. and Great

Britain. Born to poor gypsy parents near London, he gave his life to Christ when he was sixteen years old. Immediately he wanted to learn more about Christ and to see others know the Lord. The teenager began faithfully praying for his favorite Uncle Rodney's salvation.

One Sunday Uncle Rodney noticed Gipsy's trousers were worn at the knees. "Laddie, how do you account for the fact that the knees of your trousers have worn nearly through while the rest of the suit is almost like new?" Surprised at the question the boy said, "I have worn the knees through, praying for you Uncle Rodney." With tears he added, "I want so much to have God make you a Christian."

Rodney's soul was touched. He had seen the changes Christ had made in Gipsy's life and in the lives of Gipsy's father and mother. Now he knew that they loved him so much that they were earnestly praying for his salvation. So Rodney did the only thing he could do. He bent his own knees and asked Christ into his life.

Christ desires us to pursue His will. Do you give up on prayer if you do not receive an instant answer? Today thank Christ that He rewards persistent prayer.

We assert, therefore, that perseverance, by which one perseveres in Christ even to the end, is a gift of God.
—Augustine

Day 152
YOU ARE SAFE IN CHRIST

The LORD is gracious and righteous; our God is full of
compassion. The LORD protects the simplehearted;
when I was in great need, he saved me.
Psalm 116:5–6

In 1899, at the onset of the Boer War in South Africa, the twenty-five-year-old Winston Churchill was a journalist for the *London Morning Post*. He immediately went to the front lines and made a name for himself writing morale-building stories of the heroics of the British Army. Once while he was riding on an armored train, the advancing Boer army ambushed the train and cut off any possible retreat. The British soldiers were shot helplessly in their cars. Churchill rallied the wounded engineer who disconnected the engine from the train and escaped with the wounded. Churchill remained and was captured.

Taken to a military prison in Pretoria, he made a daring escape and wandered around the area for several days. He was at the end of his rope when he decided to present himself at the door of one of the houses in the valley. Although the price of twenty-five pounds had been set upon his head to be captured dead or alive, Churchill thought there was a chance of some friendly soul in the heart of this unfriendly area who might help him. He prayed, approached the home, and knocked. A man answered the door and the journalist said, "I am Winston Churchill." The friendly voice said, "Come in, this is the only house for miles in which you would be safe."

Do you tend to become paralyzed when fear strikes you? Today in prayer give thanks to the Lord that He is your protector, your shield. In Him you are safe.

> When God gives a man a task to do, he also gives
> him the power to do it.
>
> —William Barclay

WORKERS DESERVE THEIR WAGES

The elders who direct the affairs of the church well are worthy of double honor, especially those whose work is preaching and teaching. For the Scripture says, "Do not muzzle the ox while it is treading out the grain," and "The worker deserves his wages."
1 Timothy 5:17–18

One of John Wesley's most famous sermons is about stewardship. Its three points are: "Earn all you can, save all you can, give all you can."

A farmer who had never heard Wesley preach was enjoying this sermon as it unfolded. After Wesley made his first point the farmer nudged his neighbor, "I have never heard preaching like this before. This man has some good things in him." Then Wesley launched into his second point—the abhorrence of wastefulness. He concluded this point by saying, "Save all you can!" The farmer responded with an "Amen!"

John Wesley then launched into his third point and the farmer bowed and shook his head, "Aw dear, he's gone and spoiled it all!"

John Wesley proved to be a good steward of money. At the height of his income he made 120 pounds a year ($220). He lived on thirty-two pounds and gave away ninety-two pounds a year. When he died Wesley's possessions included his clothes, a carriage, and books. It is estimated he gave away over twenty-four thousand pounds in his lifetime (forty-four thousand dollars).

A majority of pastors and ministers will never come close to being materially rich. But they do have legitimate financial needs and they depend on the Lord to work through the church to provide those needs. Those who direct our congregations well deserve double honor and should not have to endure financial hardship. Today in prayer, ask Christ, "Is my minister or pastor paid as he should be? If not, what should I do?"

Giving to God has a wonderful power to bind one's life to him.

—Rev. J.B. Gambrell

Day 154
THE MAN WHO HELPED OTHERS

For you know the grace of our Lord Jesus Christ,
that though he was rich, yet for your sakes he became poor,
so that you through his poverty might become rich.
2 Corinthians 8:9

Henry Bartle Edward Frere was born in Wales and entered diplomatic service as a youth. By age thirty-five, he was the chief commissioner of Sind, an area later annexed by India. During his career Frere distinguished himself by suppressing an Indian rebellion and later eliminating the slave trade in Zanzibar. His efforts earned him knighthood. The pinnacle of his career was his appointment as governor of Bombay in 1862.

While serving as governor, he returned to Great Britain for an extended stay. His aged mother sent a carriage driver to pick up her son at the railroad station. The driver asked his mother how he could recognize her son. "Look for a man who is helping someone else," she replied. Following her advice, the driver carefully observed the people as they left the train. It didn't take long until he noticed a middle-aged man helping an elderly lady to the station platform, and then he returned to the train to carry her luggage for her. His kindness stood in contrast to all the others who were concerned with their own affairs. The driver approached the man and asked, "Sir, are you Sir Bartle?" The driver had correctly recognized the governor because of his helpful nature.

Christ left the splendor of heaven to serve us. He became poor so that we can inherit the riches of God. Today in prayer thank God for this incomprehensible gift.

No person was ever honored for what he received.
Honor has been the reward for what he gave.
—Calvin Coolidge

Day 155
A HEEL ON ENVY'S HEAD

*And I saw that all labor and all achievement spring
from man's envy of his neighbor.
This too is meaningless, a chasing after the wind.*
Ecclesiastes 4:4

G. Campbell Morgan was sixteen years younger than F. B.
Meyer and one of the most gifted preachers of all time. In
1904 Meyer, himself a renowned preacher, was the pastor of
Christ Church on Westminster Bridge Road in London when
Morgan accepted the pastorate at nearby Westminster Chapel.
Meyer related the following experience to a few personal
friends: "It was easy to pray for the success of Morgan when he
was in America. But when he came back to England and took
a church near to mine it was something different. The old
Adam in me was inclined to jealousy but I got my heel upon
his head and whether I felt right toward my friend, I determined to act right.

"My church gave a reception for him and I acknowledged
that if it was not necessary for me to preach Sunday evenings
I would dearly love to go and hear him myself. Well, that made
me feel right toward him. But just see how the dear Lord
helped me out of my difficulty."

You cannot help but enjoy the gifts God has given to you.
But envy takes root when that same gift is found in greater
abundance in someone else. Are you tempted to envy? Today
ask God to crucify those thoughts and seek to demonstrate
love toward that person.

One can not be envious and happy at the same time.

—Henry Gerber

Day 156
GOD MOVES IN A MYSTERIOUS WAY

*Then Daniel returned to his house and explained the matter
to his friends Hananiah, Mishael and Azariah.
He urged them to plead for mercy from the God
of heaven concerning this mystery,
so that he and his friends might not be executed
with the rest of the wise men of Babylon.*
Daniel 2:17–18

William Cowper (1731–1800) was a brilliant British poet, writer, and hymn writer. He translated Homer and collaborated with John Newton to write the Olney Hymns. Cowper often suffered great mental anguish. At times he even considered suicide. Though his father was a minister and he himself was a Christian, Cowper often lacked the comforting assurance of salvation. He twice refused appointments to administrative posts in the House of Lords because he was too frightened to take the required oral examination.

One night Cowper was suicidal. He hailed a cab and asked to be taken to the Thames River. London was blanketed with a thick fog and the driver lost his way. Cowper leaped impatiently from the buggy, determined to find his watery grave unassisted. As he groped through the fog he was astonished to discover that he was back at his own doorstep. Falling to his knees he thanked the Lord for the fog which had prevented his suicide.

Cowper knew that the Lord had misdirected the cab driver. This event caused him to write the hymn "God Moves In A Mysterious Way." The poet lived to an advanced age and on his deathbed his last words were, "I am not shut out of heaven after all."

Do you ever feel like the Lord has turned His back on you? Today in prayer pour out your heart to Him. God does move in a mysterious way!

God moves in a mysterious way his wonders to perform; he plants his footsteps in the sea, and rides upon the storm. You fearful saints, fresh courage take; the clouds you so much dread are big with mercy, and will break in blessing on your head!
—William Cowper

Day 157
THE MINTING HOUSE OF GOD'S WORD

In the first year of his reign, I, Daniel,
understood from the Scriptures, according to the word
of the LORD given to Jeremiah the prophet,
that the desolation of Jerusalem would last seventy years.
Daniel 9:2

In 1628, John Bunyan was born in Elstow, England, where he spent most of his life. Even though today he is regarded as a literary genius, he had little formal education. Early on, he was known as a profane young man in Elstow and a bad influence on children.

John Bunyan went on to be a preacher and an author of more than sixty books including the classic *The Pilgrim's Progress.* His changed life was due to the power of the Word of God. People would often come to him discouraged that they couldn't understand a particular passage of Scripture. He would reply, "Although you may have no commentaries at hand, continue to read the Word and pray; for a little from God is better than a great deal received from man. Too many are content to listen to what comes from men's mouths without searching and kneeling before God to know the real truth. That which we receive directly from the Lord through the study of his Word is from the 'minting house' itself. Even old truths are new if they come to us with the smell of heaven upon them."

John Bunyan knew that the Word of God has the power to "mint" us into God's image. Do you spend time studying the Bible? When you do, ask Christ to give you understanding.

> For instance, if a man doth delight to talk of the history, or the mystery of things; or if a man doth love to talk of miracles, wonders, or signs, where shall he find things recorded so delightful, and so sweetly penned, as in the holy Scripture?
>
> —John Bunyan

Day 158
THE FIRST GOOD WORK

Before this faith came, we were held prisoners by the law,
locked up until faith should be revealed.
So the law was put in charge to lead us to Christ
that we might be justified by faith.
Now that faith has come,
we are no longer under the supervision of the law.
Galatians 3:23–25

Albert Benjamin (A. B.) Simpson grew up in a Christian home in Ontario, Canada. He studied for the ministry at Knox College and went on to minister in churches in Louisville, Kentucky, and New York City. He was an excellent preacher who practiced pastoral visitation and evangelism. He helped establish what today is known as the Christian and Missionary Alliance and the Missionary Training College. He authored over seventy books on Christian themes.

Simpson came to know the Lord as a young man. While reading a book called *Marshall's Gospel Mystery of Sanctification* his eyes fixed on this passage: "The first good work you will ever perform is to believe on the Lord Jesus Christ. Until you do this, all your works, your prayers, tears, and good resolutions are vain. To believe on the Lord Jesus Christ is to believe that he saves you here and now, for he has said, 'Him that cometh to me I will in no wise cast out.' " That did it. Simpson knew what he had to do. He bowed his knees and performed the first good work in his life—he trusted Jesus Christ as Lord.

The first good work any of us can do is to trust Jesus Christ. Do you know someone who has yet to take this step? Today in prayer ask the Lord to show you someone who needs to hear the freeing words of the gospel. Pray they will be saved by faith in Him.

> 'Til men have faith in Christ, their best services are but glorious sins.
>
> —Thomas Brooks

Day 159
THE BEGINNING OF BIRTH PAINS

When you hear of wars and rumors of wars, do not be alarmed.
Such things must happen, but the end is still to come.
Nation will rise against nation, and kingdom against kingdom.
There will be earthquakes in various places, and famines.
These are the beginning of birth pains.
Mark 13:7–8

The U.S. Geological Survey reported the following earthquakes worldwide during the two-day period of August 29–30, 1996. All times are Greenwich Mean Time:

Date	Time	Magnitude	Location
08/29/96	06:22	4.6	Greenland Sea
08/29/96	09:24	5.0	Aegean Sea
08/29/96	13:44	3.3	California-Nevada Border
08/29/96	14:10	4.6	Tonga Islands
08/29/96	15:49	3.0	Near Coast of Northern California
08/29/96	20:22	4.9	Central Mid-Atlantic Ocean Ridge
08/29/96	22:05	4.5	Andreanof Island, Aleutian Islands
08/30/96	02:11	5.2	Chagos Archipelago Region
08/30/96	02:12	4.0	Near Coast of Northern California
08/30/96	05:30	4.3	Andreanof Island, Aleutian Islands
08/30/96	06:58	4.7	Malawi
08/30/96	11:41	5.1	Central Mid-Atlantic Ocean Ridge
08/30/96	12:10	3.1	California, Baja California Region
08/30/96	13:01	4.0	Andreanof Island, Aleutian Islands
08/30/96	21:13	5.4	Sea of Okhotsk
08/30/96	22:50	3.2	Off of Coast of Northern California
08/30/96	23:00	5.1	North of Ascension Island

The above information is not intended to alarm you. But it is informative.

War, famine, and earthquakes are only the start of the times which precede Christ's return. Do not fear—prepare. Today place Christ first in all that you do, knowing that Jesus will return one day in glory.

It has been said by scholars that the second coming of Christ is mentioned no less than 1,200 times in the Old Testament and 300 times in the New Testament.

—Francis W. Dixon

Day 160
BELIEVERS ARE NOT BYSTANDERS

*This is a trustworthy saying that deserves full acceptance
(and for this we labor and strive),
that we have put our hope in the living God,
who is the Savior of all men,
and especially of those who believe.*
1 Timothy 4:9–10

In the spring of 1859, the Frenchman Charles Blondin advertised in the *New York Times* that he was going to cross Niagara Falls on a tightrope. On June 30 over six thousand people gathered on the banks of the Niagara River to watch him attempt this acrobatic stunt. The "Great Blondin" stretched the tightrope across the American side of the falls. The distance was 1,060 feet and the rope was 160 feet above the river. Immediately downstream was the falls, a 190-foot vertical plunge.

"How many of you believe I can cross Niagara Falls on the tightrope pushing this wheelbarrow?" Blondin asked. The crowd responded with light applause. Blondin made his way across and back with the wheelbarrow. He then crossed on stilts and followed that by crossing blindfolded.

Then the Great Blondin asked, "How many of you believe I can cross with someone on my back?" Everyone responded, "Yes, we believe. Sure, you can do it!"

"Who will volunteer?" Silence came over the crowd. Blondin's promotion manager volunteered. The two went across and returned safely without incident. Blondin again asked, "Any volunteers?" No one came forward.

Our trust in Jesus Christ must be like that of Blondin's manager. We cannot be bystanding believers. Believing is active trust. If you have never actively put all of your life in Christ's hands, come to Him in prayer. He will not let you down.

> I always come back to two basic factors: the objective, external, historical facts of the resurrection, and the subjective, internal personal experience of Christ that I have known.
>
> —Paul E. Little

Day 161
NO PIT SO DEEP

So do not be ashamed to testify about our Lord, or ashamed
of me his prisoner. But join with me in suffering
for the gospel, by the power of God, who has saved us
and called us to a holy life—not because of anything
we have done but because of his own purpose and grace.
2 Timothy 1:8–9

In May 1942, Corrie ten Boom and her family began taking in Jews who were fleeing Nazi Germany. In February 1944, Corrie and her family were arrested. Corrie was fifty-two years old when she endured the cold, cramped, flea-infested quarters at the Ravensbruck concentration camp.

Corrie later wrote to the man who had betrayed her family which led to their imprisonment:

"Dear Sir, Today I heard that most probably you are the one who betrayed me. I went through ten months of concentration camp. My father died after nine days of imprisonment. My sister died in prison too. The harm you planned was turned into good for me by God. I came nearer to him. . . .

"I have forgiven you everything. God will also forgive you everything if you ask him. He loves you and he himself sent his Son to earth to reconcile your sins, which meant to suffer the punishment for you and me. You, on your part, have to give an answer to this. If he says: 'Come unto me, give me your heart,' then your answer must be: 'Yes, Lord, I come, make me your child.' If it is difficult for you to pray, then ask if God will give you his Holy Spirit, who works the faith in your heart."

Today in prayer remember Corrie's words to her betrayer: "Never doubt the Lord Jesus' love. He is standing with his arms spread out to receive you. I hope that the path which you will now take may work for your eternal salvation."

There is no pit so deep that God is not deeper still.
—Corrie ten Boom

Day 162
ALL THE KINGS WILL PRAISE HIM

May all the kings of the earth praise you, O LORD, when
they hear the words of your mouth. May they sing
of the ways of the LORD, for the glory of the LORD is great.
Psalm 138:4–5

On June 11, 1788, King George III, the British king who ruled when America won its independence, was seized with a fever and spasms of the stomach and bowels. For months the king was afflicted. All of Great Britain expected him to die. This was a tragedy which caused the country to pray for its king. By February, 1789, King George, slowly recovering, declared a time of national thanksgiving. In March the people began giving public thanks for the king's recovery. This time of thanksgiving culminated on April 23 with a service at St. Paul's Cathedral.

That day the king's advisors were afraid that if the king were to participate he would suffer a relapse. The king replied, "I have twice read over the evidence of the physicians on my case and if I could stand that I can stand anything." As he rode to St. Paul's there was a large public support for his return. "I now feel that I have been ill," he said, greatly moved by the crowd.

The service at St. Paul's lasted three hours. Some of the dignitaries were conspicuously bored. But the king was involved in worship. Near the end of the service he raised both arms upward and looked toward heaven. He maintained that position for about a minute and then put both hands on his heart and began to weep.

If a powerful king can give thanks to God is there any reason why you cannot do the same? Today thank God for His mercy upon you and your family.

Praise ye the Lord, the almighty, the king of creation!
O my soul, praise him, for he is thy health and salvation! All ye who hear, now to this temple draw near; join me in glad adoration.

—Joachim Neander

Day 163
PUT AWAY EVIL WAYS

*Many of those who believed now came and openly confessed
their evil deeds. A number who had practiced sorcery brought
their scrolls together and burned them publicly. When they
calculated the value of the scrolls, the total came to
fifty thousand drachmas. In this way the word
of the Lord spread widely and grew in power.*
Acts 19:18–20

Anand Chaudhari grew up in Rajasthan, central India. His family was extremely superstitious and worshipped various deities. Young Anand was a practicing Brahman priest when he went to the University of Bombay in 1950. But through the patient love of a classmate Anand began reading and studying the Gospel of Matthew and learned about Jesus Christ. He committed his life to the Savior and put away his former ways. But immediately his family disowned him. They feared that he was cast under a spell.

In 1954 a series of celestial events occurred and a great many worshipers made a pilgrimage to the Ganges River. Anand's parents were there. The highlight of the celebration came when the moon and Jupiter were in alignment and all of the worshipers were to bathe together in the holy waters. Millions had thronged to the banks of the river and as the moment approached a wave of humanity moved toward the river's banks. In the commotion hundreds were crushed and drowned, including Anand's parents.

As a result of their death Anand became more committed to the Lord. He went to a Bible college, became an effective evangelist, and led others to life in Christ. He went on to become president of the Rajasthan Bible Institute.

When you grow in Jesus Christ evil ways are cast away. Are you holding onto something in your past which should be discarded? Today give thanks to Christ. Honor Him in your heart so He will be glorified in your life.

The books you read may have much to do with your choosing of the road.

—Katherine Logan

ACCEPT THE PARDON

If we confess our sins, he is faithful and just and
will forgive us our sins and purify us from all unrighteousness.
1 John 1:9

In 1829 George Wilson was indicted in Philadelphia for robbing the mail and putting the life of the carrier in jeopardy. He was found guilty of the crime and was sentenced to hang. But President Andrew Jackson granted Wilson a pardon.

However George Wilson refused the pardon and the case went to the Supreme Court. Chief Justice John Marshall wrote the opinion for the majority of the court: "A pardon is an act of grace proceeding from the power entrusted with the execution of the laws which exempts the individual, on whom it is bestowed, from the punishment the law inflicts for a crime he has committed. A pardon is a deed, to the validity of which delivery is essential, and delivery is not complete without acceptance. It may then be rejected by the person to whom it is tendered; and if it be rejected we have discovered no power in a court to force it on him." George Wilson was hanged for his crimes.

Sin separates us from God. But God has pardoned us in Christ. The only requirement is that we accept this pardon in order to regain our relationship with God. Christ died for sin. Therefore confess, turn from sin, and accept full pardon in Christ.

> Fellowship with God and the forgiveness of sin are never separated in Christian experience.
>
> —Dale Moody

FORGIVENESS FIRST

And when you stand praying,
if you hold anything against anyone, forgive him,
so that your Father in heaven may
forgive you your sins.
Mark 11:25

John Wesley, the English evangelist and founder of the Methodist Church, met an acquaintance on the street one day. "I heard that you and Mr. So-and-so have become enemies," said Wesley. "Have you come to terms with him?"

"No, I haven't," the friend replied. "Why should I? He's the one who should be blamed. I'll never forgive him for I am the one who was hurt."

Looking directly into the man's eyes, Wesley said, "Then you should never again commit sin. I don't think you can say you have never committed a sin. You have so far because somebody has forgiven your faults. But if you say that you don't want to forgive someone who has wronged you, from now on don't expect to be forgiven by anyone else either." At this, the man lowered his head and repented bitterly of his faults.

Christ was so broken by our sin that He left His heavenly home to come to us and offer forgiveness. If someone has hurt you and there is a broken relationship, in prayer ask Christ to give you the strength to forgive. Then contact that person and let them know you miss them and want to restore the friendship.

He who cannot forgive others breaks the bridge over which he must pass himself.

—George Herbert

THE ROAD OF THE LOVING HEART

But by faith we eagerly await through the Spirit the
righteousness for which we hope. For in Christ Jesus
neither circumcision nor uncircumcision has any value.
The only thing that counts is faith expressing itself through love.
Galatians 5:5–6

*R*obert Louis Stevenson was born in Scotland. He endured tuberculosis as a child and was in poor health his entire life. His novels *Treasure Island* and *The Strange Case of Dr. Jekyll and Mr. Hyde* are classics.

In 1889 Stevenson moved to the island of Samoa. This was not only the fulfillment of a lifetime dream—the tropical island was excellent for his health.

Stevenson's kindness won the affection of the native Samoans. They called him "Tusitala," teller of tales. They built a road to his plantation home and called it "The Road of the Loving Heart."

One day Stevenson asked his servant Sosimo to bring some bread and cheese to him while he worked. To his surprise the servant fixed a beautiful omelet, a great salad, and a cup of Stevenson's favorite coffee. "Who made this?" Stevenson asked, knowing that the cook was away for the day. "I did," said the servant. "Well then, great is your wisdom," Stevenson said complementing the man's gracious act. "Great is my love!" answered the servant.

If someone were to name the street that leads to your door would it be "The Road of the Loving Heart"? Today give thanks to Christ that you have love because He loved you first.

Lord, it is my chief complaint; that my love is weak
and faint; yet I love Thee and adore, Oh for grace to
love Thee more!

—William Cowper

Day 167
THANK THE LORD ALL LIFE LONG

Praise the LORD. Praise the LORD,
O my soul. I will praise the LORD all my life;
I will sing praise to my God as long as I live.
Psalm 146:1–2

In the 1850's in Edinburgh, Scotland, there was a good-hearted shepherd named Jock Gray who made his way in from the meadows daily with his Skye terrier, Bobby. Jock would stop off at the Traills Coffee House and pick up lunch and a bone for Bobby. They would eat lunch together—Jock a sandwich and Bobby a bone. This went on daily for several years until one day Jock collapsed and died. He was buried in the Greyfriars Kirk Church Cemetery.

After Jock was buried his dog Bobby showed up at the door of the Traills Coffee House at one o'clock as he had before with Jock. This continued each day and the proprietor would give Bobby a bone. One day the owner followed Bobby through the town. The dog led him to Jock's grave where Bobby laid down and quietly chewed his bone. For the next fourteen years, until his own death, Bobby continued to quietly have his lunch at his master's grave. Some townspeople built a little doghouse for him in the cemetery and the Traills Coffee House continued to feed Bobby. The Lord Provost personally paid for Bobby's dog license. When Bobby died he was buried near his master.

In 1873 Baroness Burdett-Coutts was so charmed by Bobby's faithfulness to his master that she had a bronze monument erected outside the Traills Coffee House for the little Skye terrier.

A little dog never forgot his faithful master. Do you take the Lord's care and faithfulness for granted? Today pray for the Lord's promised return. He is faithful.

I'll praise my Maker while I've breath, and when my voice is lost in death, praise shall employ my nobler powers; My days of praise shall ne'er be past, while life, and thought, and being last, or immortality endures.

—Isaac Watts

Day 168
THE NEIGHBOR

"Which of these three do you think was a neighbor to the
man who fell into the hands of robbers?"
The expert in the law replied,
"The one who had mercy on him."
Jesus told him, "Go and do likewise."
Luke 10:36–37

In the late 1790s, a tall middle-aged man arrived alone on horseback at one of Baltimore's most prestigious inns. He was a frequent traveler between Washington D.C., and Philadelphia but this was the first time he had visited this inn. He looked forward to changing his clothes and relaxing after a difficult day of travel. He had ridden a long distance on that rainy day. The man's simple clothing was soaked with clay from the ride. His weather-beaten face identified him as a someone who had spent long hours under the sun—perhaps a farmer. The manager of the inn looked over the man, considered his Virginia accent, and then refused him lodging. "Your farmer's appearance would discredit this inn," he said. The man, shocked at such poor treatment, quietly left. Later that same evening the innkeeper discovered that he had turned away Thomas Jefferson!

He immediately sent a messenger with an apologetic note to the distinguished gentleman urging him to return and be a guest at the inn. Mr. Jefferson replied to the messenger, "Tell him I have already engaged a room. I value his good intentions highly but if he has no place for a dirty American farmer he has none for the vice president of the United States."

Are you color-blind when it comes to helping others? In prayer give thanks for the parable of the Good Samaritan and ask God to lead you in a life that loves your neighbor as yourself.

> Your neighbor is the man who needs you.
> —Elbert Hubbard

Day 169
THE TOUGHEST PEOPLE TO FORGIVE

When they came to the place called the Skull,
there they crucified him, along with the criminals—
one on his right, the other on his left.
Jesus said, "Father, forgive them,
for they do not know what they are doing."
And they divided up his clothes by casting lots.
Luke 23:33–34

Louis was born the son of the Duke of Orleans. Though he was cousin to the King of France he involved himself in a revolt against King Charles VIII. The king was oppressing the people of France and Louis sought reforms. He was imprisoned for his rebellion for three years. He ascended to the throne in 1498 when Charles died.

Soon after being freed from prison the king made a list of those who had persecuted him and marked against each of their names a large black cross. When this became known the king's enemies fled. But Louis, learning of their fears, found them and recalled them with the full assurance of pardon and said that he had put a cross beside each name to remind them of the cross of Christ. He intended to follow the example of Jesus Christ who prayed for his murderers, "Father, forgive them, for they do not know what they are doing." Louis followed this same pattern during his reign when he sought peace with his former enemies Henry VIII of England and Emperor Maximilian I of Austria.

It isn't easy to pray for those who desire to see you fall. They are tough people to forgive. Do you pray for those who don't like you? Today thank Jesus Christ that He prayed for His enemies. Ask Him to give you a loving heart toward those who do not like you.

> Remember then the Cross. Christ prayed for his ene-
> mies. Learn then not to look on any as beyond the
> reach of prayer.
>
> —A. W. Pink

Day 170
YOUR HEART AND YOUR MOUTH

That if you confess with your mouth, "Jesus is Lord,"
and believe in your heart that God raised him
from the dead, you will be saved.
For it is with your heart that you believe and are justified,
and it is with your mouth that you confess and are saved.
Romans 10:9–10

The Greek philosopher Socrates lived from 469–399 B.C. Though he was the son of a sculptor, Socrates deplored the art. He saw sculptors taking great pains to make a block of marble into a human likeness rather than chiseling away at their own imperfections to refine their own character. He lived simply and never took a fee for his teaching.

The wisdom of Socrates attracted many young men who wanted to study under his direction. Aeschines was one such man. But he was poor and only had himself to give to Socrates.

The philospher told him, "No, don't you see. You are offering me the greatest gift of all." Another young man came to him but was overwhelmed by being in the presence of the great intellectual. So the two walked along in silence. Finally Socrates broke the silence and said him, "Speak, that I may see you."

This short sentence expresses truth—our deepest being is seen in the words we speak. There is a connection between the belief in our heart and the words from our mouth. Thus the Christian confession: "Jesus is Lord."

Since we believe in our hearts that Jesus is Lord we must be willing to say it. Do you shy away from sharing your faith in Christ? Today praise Jesus Christ. He is Lord! Ask God for the opportunity to tell someone about the Son.

> When the heart is afire, some sparks will fly out of the mouth.
>
> —Thomas Fuller

Day 171
THE PATH OF LIFE

David said about him: "I saw the Lord always before me. Because he is at my right hand, I will not be shaken. Therefore my heart is glad and my tongue rejoices; my body also will live in hope, because you will not abandon me to the grave, nor will you let your Holy One see decay. You have made known to me the paths of life; you will fill me with joy in your presence."
Acts 2:25–28

Grace Weiser Davis was a noted evangelist of the nineteenth century. She gives an account of her mother's last days before death: "One day my mother prayed, 'Dear Lord, prepare me for the country to which I am going!' Before the close of that day she was shouting the praises of God. From that time on she talked of her coming translation and her faith was gloriously triumphant. . . .

"One afternoon she said, 'I am homesick for heaven.' She told the doctor, 'Sometimes my way has seemed dark but it was like the Ferris wheel—it always came round to a point of light.' Again she said, 'I believe I will awake sometime and find myself in a strange country to which I shall be translated.' The night previous to her death she said, 'There is light all around me.'

"Until the last she gave evidence of hearing, seeing, and understanding. I knelt within fifteen minutes of her passing and said, 'Mother, though you walk through the valley of the shadow of death, you need fear no evil, for God is with you. Surely goodness and mercy shall follow you, and you are going to dwell in the house of the Lord forever.' There came a responsive smile. In a few minutes she drew a gentle breath and was gone."

In the face of death Christ remains our shepherd and guide. Are you discouraged about death? Take heart and give thanks that when you pass through death you will be forever with the Lord.

> If God hath made this world so fair where sin and death abound, how beautiful beyond compare will paradise be found.
>
> —James Montgomery

Day 172
YOU ARE GOD'S BUILDING

The man who plants and the man who waters
have one purpose, and each will be rewarded according
to his own labor. For we are God's fellow workers;
you are God's field, God's building.
1 Corinthians 3:8–9

In 1293, the people of Florence, Italy, began to build a cathedral that would surpass all other buildings. Over 140 years the beautiful monument slowly rose from the Tuscany marshland. Florence numbered less than one hundred thousand citizens yet the people gave liberally to the cathedral. Beautiful frescoes, ornate stained glass, statues by Michelangelo, wood carvings by Donatello—all these grace the magnificent cathedral.

But the distinctive part of the cathedral of Florence is the dome designed and built by Filippo Brunelleschi. It is 130 feet in diameter and 185 feet in height. Special equipment was needed to raise the twenty-five thousand tons of material into place. So special is the design of this dome that it wasn't until 1985 that the secret of its strength and beauty was discovered: The dome's curved panels are shaped like flower petals. Brunelleschi borrowed his design from God the Creator.

Brunelleschi designed a small opening in the dome to allow a shaft of sunlight to stream through on one day a year—June 21. At just the right spot on the floor of the sanctuary he placed a brass plate. If the sunlight fails to cover this plate completely engineers are alerted that the cathedral has shifted its center of gravity.

The church is God's building composed of many brothers and sisters in Christ. This multitude brings strength and beauty to the church. They also focus God's light on any dangerous shifting of our foundation. Today in prayer give thanks that the Lord uses others to strengthen and adjust your life in Christ.

> We are not told that we are going to have the privilege of being coworkers in the future but we know it is our privilege today.
>
> —D. L. Moody

Day 173
TURN OVER YOUR FEARS TO GOD

For God did not give us a spirit of timidity,
but a spirit of power, of love and of self-discipline.
2 Timothy 1:7

Peter Cartwright gave his life to Jesus Christ at a camp revival at age sixteen. One year later he became a preacher and rode a circuit through Illinois, Indiana, Ohio, Kentucky, and Tennessee. He was a hellfire and brimstone preacher, a man who did not mince words. In over fifty years of traveling Cartwright received over ten thousand members into the Methodist church and preached over fifteen thousand sermons.

Just prior to a Sunday morning service in Nashville, Tennessee, the local preacher whispered in Cartwright's ear that the famous General Andrew Jackson was in the congregation. The pastor asked Cartwright not to say anything out of line. Cartwright stood to preach and said, "I understand Andrew Jackson is here. I have been requested to guard my remarks. And who is General Jackson? If General Jackson doesn't get his soul converted, God will damn him as quickly as anyone else!" Jackson smiled and later told Cartwright: "Sir, if I had a regiment of men like you, I could whip the world."

Your manner may not be "knock them over the head" but people should know where you stand with Jesus Christ. The Lord has not given us a spirit of timidity. Speak openly and clearly about the hope you have in Christ. Today in prayer turn over your fears to God and ask Him to prepare someone with whom you can share the good news.

> We do not need to be ashamed of our fear, but we can rest assured that he will give us strength when we have none of our own, courage when we are cowardly, and comfort when we are hurting.
>
> —Billy Graham

A CALL TO SERVICE

Jesus went up on a mountainside and called to him
those he wanted, and they came to him.
He appointed twelve—designating them apostles—
that they might be with him
and that he might send them out to preach.
Mark 3:13–14

Amanda Smith was born a slave in Maryland in 1837. One of thirteen children, Amanda had only a few months of formal education. Her father's hard work had purchased freedom for the family. Amanda worked as a maid and a washerwoman. She had two marriages and five children. Untimely deaths claimed her second husband and all five of her children. By 1869 she was alone except for God.

Amanda became an effective speaker and her reputation spread beyond her community. She soon received invitations not only to give her testimony but also to preach. In 1870 she became a full-time evangelist. For eight years she was a familiar figure in churches from Knoxville, Tennessee to Kennebunk, Maine. Amanda Smith received invitations to minister in England and then India from 1878 to 1881. So effective was Smith that the Methodist Episcopal bishop of India said that he learned more that was "of actual value to me as a preacher of Christian truth from Amanda Smith than any other person I had ever met."

On her return to the United States, Amanda Smith continued to preach and became burdened by the suffering of black orphans. In 1899, she opened up an orphan's home and she continued to fund it from her preaching until her death in 1915.

Is Christ calling you to His service? The apostles weren't born leaders; they were born babies. But they were available to God. If you aren't active in a ministry pray that Christ would show you how you can make a difference in your church and the world.

It is not God who does not call. It is man who will not respond!

—Isobel Kuhn

Day 175
HIS STRENGTH IN OUR WEAKNESS

Three times I pleaded with the Lord to take it away from me. But he said to me, "My grace is sufficient for you, for my power is made perfect in weakness." Therefore I will boast all the more gladly about my weaknesses, so that Christ's power may rest on me. That is why, for Christ's sake, I delight in weaknesses, in insults, in hardships, in persecutions, in difficulties. For when I am weak, then I am strong.
2 Corinthians 12:8–10

Admiral Lord Horatio Nelson is one of England's greatest heros. At the Battle of Cape St. Vincent his ship valiantly fought seven Spanish ships and successfully captured two of them. At the battles of the Nile and Copenhagen he displayed brilliant courage in triumphantly leading his fleet. Nelson's crowning achievement was at Trafalgar, where his smaller, less-armed British fleet won a decisive victory over the French and Spanish. After Trafalgar, Britain remained secure from invasion and exercised supremacy at sea for over a century.

But Nelson's road to greatness was difficult. He was one of eleven children of Reverend Edmund Nelson. His mother died when he was nine. He was a sickly child who had poor digestion and chest pains. For his entire life Nelson suffered from seasickness. The last words penned in his diary before he died at Trafalgar were: "For myself, individually, I commit my life to Him who made me, and may His blessing light my endeavors for serving my Country faithfully. To Him I resign myself, and the just cause which is entrusted to me to defend. Amen. Amen. Amen."

When your human strength comes to its end, Christ's strength can be shown in your life. Do you let your short-comings stop Christ from working in your life? Today thank Jesus Christ that in your weaknesses His love and compassion can be seen.

> Many of our prayers fail to enter heaven for the same reason that a whole generation of Israelites failed to enter Canaan—because of unbelief.
> —William Proctor

Day 176
PRAISE GOD FROM WHOM ALL BLESSINGS FLOW

Now to him who is able to do immeasurably more than all we ask or imagine, according to his power that is at work within us, to him be glory in the church and in Christ Jesus throughout all generations, for ever and ever! Amen.
Ephesians 3:20–21

Thomas Ken was orphaned early in his childhood and raised by an older sister. He graduated from Oxford University, was ordained and went into the ministry. As chaplain at the royal court at the Hague he unabashedly spoke out against sin. He soon was appointed as chaplain to King Charles II who welcomed Ken's boldness and said, "I must go in and hear Ken tell me about my faults."

Under King James II, who followed Charles II, Ken was

imprisoned for his refusal to swear allegiance to the king. After his release from prison, he lived the remainder of his life in obscurity.

Ken was author of several devotional books and hymns including "Awake, My Soul, And with the Sun" and "Glory to Thee, My God, This Night." He also wrote three hymns entitled "Morning Hymn," "Evening Hymn," and "Midnight Hymn." These three hymns all close with the familiar lines we know as the Doxology:

> *Praise God from whom all blessings flow;*
> *Praise Him, all creatures here below;*
> *Praise Him above, ye heavenly host;*
> *Praise Father, Son, and Holy Ghost. Amen.*

Everyone will eventually come to the point where they must use every superlative to praise God. He must be praised! Today praise Christ that He is God and the giver of every good and perfect gift.

I am suggesting that the Apostle ended with this doxology because he could do nothing else. What he had been requesting for these Christians was such a glorious possibility that he involuntarily burst forth into this great hymn of praise, worship, and adoration.
—D. M. Lloyd-Jones

THE TOOLS OF THE TRADE

Take the helmet of salvation and the sword of the Spirit,
which is the word of God. And pray in the Spirit on all
occasions with all kinds of prayers and requests. With this in
mind, be alert and always keep on praying for all the saints.
Ephesians 6:17–18

Henry Martyn served as a chaplain with the East India Company. Though his congregation was primarily European he learned the native language and then reached out to the native people. He soon translated the New Testament and the *Anglican Book of Common Prayer* into Hindustani.

In 1809 Martyn traveled through Persia and there translated the New Testament into Persian. But Henry Martyn died in 1812. In his short life he gave his all for Jesus Christ. He once said, "With thee, O my God, is no disappointment. I shall never have to regret that I have loved thee too well."

"A workman in time of need would part with everything but his tools," Martyn wrote, "for to lose them would be to lose all. Reading the Word of God and prayer are the tools of the Christian's craft; without them he is helpless. How is it, then, that when time presses, he so often foregoes these, or shortens them? What is this but to sell his tools? If there be anything I do, if there be anything I leave undone, let me be perfect in prayer."

The Bible and prayer work together to mold us into Christ's likeness. Are you using the "tools of the trade"? Today thank Christ that He has given us His Word and He is always ready to hear our prayers.

> The equipment has to be "put on." There has to be
> a definite action on the part of the believer in carefully dressing for battle.
>
> —Dr. Stuart Briscoe

GODLY SORROW

Godly sorrow brings repentance that leads to salvation and leaves no regret, but worldly sorrow brings death.
2 Corinthians 7:10

Horatio Spafford was a Christian who built a successful legal practice in Chicago. He invested heavily in real estate but lost most of his wealth in the Chicago Fire of 1871. Though he was overwhelmed by the loss of his fortune, Spafford became involved with the ministry of D. L. Moody and planned to accompany Moody on a European campaign.

Spafford sent his wife and four daughters ahead aboard the ship *Ville du Havre.* He expected to take a later ship and join them in a few days. While crossing the Atlantic the *Ville du Havre* was struck by another ship. Of the 225 passengers onboard, only eighty-seven were rescued.

Mrs. Spafford survived but their four daughters drowned. Upon reaching land she cabled her husband: "Saved alone. Children lost. What shall I do?" Spafford left immediately to join his wife. Near the area of the ocean where his daughters lost their lives he was filled with grief. There the words to the hymn "It is Well with My Soul" came to him. Though he was experiencing sorrow he looked forward to the future joy of Christ's second coming.

Sorrow touches everyone. But everyone does not react in the same way. Do you look to Christ in times of sorrow? Today in prayer thank the Lord for His control of your life. Pray for the joy of His second coming.

There is a sweet joy which comes to us through sorrow.

—Charles Spurgeon

PAYING ATTENTION

This is why I speak to them in parables: "Though seeing, they do not see; though hearing, they do not hear or understand."
Matthew 13:13

Franklin D. Roosevelt came to office during one of the most stressful eras of American history. He began his four terms as president during the worst of economic depressions and died in office during the final days of World War II. He survived an assassination attempt and battled polio. Through it all Roosevelt's poise, ease, and confidence made him a popular president. He had a playful mood and was eager to display his sense of humor.

Once while in the receiving line at a White House reception, Roosevelt grew tired of smiling and of not having anyone listen to what he said. So to test his theory that people really don't listen to the president of the United States he gave a warm handshake and said with a grin, "I murdered my grandmother this morning." People would automatically respond with comments such as, "How lovely!" or, "Just continue with your great work!" To his amazement nobody listened to what he was saying. Then a foreign diplomat shook Roosevelt's hand. When the president said, "I murdered my grandmother this morning," the diplomat responded softly, "I'm sure she had it coming to her."

We are often lulled into ignoring important words, even the Word of God. Are you paying attention, sitting on the edge of your seat when reading or hearing God's Word? Today in prayer give thanks to Christ for what we know by the Word.

> Are we disposed to be the number of those who, having eyes, see not, and having ears, hear not, the things which so nearly concern their temporal salvation? For my part, whatever anguish of spirit it may

cost, I am willing to know the whole truth; to know
the worst, and to provide for it.

—Patrick Henry

Day 180
THE EXPOSING WORD

For the word of God is living and active.
Sharper than any double-edged sword,
it penetrates even to dividing soul and spirit,
joints and marrow;
it judges the thoughts and attitudes of the heart.
Hebrews 4:12

Knute Rockne was head football coach of the
Notre Dame "Fighting Irish" from 1918–1930. During that
period his teams had 105 victories, 12 loses, and 5 ties. Rockne
often said, "Football is a game played with the arms, legs, and
shoulders but mostly from the neck up."

During his coaching days at Notre Dame a sports columnist in a South Bend newspaper earned the reputation of being
the meanest, most cutting writer in the country. The anonymous writer knew Notre Dame well and wrote about the team's
weaknesses. He pointed out the mistakes of individual players
and described some as lazy and undisciplined. The column
enraged the football players. Though all that was written was
true they disliked having their weaknesses exposed. They com-
plained to Rockne and he patiently listened and told his players
the best way to silence their critic was to prove him wrong. He
told them to train and play in such a way as to stop fueling the
columnist's criticism. And that is what the team did. Later it
became known that the writer of the column was Knute
Rockne himself. He used the newspaper column as a device to
sharpen his team to its full potential.

God tells the truth because He loves us and wants to make

us winners. Does a certain passage of Scripture expose your sin? Today thank Christ for His Word. Ask Him to give you the strength to discipline yourself to obey it.

> I know the Bible is inspired because it finds me at greater depths of my being than any other book.
> —Samuel Taylor Coleridge

Day 181
THE CRITICAL PHASE

Jesus took the Twelve aside and told them, "We are going up to Jerusalem, and everything that is written by the prophets about the Son of Man will be fulfilled. He will be handed over to the Gentiles. They will mock him, insult him, spit on him, flog him and kill him. On the third day he will rise again.
Luke 18:31–33

As a young man Frank Morison studied the life of Christ, thinking that the history of Jesus Christ rested on insecure foundations. He decided to write a book entitled *Jesus, the Last Phase* to examine the last seven days of the life of Jesus Christ. "It seemed to me," said Morison, "that if I could come at the truth why this man died a cruel death at the hands of the Roman power, how he himself regarded the matter, and especially how he behaved under the test, I should be very near to the true solution of the problem. . . . I wanted to take this last phase of the life of Jesus, with all its quick and pulsating drama, its sharp, clear-cut background of antiquity, and its tremendous psychological and human interest—to strip it of its overgrowth of primitive beliefs and dogmatic suppositions, and to see this supremely great person as he really was."

Frank Morison never wrote *Jesus, the Last Phase.* As he was studying Jesus' death the insecure foundation of the historical

Jesus became a solid rock. Doubts evaporated as Morison wrestled with the truth and so he wrote *Who Moved the Stone?* This book is a classic defense of the historical accuracy of the biblical account of the crucifixion and resurrection of Jesus Christ.

The Christian faith rests upon the crucifixion and resurrection of Christ. Today in prayer consider these things and give thanks to Christ that He fulfilled the prophesies of the Old Testament, suffered, died, and rose from the dead.

> The Bible is true. Upon that sacred volume I rest my hope of eternal salvation through the merits of our blessed Lord and Savior Jesus Christ.
> —Andrew Jackson

Day 182
THE BIRTHPLACE OF THANKS

Give thanks to the LORD, call on his name; make known among the nations what he has done. Sing to him, sing praise to him; tell of all his wonderful acts. Glory in his holy name; let the hearts of those who seek the LORD rejoice. Look to the LORD and his strength; seek his face always.
Psalm 105:1–4

In Daniel Defoe's novel *Robinson Crusoe,* Crusoe is the sole survivor of a shipwreck on a deserted island. After being on the island for several days, Robinson Crusoe begins to exercise new thoughts about his situation.

"I daily read the Word of God and applied all the comforts of it to my present state. One morning, being very sad, I opened the Bible upon these words, 'I will never, never leave thee, nor forsake thee.' Immediately it occurred that these words were to me; why else should they be directed in such a manner, just at that moment when I was mourning over my condition, as one forsaken of God and man? 'Well, then,' said I, 'if God does not forsake me, of what ill consequence can it, or what matters it, though the world should all forsake me, seeing on the other hand, if I had all the world, and should lose the favor and blessing of God, there would be no comparison in the loss?'

"From this moment I began to conclude in my mind that it was possible for me to be more happy in this forsaken, solitary condition than it was probable I should ever have been in any other particular state in the world; and with this thought I was going to give thanks to God for bringing me to this place."

The heart is the birthplace of thanks. Look only at Jesus Christ and realize that life is a gift from Him. Today ask Jesus to fill your heart with thanksgiving.

> He who thanks with the lips thanks but in part; The
> full, the true thanksgiving, comes from the heart.
> —Anonymous

Day 183
FELLOWSHIP IN CHRIST

*They devoted themselves to the apostles' teaching and
to the fellowship, to the breaking of bread and to prayer.
Everyone was filled with awe, and many wonders
and miraculous signs were done by the apostles.*
Acts 2:42–43

James Garfield was the twentieth president of the United States. He was born in a cabin near Cleveland, Ohio, and raised by a widowed mother. In 1854 he attended Williams College in Massachusetts. John J. Ingalls, future senator from Kansas, was a student with Garfield there. Ingalls described Garfield's faith: "There was nothing of gloomy bigotry or monastic asceticism about his religion. He never held himself aloof from the society of intelligent and vivacious sinners, while enjoying the fellowship and communion of the saints."

Garfield went from Williams to become a Civil War hero, member of the U.S. House of Representatives, and president of the United States. On July 2, 1881, six months after taking office, he was assassinated.

In a meeting to pray for Garfield's recovery a college class-mate said, "Twenty-six years ago tonight, and at this very hour, our class was on the top of Mount Greylock to spend the Fourth of July. As we were about to lie down to sleep, Garfield took out his pocket Testament and said, 'I am accustomed to read a chapter with my absent mother every night: Shall I read aloud?' We all agreed, and when he had read he asked the old-est member of our class to pray. And there, in the night, and on the mountaintop, we prayed with him for whom we are now assembled to pray."

Do you share your faith with other believers? Today give thanks for the believers. Ask that you may share Christ with someone who needs encouragement.

> Things can happen when we come together. God's Spirit moves upon his worshipping people.
> —William Barclay

Day 184
FREEDOM TO SERVE

> *You, my brothers, were called to be free.*
> *But do not use your freedom to indulge the sinful nature;*
> *rather, serve one another in love.*
> *Galatians 5:13*

*S*amuel Francis Smith was born in Boston, Massa-chusetts, graduated from Harvard University, studied for the ministry at Andover Theological Seminary and went on to serve as a Baptist pastor and on various missionary boards.

In 1824 Smith came across a German song entitled "God Bless Our Native Land." He thought that America needed a similar song to thank the Lord for freedom and also pay tribute to the founding fathers who used their liberty to serve the generations to follow.

Smith wrote the verses to "My Country, 'Tis of Thee" in a half an hour. The following Fourth of July, Boston's Park Street Congregational Church children's choir sang the song for the first time. It became an immediate American favorite. One leader at the time proclaimed, "Strong in simplicity and deep in its trust for God, children and philosophers can repeat the hymn together. Every crisis will hear it above the storm." Here are the words to the first verse of the song:

"My country, 'tis of thee, sweet land of liberty, of thee I sing: Land where my fathers died, land of the pilgrim's pride, from every mountain side, let freedom ring!"

Freedom is a precious gift given to us by Christ. The Son of Man came to serve others. So we should use our freedom in Christ to serve others. Today thank Jesus Christ for the freedom you find in him and ask whom you can serve in God's love.

He climbs highest who helps another up.

—Zig Ziglar

Day 185
THE LIFE OF A FREE MAN

Live as free men, but do not use your freedom as a cover-up for evil; live as servants of God. Show proper respect to everyone: Love the brotherhood of believers, fear God, honor the king.
1 Peter 2:16–17

And for the support of this Declaration. . .we mutually pledge to each other our Lives, our Fortunes and our sacred Honor." This is the last line of the Declaration of Independence. Fifty-six men signed the document. Here is what happened to some of them:

Five were captured as traitors to Britian and tortured before they died. One was wounded, taken prisoner, and released in a prisoner exchange. Two lost their sons in the war; another had two sons captured. Another saw his ships destroyed by the British Navy, sold his home and property to pay his debts, and died in rags. Yet another was pursued by British troops—forced to move his family constantly, he lost all of his possessions.

British General Cornwallis used one signer's farm for his headquarters at Yorktown. George Washington opened fire and the farm was destroyed. Its owner died bankrupt. Another had his home and properties destroyed and his wife jailed. She died within a few months. One man who signed the historic document was driven from his wife's sickbed as their thirteen children fled for their lives. His fields and his gristmill were laid waste. For a year he lived in forests and caves. When he returned his wife was dead; his children missing. A few weeks later he died.

The price of political freedom is high. So is a life free from sin. Our freedom is always threatened by God's enemy. Today in prayer thank the Lord for freedom and deliverance from the evil one.

> We have this day restored the Sovereign of Whom all men ought to be obedient. He reigns in Heaven and from the rising to the setting of the sun, let His Kingdom come!
>
> —Samuel Adams

THE STARTING POINT OF PRAYER

*So I turned to the Lord God and pleaded with him in prayer
and petition, in fasting, and in sackcloth and ashes.*
Daniel 9:3

Jonathan Edwards is regarded as one of the most brilliant theologians that the United States has ever produced. Under the influence of Edwards' preaching at Northampton, Massachusetts, and neighboring parishes experienced a powerful spiritual awakening in 1734–1735. On July 8, 1741, in Enfield, Connecticut, Jonathan Edwards preached a sermon titled, "Sinners in the Hands of an Angry God." The sermon is the most widely known from the period called The Great Awakening when thousands came to know Christ.

Edwards was not a dynamic preacher, though he was a well-versed, sincere man. But his sermon preparation was notable. John Chapman gives us the story: "For three days Edwards had not eaten a mouthful of food; for three nights he had not closed his eyes in sleep. Over and over again he was heard to pray, 'O Lord, give me New England! Give me New England!' When he arose from his knees and made his way into the pulpit that Sunday he looked as if he had been gazing straight into the face of God. Even before he began to speak, tremendous conviction fell upon his audience."

The starting point for those who wish to be used by the Lord is prayer and petition. What is on your heart? Today come before the Lord Jesus and ask Him to do only what He can do to bring glory and honor to Himself.

> The assembly in general were, from time to time, in tears while the word was preached, some weeping with sorrow and distress, others with joy and love, others with pity and concern for their neighbors.
> —Jonathan Edwards

THE SLOUGH OF DESPOND

The Spirit of the Sovereign LORD is on me, because the LORD
has anointed me to preach good news to the poor. He has sent
me to bind up the brokenhearted, to proclaim freedom for
the captives and release from darkness for the prisoners,
to proclaim the year of the LORD'S favor and the day
of vengeance of our God, to comfort all who mourn.
Isaiah 61:1–2

In *The Pilgrim's Progress* by John Bunyan, the main character, Christian, falls into a bog called the Slough of Despond. Here he wallows, trapped by the burden that is on his back.

A fellow named Help happens along and pulls Christian to solid ground. "This miry slough is such a place as cannot be mended," said Help. "It is the descent whither the scum and filth that attends conviction for sin doth continually run, and therefore it is called the Slough of Despond; for still, as the sinner is awakened about his lost condition, there arise in his soul many fears and doubts, and discouraging apprehensions, which all of them get together, and settle in this place: and this is the reason of the badness of this ground. It is not the pleasure of the King that this place should remain so bad. . . . To my knowledge," said he, "there have been swallowed up at least twenty thousand cart loads, yea, millions of wholesome instructions, that have at all seasons been brought from all places of the King's dominions. . .if so be it might have been mended; but it is the Slough of Despond still, and so will be when they have done what they can."

Nothing can overcome our own Slough of Despond except the One who has overcome everything. In Christ we can rise above our broken hearts. In Christ we are set free. Today if you are in despair remember Christ and the liberty of the gospel.

Art thou weary? Heavy laden? Distressed? Come to the Savior. Come immediately, come repeatedly, come boldly. And be at rest.

—Charles Swindoll

Day 188
DARE TO USE YOUR GIFT

Do not neglect your gift, which was given you
through a prophetic message when the body
of elders laid their hands on you.
1 Timothy 4:14

Some great Christian work has been done under less than ideal conditions. John Bunyan was wrongfully jailed and then wrote *The Pilgrim's Progress.* Sir Walter Scott authored some of his most famous classics at an advanced age because he had to pay off more than a half million dollars of debt for which he was not legally responsible. William Carey had no formal schooling after twelve years of age yet he is considered the father of modern missions. Martin Luther was hiding from enemies in Wartburg Castle when he translated the Bible into German. Mary Slessor was born into extreme poverty to an alcoholic father. Although she was a single woman, Slessor became a missionary to Africa.

Beethoven composed some of his best symphonies when he was totally deaf. John Calvin continued to write and preach while suffering from tuberculosis. Blind from childhood, Fanny Crosby became one of the most prolific hymn writers in history. Today, Joni Eareckson Tada, a quadriplegic from her youth, is an outstanding artist, author, and speaker.

What gifts has the Lord given to you? Everyone has at least one spiritual gift to build up the body of Christ. Don't let circumstances prevent you from using the gift Christ has given

217

you. Today in prayer ask the Lord to open doors for you to use your spiritual gifts.

> Expect great things from God. Attempt great things for God.
>
> —William Carey

Day 189
SO STRONG IN CHRIST

But it has now been revealed through the appearing of our Savior, Christ Jesus, who has destroyed death and has brought life and immortality to light through the gospel.
2 Timothy 1:10

Adoniram Judson was an extremely gifted individual. He taught himself to read at age six, learned Latin and Greek by age ten, and enrolled in Brown University in Providence, Rhode Island, by age sixteen. This son of a Congregational minister went on to Andover Theological Seminary and left with his wife Ann as a missionary to India in 1812.

Judson was not welcomed in British-occupied India because of the War of 1812. So he and his wife sailed on to Burma. There Judson learned the language and began translating the New Testament. After six years of sharing his faith in Christ he saw his first convert. After two more years a Burmese church was formed and the translation work continued.

In 1824 Adoniram Judson was arrested and imprisoned for eighteen months. He endured beatings and disease with little food or water. Ann bolstered his faith and smuggled food to him. Ann died in 1826. A few months later his third child died. But Judson continued to preach and translate. He eventually left a heritage of over seven thousand believers in Burma.

Despite the sadness of his life Judson remained confident

in Christ. In April 1850 his dying words were: "I go with the gladness of a boy bounding away from school. I feel so strong in Christ."

Today in prayer thank the Lord for conquering death and giving you eternal life.

> I shall see Jesus, and this will be grand. I shall see him who made the worlds.
>
> —Sir David Brewster

Day 190
THE RIGHT OF RIGHTEOUS ANGER

I am a stranger to my brothers,
an alien to my own mother's sons;
for zeal for your house consumes me,
and the insults of those who insult you fall on me.
Psalm 69:8–9

When Robert E. Lee joined the Confederacy he left his home in northern Virginia never to return. The North seized his plantation and made it a burial ground. Today that estate is known as Arlington National Cemetery. Lee was indicted for treason after the war. His friends were indignant that anyone would bring the beloved general to trial. But Lee calmly spoke, "I have never cherished toward them bitter or vindictive feelings, and I have never seen the day when I did not pray for them."

General Lee was a mature, Christian gentleman. He often turned the other cheek when wronged. But one incident did incite his anger. After the Civil War, managers of the Louisiana Lottery approached Lee and asked if he'd let them use his name in their scheme. They promised that if he did he would become rich. Astounded, Lee straightened up, buttoned his gray coat, and shouted, "Gentlemen, I lost my home in the war. I lost my fortune in the war. I lost everything except my name. My name is not for sale and if you fellows don't get out of here I'll break this crutch over your heads!"

Today, jot down a list of things that make you angry. Then study the Bible to learn what makes God angry. Finally, in prayer ask Christ to give you the patience and peace, the courage and conviction when it is necessary to stand in righteous anger.

> A man that does not know how to be angry does not know how to be good. A man that does not know how to be shaken to his heart's core with indignation over things evil is either a fungus or a wicked man.
> —Henry Ward Beecher

Day 191
THE THREAD OF LOVE

The end of all things is near. Therefore be clear minded and self-controlled so that you can pray. Above all, love each other deeply, because love covers over a multitude of sins.
1 Peter 4:7–8

Frances Hodgson Burnett wrote the children's book *Little Lord Fauntleroy.* It vividly illustrates the positive influence of a person who expresses a warm and trusting attitude toward others. The story is about a young American boy named Cedric who goes to stay with his British nobleman grandfather. The man had a reputation for being extremely mean and selfish but the lad could see nothing but good in him. He said over and over again, "Oh, Grandpa, how people must love you! You're so good and kind in all you do."

No matter how disagreeable the elderly man was, the grandson saw the best in everything he did. Finally the youngster's unquestioning love softened the old man's heart. He couldn't resist the boy's unwavering trust. As a result he gradually began to change his ways. In time he became the unselfish and kind person his grandson thought him to be.

It is easy to love those who love us and treat us well. Today take time to thank Christ for His love to you. Ask Jesus to teach you to love the most difficult person in your life.

No cord or cable can draw so forcibly, or bind so fast,
as love can do with a single thread.
—Robert Burton

Day 192
THE THINGS THAT ARE
IMPORTANT ARE ETERNAL

The world and its desires pass away,
but the man who does the will of God lives forever.
1 John 2:17

In the city of Milan, Italy, there stands a beautiful Gothic cathedral made of white Candoglia marble. It is the symbol of Milan. The construction of this cathedral began in 1386 and was not completed until 1887, over five hundred years later. It is extraordinarily beautiful with over thirty-four hundred statues and many stained-glass windows representing biblical passages.

There are three huge gates that lead into the cathedral from the city. Over one gate is a beautiful flower bouquet. Under it is the inscription, "The things that please are temporary." Over the second gate is a cross with the words, "The things that disturb are temporary." Over the central gate are the words, "The things that are important are eternal."

God, God's Word, and God's people. These are important. These are eternal. Today take a look at your calendar and your checkbook. Where are you investing your life? In prayer ask Jesus Christ to show you how to invest in what is eternal.

> There is one fact that we may oppose to all the wit and argument of infidelity, namely, that no man ever repented of being a Christian on his deathbed.
>
> —H. More

Day 193
WIN THE APPROVAL OF GOD

As we have already said, so now I say again: If anybody is preaching to you a gospel other than what you accepted, let him be eternally condemned! Am I now trying to win the approval of men, or of God? Or am I trying to please men? If I were still trying to please men, I would not be a servant of Christ.
Galatians 1:9–10

Thomas Wolsey received his degree from Oxford University at age fifteen. At thirty-six he was the second most powerful man in Britain after King Henry VIII. He was Archbishop of York, Cardinal to the Church, and the pope's representative to England. Wolsey was a skilled administrator but his greed and lust carried him away from the Lord. He sought to please the king and the pope in order to further his career.

Wolsey's downfall came when King Henry VIII sought to divorce Queen Catherine of Aragon so he could marry Anne Boleyn. Henry wanted Wolsey to receive permission from the pope to carry out his plans. Wolsey was unable to secure such permission. After Henry cut off relations with Rome, Wolsey continued to try to please both the pope and the king. The King saw Wolsey's communication with the pope as treasonous and sentenced Wolsey to death.

Wolsey's final words were: "But if I had served God as

diligently as I have done the king, he would not have given me over in my gray hairs. However this is the just reward that I must receive for my worldly diligence and pains that I have had to do him service, only to satisfy his vain pleasures, not regarding my godly deity."

We all want the approval of our peers but the Lord's approval must be foremost. Today ask God how you can be a better servant of Jesus Christ.

It is a hard undertaking to seek to please everyone.
—Publilius Syrus

Day 194
KNOW THE WORD

But as for you, continue in what you have learned and
have become convinced of, because you know those
from whom you learned it, and how from infancy you have
known the holy Scriptures, which are able to make
you wise for salvation through faith in Christ Jesus.
2 Timothy 3:14–15

Curtis Martin grew up in the projects of Pittsburgh where senseless murder was a way of life. His grandmother was killed when he was four years old. His best friend was gunned down in his teens.

But Martin was a running back on the high school football team and won a scholarship to the University of Pittsburgh. There he accepted Christ as Lord and was quietly transformed as he eagerly studied the Bible.

Injured during his senior year, Martin could not play the last eight games of the season. But he saw this as a blessing: "The injury brought me closer to God. It was the greatest, most crucial time of my life. I learned so many morals of life.

I had nothing to do but study my Bible."

Curtis Martin was drafted by the New England Patriots. In his rookie year he rushed for 1487 yards and fourteen touchdowns. He also started a team Bible study. In 1996 Curtis ran for 1152 yards and was chosen for the Pro Bowl.

"I'm thankful for the spiritual maturity that God has brought me to right now. It's a relationship that is more intimate than I have with any other person, including my mother, even though we are very, very close. I'm grateful he chose me."

How much time are you spending each week in the Word? Ask God to show you how you may be wasting time and resolve to increase your time reading the Bible.

> If there is anything in my thoughts or style to commend, the credit is due to my parents for instilling in me an early love of the Scriptures.
>
> —Daniel Webster

Day 195
IT IS GREAT TO PRAISE THE LORD!

Praise the LORD. How good it is to sing praises to our God, how pleasant and fitting to praise him!
The LORD builds up Jerusalem; he gathers the exiles of Israel.
Psalm 147:1–2

Henry Ward Beecher was one of the most beloved preachers in New York City during the nineteenth century. Growing up in Litchfield, Connecticut, Beecher shared his bedroom with a farmhand named Charles Smith. Charles was a former slave—a Christian who took special delight in reading his Bible. Beecher describes Smith: "He used alternatively to pray and sing and laugh, pray and sing and laugh. He had a little room, in one corner of which I had a little cot; and I used to lie and see him attend to his devotions. They were a regular thing. Every night he would set his candle at the head of his bed, and pray and sing and laugh. And I bear record that his praying made a profound impression upon my mind. I never thought whether it was right or wrong. I only thought, 'How that man does enjoy it! What enjoyment there must be in prayer as his!' I gained from that man more of an idea of the desirableness of prayer, than I ever did from my father or mother. . . . This poor man. . .led me to see that there should be real overflowing gladness and thanksgiving in prayer. I learned to feel that I was the pauper and he was the rich man."

How pleasant it is to pray! Do you enjoy giving thanks to Christ? Is it a chore for you? Today ask Christ to give you a glad heart and a willing spirit to praise and love Him.

> If gratitude is due from children to their earthly parents, how much more is the gratitude of the great family of men due to our Father in heaven.
>
> —Hosea Ballou

Day 196
A WILL TO CHOOSE

But Daniel resolved not to defile himself with the royal food and wine, and he asked the chief official for permission not to defile himself this way.
Daniel 1:8

Frederick Brotherton (F. B.) Meyer was a dynamic preacher and author of more than seventy books. Charles Spurgeon wrote: "Rev. F. B. Meyer is a great gain to the armies of evangelical truth; for his tone, spirit and aspirations are all of a fine gospel sort. In all his books there is a sweet, holy savor." How did F. B. Meyer develop such a closeness to the

Lord and accomplish so much in his lifetime?

When he was seventeen Meyer believed that the Lord was calling him into the full-time ministry. He discussed it with his mother and she pointed out that being in the ministry would involve sacrifice and many trying times. She also mentioned that if he later regretted taking such a step he could always leave the ministry. Looking her straight in the eye the young man said, "Never, Mother! That would be putting my hand to the plow and looking back." Through God's grace, F. B. Meyer did not waiver from his high calling and maintained a vigorous ministry serving Christ. Many have pointed to his decision as a seventeen-year-old as a watershed act, a resolve that carried him through a lifetime of service.

How's your resolve? Today in prayer, give thanks to Jesus Christ that He rewards those who seek Him in all that they do.

God has given us a will to choose his will.
—Henrietta C. Mears

Day 197
THE MOST BEAUTIFUL ROSE

Then he opened their minds so they could understand the
Scriptures. He told them, "This is what is written:
The Christ will suffer and rise from the dead on the third day,
and repentance and forgiveness of sins will be preached
in his name to all nations, beginning at Jerusalem.
Luke 24:45–47

*H*ans Christian Andersen wrote "The World's Most Beautiful Rose." The story goes like this:

There once was a mighty queen whose garden grew the most beautiful flowers in the world. Every season there were

226

different blooms bringing forth the sweetest smelling and loveliest of roses.

But inside the castle, the queen was dying. The wisest doctor in the land said, "There is only one cure for the queen. Bring her the most beautiful rose in the land. It must symbolize the highest and purest love, and when she sees that flower, then she will not die."

After many had tried and failed to find a rose for the queen, her young son came to her and said, "Mother, look what I have read," and he proceeded to read about Jesus who suffered death on the Cross in order to save all men. "Greater love there cannot be!" he exclaimed.

The queen's pale cheeks regained their hue and her eyes became clear and bright again. "I see it. I see the rose that grew from Christ's blood on the Cross," she cried. "And those who shall see that rose, the most beautiful rose in the world, shall not die."

Jesus Christ's love conquered death. He is the "Rose of Sharon" who gave up His life so we may have life in Him. Give thanks and praise that Jesus loves you and died for you so you may live eternally in Him.

> Without the cross, his servants would have no gospel. Having the cross, his servants are bound to publish it everywhere.
>
> —Alexander MacLaren

Day 198
THE DEEP POCKETS OF GOD

And my God will meet all your needs
according to his glorious riches in Christ Jesus.
Philippians 4:19

John Wilbur Chapman was educated at Oberlin College, Lane Seminary, and received a doctorate from Heidelberg University. He held pastorates in Ohio, New York, Indiana, and Pennsylvania and was one of the most effective evangelists of his day.

Chapman experienced sorrow when his wife of four years died. Suddenly he was a single parent. His finances became depleted yet he had responsibility for a full schedule of evangelistic meetings.

During this stressful time an elder in his church, a wealthy banker, came to Chapman's home to comfort and encourage him. As this man left he slipped a piece of paper into Chapman's hand. It was a signed check made out to Chapman. But the figures indicating the amount of the gift were missing.

"Did you really mean to give me a signed blank check?" Chapman asked. "Yes," said the man. "I didn't know how much you'd need, and I wanted to be sure you would have enough." Later Chapman said, "While I never had to use that check, it gave me a secure feeling to know that thousands of dollars were literally at my disposal." Someone has said, "God too has given us a signed check in Philippians 4:19 to provide for every genuine need that arises in our lives."

The Lord has deep pockets. Today in prayer express the deepest concerns of your heart and trust God to deliver.

His plans defy the penetration of the human mind and his ways surpass the ability of man to trace them out.

—Everett F. Harrison

KINDNESS TO STRANGERS;
SERVICE TO GOD

*The islanders showed us unusual kindness. They built a fire
and welcomed us all because it was raining and cold.*
Acts 28:2

*A*gnes Gonxha Bojaxhiu was born in Skopje, Albania, in 1910. At the age of eighteen she sensed God's call to become a missionary nun and joined the Sisters of Loreto and took the name Teresa. From 1929 to 1948 she taught geography at St. Mary's High School in Calcutta where beggars, lepers, the homeless, and the dying crowded the streets.

In 1946 the woman whom the world would come to know as Mother Teresa gave up everything to follow Jesus into the slums and there serve Him in the poorest of the poor. She began her work by caring for one dying person. She soon became a citizen of India and in 1950 founded the Missionaries of Charity.

Mother Teresa dedicated her life to helping the poor, the sick, and the dying. In 1979 she received the Nobel Peace Prize. Today, more than four thousand Missionary of Charity sisters and brothers serve the poor in at least twenty-five countries. She chose to love and show unusual kindness among the poor and suffering. Her commitment to Christ was central to all that she did and that the missionaries of charity do. "I am doing my work with Jesus, I'm doing it for Jesus, I'm doing it to Jesus," she said, "and therefore the results are his, not mine."

God has called us to be His instruments of love to the sick, the dying, and the captives not only in body but also in mind and spirit. Today in prayer ask Jesus to show you someone who needs unusual kindness.

As each sister is to become a coworker of Christ in the slums, each ought to understand what God and the missionaries of charity expect from her. Let

Christ radiate and live his life in her and through her in the slums. Let the poor, seeing her, be drawn to Christ and invite him to enter their homes and their lives. Let the sick and suffering find in her a real angel of comfort and consolation. Let the little ones of the streets cling to her because she reminds them of him, the friend of the little ones.

—Mother Teresa

Day 200
THE LORD'S BATTLE

All those gathered here will know that it is not by sword or spear that the LORD saves; for the battle is the LORD's, and he will give all of you into our hands.
1 Samuel 17:47

Soon after the beginning of the Protestant Reformation, the Netherlands embraced Protestantism. At the time King Philip of Spain ruled over much of Europe. When the people of the Netherlands revolted against Spain, Philip ordered the rebellion to be crushed. Over 100,000 Protestants died between 1567 and 1573.

In 1574 the Dutch town of Leiden was besieged by the Spanish. Three times the siege was broken when Spanish soldiers mutinied because of intolerable cold and no pay. Within the year, the Spanish abandoned Leiden to Dutch hands. Both Dutch and Spanish agreed on one thing, the freedom of Leiden came as a direct result of divine intervention.

The Dutch historian Alkamaar wrote: "Surely, gentle reader, it cannot be otherwise thought but that this dissension and disorder was even the very mighty work of God, considering the great advantage, benefit and gain that resulted in this country."

The Spanish governor Don Luis de Requesens came to the same conclusion: "When I recall the circumstances in which these mutinies broke out, I cannot but conclude that God, for some secret reason wishes to punish us by our own hands because we deserve it."

The human heart is a battlefield. Victory comes when Jesus is recognized as Lord. Are you trusting in the strength of the Lord? Today in prayer give your heart's battles to God.

> The believer today needs to recognize that the world can be overcome only by his faith and confidence in God.
>
> —J. Vernon McGee

Day 201
THE SENSITIVITY OF
THE BODY OF CHRIST

If one part suffers, every part suffers with it;
if one part is honored, every part rejoices with it.
Now you are the body of Christ,
and each one of you is a part of it.
1 Corinthians 12:26–27

Leprosy is a very visible disease of the nervous system because it affects the skin. It often damages nerves in the face, arms, and legs. Damaged nerves result in paralysis and a loss of sensation in hands, feet, and eyes. This makes everyday activities fraught with danger. Burns may go unrecognized, wounds untended, stones in shoes or grit in eyes undetected.

In 1947 Dr. Paul Brand was in India visiting a sanitarium for leprosy victims. The sanitarium was run by the Church of Scotland and was looked upon as a model facility. Leprosy victims could learn and work a trade there. They would never have had this chance outside the sanitarium.

Dr. Brand visited the weaving shop and noticed a young

231

boy working vigorously at a loom. As Dr. Brand and the director neared the boy picked up speed, probably showing off to his director. Dr. Brand noticed a trail of dark spots on the cotton cloth. "May I see your hand," Dr. Brand shouted over the noise. The boy held out a deformed, twisted hand with shortened fingers. The tip of the index finger had a bad septic wound in which the naked bone was protruding. He was bleeding on the cotton and was weaving while working with a finger cut to the bone yet he felt no pain.

No rational person enjoys pain. In the body of Christ when one person suffers we all feel that person's pain. Have you cut yourself off from the fellowship of other believers? Today in prayer give thanks to God for the encouragement, fellowship, and sensitivity of the body of Christ.

> The members [of the body of Christ] are not inter-changeable. If you subtract any one member, you have not simply reduced the family number, you have inflicted an injury on its structure.
>
> —C. S. Lewis

Day 202
TAKE TIME

Pray continually.
1 Thessalonians 5:17

D. L. Moody was a popular American evangelist who preached in Great Britain from 1873–1875. When he was on a trip across the Atlantic a fire broke out in the hold of the ship and he and other volunteers helped the crew put it out. As they stood in the bucket line someone said to Moody, "Let's go up to the other end of the ship and pray." The commonsense evangelist replied, "No, sir, we will stand right here and pass buckets and pray hard all the time we are doing so."

The words pray continually evoke an image of a person who has dropped out of the world and has developed well-callused knees. But Paul in his letter to the Thessalonians urges Christians to continually pray in all that they do. As you wake up, thank Jesus for the day. As you shower and come to grips with the concerns for the day, give those concerns to Christ. As you eat breakfast, thank God for your daily bread. As you drive to work, remember in prayer those around your town and throughout the world. As events come up at home or at work, give them over to Jesus Christ. As you spend quiet moments near the end of the day, pray that you would listen to God's voice. Prayer, like breathing, must be continual in a Christian's life.

> Many people like to talk about the great prayer meetings they used to have or about the periods of time and experiences they used to have with God. But today they are too busy to take time to experience these things. We do not depend on the good meals we had years ago for our physical strength today. We must take time to eat every day to maintain our physical strength. Just so, God wants us to take time to talk to him every day.
>
> —Peter Deyneka

Day 203
MAKE EVERY EFFORT

Be completely humble and gentle; be patient, bearing with one another in love. Make every effort to keep the unity of the Spirit through the bond of peace.
Ephesians 4:2–3

Francis was the son of a wealthy merchant in Northern Italy. While in the military he was taken prisoner. In prison he reflected on his life and after release chose to follow Jesus Christ. Francis left his wealth and home in Assisi to live a life of poverty. His primary ministry was to those in the cities, where he lived among the impoverished masses and preached the good news about Christ. Soon others started to follow him and the Franciscan Order was begun.

When asked how he could accomplish so much in his lifetime Francis of Assisi replied, "This may be why: The Lord looked down from heaven and said, 'Where can I find the weakest, littlest, meanest man on earth?' Then he saw me and said, 'I've found him; he won't be proud of it; he'll see that I am using him because of his insignificance.' "

The following prayer is attributed to Francis of Assisi: "Lord, make me an instrument of thy peace. Where there is hatred, let me sow love; where there is injury, pardon; where there is doubt, faith; where there is despair, hope; where there is darkness, light; where there is sadness, joy. O Divine Master, grant that I may not so much seek to be consoled, as to console; not so much to be understood as to understand; not so much to be loved as to love; for it is in giving that we receive; it is in pardoning that we are pardoned; it is in dying that we awaken to eternal life."

In the body of Christ we love one another and thus keep our unity in Christ. Are you humble and gentle in order to keep unity of the Spirit? Today in prayer, ask the Lord to strengthen you and grant you the peace you need to love others.

I believe the first test of a truly great man is his humility.

—John Ruskin

THE REPLENISHMENT OF PRAYER

Very early in the morning, while it was still dark, Jesus got up,
left the house and went off to a solitary place, where he prayed.
Mark 1:35

Billy Graham tells a story about the young president of an East Coast company who "instructed his secretary not to disturb him because he had an important appointment. The chairman of the board came in and said, 'I want to see Mr. Jones.' The secretary answered, 'I'm terribly sorry, he cannot be disturbed; he has an important appointment.' The chairman became very angry, opened the door, and saw the president of his corporation on his knees in prayer. The chairman softly closed the door and asked the secretary, 'Is this usual?' She responded, 'Yes, he does that every morning.' The chairman of the board said, 'No wonder I come to him for advice.' "

Jesus knew he needed to spend time with the Father to gain strength for the busy days of ministry. Times have not changed. Life in this world is draining. Demands for our time and talents seem to come from every direction. Where are you going for replenishment? Like the young company president, spend some time today with the Father. Let Him restore your strength and give you wisdom. If Jesus needed this, how much more do we?

> Feeling crushed by the crowd these days? Pushed into a corner from which there is no escape? Anxiety reaching a fever pitch? Stop. Pray. Try turning it over to One who can handle your load.
>
> —Charles Swindoll

THE JOY OF GIVING

Out of the most severe trial, their overflowing joy
and their extreme poverty welled up in rich generosity.
2 Corinthians 8:2

The man known as Saint Nicholas was born in A.D. 280 in what is modern-day Turkey. He came from a wealthy family, decided to follow Christ at a young age, and became a monk in the monastery at Myra. During his early years in ministry Nicholas found joy in giving to others. He gave away his inheritance and was particularly charitable in giving to the poor and to children. Nicholas was esteemed by the church for his selfless acts and became the Bishop of Myra.

When the Roman Emperor Diocletian came to power in A.D. 284 he sought to consolidate power throughout the Empire. In A.D. 303 he attempted to use a state religion as a unifying element. He issued four harsh decrees designed to compel Christians to take part in this imperial cult. During a two year period known as the "Great Persecution," Nicholas was imprisoned for his faith. While in chains Nicholas continued giving—now to his fellow prisoners. Though he had little he continued to give whatever he could.

What does it take to start giving? A willing heart. Are you a joyful giver? Today thank the Lord that you are able to participate in His work through your giving.

Blessed are those who can give without remembering, and take without forgetting.

—Elizabeth Bibesco

Day 206

IT IS ONLY GOODNESS
WHICH GIVES EXTRAS

Give thanks to the LORD,
for he is good; his love endures forever.
Psalm 118:1

In *The Memoirs of Sherlock Holmes,* Sir Arthur Conan Doyle tells of the "Case of the Naval Treaty." In this story Holmes is reviewing the facts surrounding the theft of important diplomatic papers when he is struck by the beauty of a rose.

"What a lovely thing a rose is!" he said, holding the drooping stalk of a moss rose. This revealed a new aspect of the Holmes character. He had never before shown any keen interest in natural objects.

"There is nothing in which deduction is so necessary as in religion," said Holmes. "It can be built up as an exact science by the reasoner. Our highest assurance of the goodness of Providence seems to me to rest in the flowers. All other things, our powers, our desires, our food, are really necessary for our existence in the first instance. But this rose is an extra. Its smell and its colour are an embellishment of life, not a condition of it. It is only goodness which gives extras, and so I say again that we have much to hope from the flowers."

Though we often take much for granted in life, Jesus Christ continues to lavishly give good things. Flowers are a symbol of love not because they are necessary but because they are beautiful and extra. Today, thank Christ that He gives in abundance above what is needed—He gives the beautiful, extra things which bring joy to daily life.

The backward-looking act of thanksgiving in itself it
is quite selfless. Thus it is akin to love. All our love to

God is in response to his love for us, it never starts on our side.

—William Temple

Day 207
PLEASING TO GOD

The LORD detests the sacrifice of the wicked,
but the prayer of the upright pleases him.
Proverbs 15:8

While crossing the Atlantic F. B. Meyer was asked to preach to those onboard ship. He gave a message on answered prayer. An agnostic who was asked what he thought of the preaching responded that he did not believe a word of it.

Later Meyer gave the same sermon again in another part of the ship. The agnostic attended. Before starting for the service the agnostic put two oranges in his pocket. On his way he passed an elderly woman sitting in her deck chair fast asleep. Her hands were open. In the spirit of fun the agnostic put the two oranges in her outstretched palms. After the meeting he saw the old lady eating one of the oranges. "You seem to be enjoying that orange," he remarked with a smile. "Yes, sir," she replied, "my Father is very good to me."

"You are an older woman, surely your father can't still be alive!" said the man. "Praise God," she replied, "He is very much alive."

"What do you mean?" asked the agnostic. She answered, "Sir, I have been seasick for days. I was asking God somehow to send me an orange. I suppose I fell asleep while I was praying. When I awoke, I found he had not only sent me one orange but two!" The stunned agnostic realized he had been part of an answer to prayer. He later gave his life to Christ.

What can you give a person who has everything? Time.

Time spent alone praying to Christ is the perfect gift to our Lord.

> The godly man's prayers are his best biography, his most excellent portrait. People who do a lot of kneeling don't do much lying.
>
> —*Moody Church News*

Day 208
THE VALUE OF PATIENCE

*You, however, know all about my teaching, my way of life,
my purpose, faith, patience, love, endurance, persecutions,
sufferings—what kinds of things happened to me in Antioch,
Iconium and Lystra, the persecutions I endured.
Yet the Lord rescued me from all of them.*
2 Timothy 3:10–11

Abraham Lincoln first met Edwin Stanton in 1850 when they were opposing counsel in the McCormick Reaper patent case. Stanton referred to Lincoln as "the giraffe" and "the creature from Illinois." He considered Lincoln nothing more than a backwoods hick.

When Lincoln became a congressman in the U.S. House of Representatives, Stanton denounced Lincoln as a "low cunning clown." He said that explorer Paul Du Chaillu did not need to go to Africa to capture a gorilla because Lincoln was "the original gorilla." Despite Stanton's taunting, Lincoln remained unflappable and never retaliated with similar comments.

After Lincoln was elected president of the United States he chose Stanton to be Secretary of War. The War Department was in disarray at the beginning of the Civil War and Stanton was a highly capable administrator who could straighten it out. Throughout the war years Lincoln and Stanton spent many hours together. Stanton became a trusted advisor and a friend.

He put aside his own ambition to be a Supreme Court judge because Lincoln needed him as Secretary of War.

When Lincoln was shot Stanton was next to him. When Lincoln died he sobbed, "He now belongs to the ages."

Patience and love can prevail in difficult relationships. For example, the apostle Paul remained loving and a faithful witness for Christ despite his persecution. Are you patient and loving when you are criticized? Today ask Christ to be your peace, patience, and wisdom in all your relationships.

The principal part of faith is patience.
—George MacDonald

Day 209
SPIRITUAL BROTHERS

After David had finished talking with Saul, Jonathan became one in spirit with David, and he loved him as himself.
1 Samuel 18:1

*C*yril and Methodius were brothers. Methodius followed his father's footsteps and became a regional governor near Thessalonica. The younger, Cyril, was a gifted scholar who excelled in all the sciences, poetry, dialectics, rhetoric, and mathematics. His scholarly achievements earned him the nickname "the Philosopher."

While in his thirties, Methodius came to a spiritual crossroad. He relinquished his post as governor and joined a monastery. A few years later, Cyril felt God's calling and joined his brother in the same monastery. Together, they studied the Bible and grew in Christ's love.

In A.D. 862, the Moravian Prince Rostislav desired to have a church that was Slavic in character. He wanted a Slav liturgy and he sent emissaries to Constantinople to have teachers and ministers sent to him who would preach the gospel. The brothers answered the call and together built a church and school in Moravia. Cyril developed an alphabet for the Slavic people. Today it is known as the Cyrillic alphabet. Using this alphabet the brothers translated the Gospels and liturgy books into the Slavic language. When Cyril suffered an untimely death, he urged his brother to continue the work they had started together. Methodius resumed his ministry in Moravia and before his own death almost completed translating the Bible into the Slavonic language.

Is there someone in your life with whom you are one in spirit? Today ask the Lord to bring you someone who has a heart to serve Him as you do or thank Him for that person He has already brought into your life.

> True friendship is a gift of God, and God grants it to those who fear him.
>
> —J. Schlier

Day 210
THE ART OF IMITATION

Therefore I urge you to imitate me.
1 Corinthians 4:16

Peter Paul Rubens—an artist's artist; born in Westphalia, Germany, 1577; a leader in the Flemish school of art; influenced Van Dyck, Delacroix, and Renoir; a diplomat; knighted by Charles I of England; a dedicated family man; a Christian. "Of all his talents, painting is the least," said Ambrogio Spinola.

Rubens studied under Otto van Veen, the dean of Flemish painters. The nineteen-year-old Rubens often finished the work van Veen started. European royalty soon employed him to copy the works of Michelangelo and Raphael for their estates. He borrowed liberally from the style of Titian, and Rubens' own style was adapted by his students.

The process of imitation is dramatically illustrated in Rubens' work at the Jesuit House in Antwerp. Reubens signed a contract to deliver paintings to grace the ceilings of the building. Van Dyck and other students were contracted with Rubens to complete the work. Rubens used the technique of "looking from the steps below" he had learned from van Veen and the angles in a painting of Abraham and Melchizedek are similar to Titian's work. Imitation in art builds upon the artistry of the past.

You can work out your faith by imitating Christlike qualities in others. Do you need patience? Find a patient believer for a model. Today in prayer ask for eyes to see Christ's qualities in others. Pray you may grow in Him because of their example.

> Man is a creature that is lead more by patterns than by precepts.
>
> —George Swinnock

Day 211
HOW TO BE SUCCESSFUL

So he sent David away from him and gave him command over a thousand men, and David led the troops in their campaigns. In everything he did he had great success, because the LORD was with him.
1 Samuel 18:13–14

At the turn of the century Eddie Rickenbacker successfully raced automobiles in major events. When World War I erupted he became a pilot and finished the war with twenty-six victories in 134 air battles. He was awarded America's highest military honor, the Congressional Medal of Honor. He returned to auto racing and bought the Indianapolis Motor Speedway.

While serving in World War II, Rickenbacker's aircraft was shot down in the Pacific. He survived three weeks in a life raft.

He led two of the men with him to Christ. In his later years, he was named chairman of the board of Eastern Airlines.

Eddie Rickenbacker had an active faith. He prayed daily and regularly read the Bible. While his son Bill was attending Harvard University, Rickenbacker wrote "Frankly, Bill, only life and it's many experiences—good and bad—will bring you to the same conclusion sooner or later that there is a God in heaven." When Bill wrote back saying there have been no useful prophets or leaders in religion, Rickenbacker wrote back disagreeing that "Jesus Christ's own record is the greatest of them all."

Rickenbacker kept his priorities straight. Is Jesus Christ first in your life? If so, this is success. Today thank Christ that in Him you have victory and in Him you have success.

> Success is living in such a way that you are using what God has given you—your intellect, abilities, and energy—to reach the purpose that he intends for your life.
>
> —Kathi Hudson

Day 212
DEVOTION MEANS REGULAR ATTENTION

For Ezra had devoted himself to the study and observance of the Law of the LORD, and to teaching its decrees and laws in Israel.
Ezra 7:10

By age twelve Henry Allan (H. A.) Ironside had read the entire Bible twelve times. He continued to read the Bible cover-to-cover at least once each year. He gave his life to Jesus Christ when he was fourteen and received much of his early Christian training as an officer in the Salvation Army. He went on to be a pastor and led Moody Memorial Church in Chicago. He was one of the most gifted of the early twentieth-century preachers.

Ironside devoted the first hour of the day to Christ. His "morning watch" was a time of prayer and personal Bible reading. He regarded this habit as essential as regular eating or sleep.

Once Ironside was guest lecturer at Evangelical Theological College (later Dallas Theological Seminary) and a student asked him, "Dr. Ironside, I understand you get up early every morning to read and study your Bible."

"Oh," he said, "I've been doing that all my life."

"Well, how do you manage to do it?" the student asked. "Do you pray about it?"

"No," he replied, "I get up."

Devotion means regular attention to a loved one. Has your busy life eliminated the time you spend with your first love? Today give thanks for the love you have for Jesus Christ and resolve to regularly meet Him in a private time of devotion.

> The only spiritual light in the world comes through Jesus Christ and the inspired Book; redemption and forgiveness of sin alone through Christ. Without His presence and the teachings of the Bible we would be enshrouded in moral darkness and despair.
> —Samuel Colgate

Day 213
FORGIVE LIKE THE LORD FORGIVES

So Jonathan called David and told him the whole conversation. He brought him to Saul, and David was with Saul as before.
1 Samuel 19:7

Bill McCartney was the most successful football coach in the history of the University of Colorado. In 1994 he walked away from football to lead the Promise Keepers men's ministry. At first his wife Lyndi thought Bill was trading the activity of football for the activity of men's ministry.

"It was like Bill was saying to me, 'I don't like you because you are another thief in my life.' " she said. Bill had been an absentee husband and father for much of their marriage. Lyndi was often left lonely and depressed. She was weary of competing against football and ministry for Bill's time. Bill saw the pain in his wife's face but somehow his promises of doing better always fell short.

In 1994 Lyndi forgave Bill without expecting him to change. The pain and resentment she felt towards him started to dissipate. "When you're able to forgive like the Lord forgives, it sets you free," she said.

Bill and Lyndi are still putting their marriage back together. He works full-time for Promise Keepers but is home by four o'clock. They travel and speak together at churches on the importance of forgiveness. And Bill will often publicly renew his wedding vows to remember to keep his promises to his wife.

Forgiveness with no strings attached is Christ's way to restore relationships. Do you forgive like the Lord forgives? Today thank Christ that He has forgiven you and gives you the strength to forgive others.

> If you are suffering from a bad man's injustice, forgive him lest there be two bad men.
>
> —Augustine

Day 214
DEFEAT THE FEAR OF FAILURE

So keep up your courage, men, for I have faith in God that it will happen just as he told me.
Acts 27:25

The 1992 Barcelona Olympics was Derek Redmond's last shot at Olympic glory. At the 1988 games he was a potential 400-meter medal winner but the young British runner suffered a pulled Achilles tendon during a qualifying heat. On May 2, 1992, he lined up for the 400-meter semifinal race. Healthy and full of confidence, he was the man to beat. Derek ran fluidly off the starting line. Near the halfway point, as he pulled away from the other runners, Derek tore the hamstring muscle in his right leg. The other seven runners raced on while Derek stood dazed on the track. He then began limping toward the finish.

A man bolted from the stands to the injured runner. "You don't have to finish the race," Jim Redmond said to his son. "Yes, I do," Derek replied. "Well, if you're going to finish this race, we'll finish it together," his father replied. Then occurred a truly dramatic scene: Supported by his father, Derek Redmond hobbled through the remainder of the course while the crowd roared their approval.

We have a heavenly Father who will not let us succumb to our fears. His word is good and we can depend on it. Christ has already won the race and through faith in Him, we will be victorious. Do you have a fear of failing? Today in prayer give thanks that Jesus Christ can strengthen us and lead us to the finish line of faith.

> I learned very early in my life never to take counsel of my fears.
>
> —General George Patton

Day 215
A BIT OF LOVE TO BRIDLE THE TONGUE

For, "Whoever would love life and see good days must keep
his tongue from evil and his lips from deceitful speech.
He must turn from evil and do good; he must seek peace
and pursue it. For the eyes of the Lord are on the righteous
and his ears are attentive to their prayer, but the face of
the Lord is against those who do evil."
1 Peter 3:10–12

In 1776 General Washington and his troops were defending Manhattan Island, New York. But by August the British Navy had fortified Staten Island with fifteen thousand troops. Desertion and drunkenness in the American army were rampant. When Washington moved his army to Long Island the British were poised to cut him off from the rest of the Continental Army.

Washington gave the following order on August 3: "The General is sorry to be informed that the foolish and wicked practice of profane cursing and swearing, a vice heretofore little known in the American army, is growing into fashion; he hopes the officers will by example as well as by influence endeavor to check it, and that both they and the men will reflect that we can have little hope of the blessings of heaven on our arms if we insult it by our impiety and folly; added to this, it is a vice so mean and low, without any temptation, that every man of sense and character detests and despises it."

On August 27 wind and rain prevented the British from advancing on Washington's position. For two days the weather kept the British pinned down. On the evening of August 29, Washington ferried his ten thousand troops from Long Island to safety under the cover of fog.

A victorious life in Christ includes a pure tongue. Today in prayer ask the Lord to watch over your speech that He would not be dishonored.

A bit of love is the only bit that will bridle the tongue.

—Fred Beck

Day 216
APPROACH THE THRONE OF GRACE

Let us then approach the throne of grace with confidence,
so that we may receive mercy and
find grace to help us in our time of need.
Hebrews 4:16

Sir Walter Raleigh was an English explorer, writer, and colonizer in the late 1500s and early 1600s. He explored the eastern seaboard of the United States and named it "Virginia" after the "Virgin Queen" Elizabeth I who gave Raleigh the first colonial grant to America in 1584. This allowed him to govern the colony as he saw fit, provided that the laws were not against the "true Christian Faith." Raleigh once came to the queen with a petition. Elizabeth indignantly remarked, "Sir Walter, when will you ever stop to approach me with petitions?" Raleigh replied, "When the queen will stop to grant me my petitions."

Jesus Christ does not become weary from hearing our petitions as do earthly kings and queens. In fact He wants to hear more from us. Raleigh was confident his petitions would be answered because they were in keeping with the queen's desires. As Christians we can be confident as we approach the throne of grace. We are approaching our God who is ready, willing, and able to address all that we bring before Him. Christ is the eternal King, the merciful King, the loving King. Even if words are difficult to utter, come before Christ and let the groaning of your heart be heard.

Prayer is a rising up and a drawing near to God in mind, and in heart, and in Spirit.

—Alexander Whyte

JUSTIFIED BY FAITH

Therefore, my brothers, I want you to know that through
Jesus the forgiveness of sins is proclaimed to you.
Through him everyone who believes is justified from everything
you could not be justified from by the law of Moses.
Acts 13:38–39

R. A. Torrey was one of the most brilliant Christians of the twentieth century. A graduate of Yale University and Yale Divinity School, he daily read the Bible in four languages. He was gifted as a pastor, educator, evangelist, and author.

Once he talked with a young woman who had no assurance that her sins were forgiven. He asked her to read aloud Acts 13:39, "Through him everyone who believes is justified from everything." Torrey inquired, "Who does God say is justified?"

"Everyone who believes," she replied.

"Believes on whom?"

"Believes on Christ," she countered.

"Have you accepted him as your Savior and Lord?"

"Yes," she affirmed.

"Then what does this verse promise?"

The doubting woman hesitated. Somehow she could not say, "I'm justified from all things." Then she wept over her many sins.

Dr. Torrey, "went over that Scripture again and again. At last the simple meaning of the word dawned upon her. And when I asked her one more time, 'Do you believe in Christ?' a glorious light suddenly spread over her face. 'Yes, praise the Lord, I do! I see it now!' she exclaimed. 'I'm justified from all things!' And so she found peace with the Lord."

Justified by faith in the work of Jesus Christ. These are beautiful words. Does the guilt of sin sometimes overwhelm you? Today give thanks to God that everyone who believes in Jesus Christ is justified from everything.

I am put right with God because prior to all, Christ died. When I turn to God and by belief accept what God reveals I can accept, instantly the stupendous Atonement of Jesus Christ rushes me into a right relationship with God; and by the supernatural miracle of God's grace I stand justified, not because I am sorry for my sin, not because I have repented, but because of what Jesus has done.

—Oswald Sanders

Day 218
ONLY THE LORD REVEALS MYSTERIES

Daniel replied, "No wise man, enchanter, magician or diviner can explain to the king the mystery he has asked about, but there is a God in heaven who reveals mysteries. He has shown King Nebuchadnezzar what will happen in days to come.
Daniel 2:27–28

Dr. Harry Rimmer was a prolific Christian writer in the first half of the twentieth century. Rimmer saw that science confirmed "the Bible is alive and more timely than it has ever been in its entire span of existence!" He often visited archeological sites at locations described in Scripture.

While traveling in Egypt he spoke with the Egyptian Secretary of State. Dr. Rimmer told the official that Christians believe God has given us three revelations of Himself.

"We Muslims believe that too," said the official.

"We believe God revealed Himself in the works of creation," said Rimmer.

"We also believe that," the man responded.

Rimmer continued, "We believe God has revealed Himself in a book—the Bible."

His host answered, "We too believe God has revealed Himself in a book—the Koran."

Rimmer declared, "We believe God has revealed Himself in a man—Jesus Christ."

"We also believe God has revealed Himself in a man," replied the official, "the prophet Mohammed." Rimmer added, "We believe that Jesus is able to substantiate his claims because he arose from the dead." The Muslim hesitated. Then his eyes fell. Finally he replied, "We have no information concerning our prophet after his death."

Have you ever wanted to know the future through horoscopes or other foolish methods? As Daniel points out, only God can reveal mysteries. Today in prayer thank the Lord for the revelation of His resurrection.

> Jesus who reveals what is hidden is Himself the light
> of the world and is declared to be the wisdom and
> power of God.
>
> —D. S. Russell

Day 219
CALL IT SIN

Now, O Lord our God, who brought your people out of Egypt with a mighty hand and who made for yourself a name that endures to this day, we have sinned, we have done wrong. O Lord, in keeping with all your righteous acts, turn away your anger and your wrath from Jerusalem, your city, your holy hill. Our sins and the iniquities of our fathers have made Jerusalem and your people an object of scorn to all those around us.
Daniel 9:15–16

Man calls it an accident; God calls it an abomination.
Man calls it a blunder; God calls it blindness.
Man call it a chance; God calls it a choice.
Man calls it a defect; God calls it death.

Man calls it an error; God calls it an enmity.
Man calls it a fascination; God calls it a fatality.
Man calls it gray; God calls it godlessness.
Man calls it habit; God calls it hate.
Man calls it an infirmity; God calls it an iniquity.
Man calls it justifiable; God calls it judged.
Man calls it kidding; God calls it killing.
Man calls it liberty; God calls it lawlessness.
Man calls it a mistake; God calls it madness.
Man calls it nothing; God calls it neglect.
Man calls it oversight; God calls it obstinate.
Man calls it a problem; God calls it a plague.
Man calls it questionable; God calls it quarrelsome.
Man calls it rights; God calls it rebellion.
Man calls it a shortcoming; God calls it sin.

There are no excuses for sin. We cannot deny it, make excuse for it or call it by any other name. Today in prayer, confess any sin in your life, turn away from it, and claim Christ's forgiveness and cleansing.

> Sin is a brat which nobody is willing to own, a sign that it is a scandalous thing.
>
> —Matthew Henry

Day 220
THE ONLY FORGOTTEN SON

O my people, hear my teaching; listen to the words of my mouth. I will open my mouth in parables, I will utter hidden things, things from of old.
Psalm 78:1–2

At the age of twenty-three Robert Laidlaw opened a mail-order business in Auckland, New Zealand, which grew to become an organization of twenty-seven hundred men and women. Because of his concern for his staff Laidlaw wrote a booklet entitled "The Reason Why"—a testimony to his faith in Jesus Christ. The booklet became well-known and Robert Laidlaw became a popular inspirational speaker.

A troubled young man once came to Robert Laidlaw. Sensing the man needed Christ, Laidlaw asked him to read John 3:16 aloud. Nervously, the man read, "For God so loved the world that he gave his only forgotten Son, that whoever. . ."

"Wait just a second," interrupted Laidlaw. "You made a mistake. Please read it again." Embarrassed that he had read "forgotten" instead of "begotten," the man apologized and read the text correctly. Then the young man saw his life in a new perspective. "I'm afraid I was right the first time. I had forgotten Jesus, but I will not forget Him again."

In the four Gospels, Jesus tells some thirty-two parables. Many Christians know these stories well and understand the truth contained in them. But Christ wants us to apply these truths to our own lives. Today reflect on one of the parables. Thank Christ for the truth it teaches and ask Him to help you apply it to your life.

> Jesus used parables to teach spiritual truths. He told stories that were true to life to make clear what life is really about.
> —A. Berkeley Mickelsen

Day 221
THE MEDALS OF ETERNAL FRIENDSHIP

The goal of this command is love, which comes from a pure heart and a good conscience and a sincere faith.
1 Timothy 1:5

At the 1936 Berlin Olympics Shuhei Nishida and Sueo Oe were Japan's representatives in the pole vaulting event.

The two athletes were in competition for second place when darkness came. Oe and Nishida returned to the Olympic village convinced that they were tied, since both had cleared identical heights.

Overnight the officials decided to award the silver to Nishida and the bronze to Oe. The reasons were never fully explained. Though he had won the silver, Nishida felt that his friend had been cheated. When they returned to Japan these athletes agreed to cut Nishida's silver medal and Oe's bronze medal in half and make two medals of half silver and half bronze. These were dubbed "The Medals of Eternal Friendship" and were as unique as their medal's winners.

How are you doing in your friendships? This year would be a great time to share your honors with your friends. Ask Christ to give you a pure heart, a good conscience, and a sincere faith to do this.

Imitating Christ is opening the door to friendship.
—Billy Graham

Day 222
LOST TIME TOGETHER

Do not rebuke an older man harshly, but exhort him as if he were your father. Treat younger men as brothers, older women as mothers, and younger women as sisters, with absolute purity.
1 Timothy 5:1–2

They sat together in the park, both staring at the ground.

"My dad's an important businessman, that's why he's not in town."

"My son is also busy, that's why he doesn't call.

"It sometimes gets real quiet when he's not home at all."

"I just want to talk to my dad when I don't know what to do."

The older man squeezed the boy's hand and whispered, "Me too."

Some people find themselves torn between career and the needs of family and friends. There is never enough time to spend with the ones who need our time. Quality time is not something that can be scheduled. It comes unexpectedly. It is saying the right word to an older man to encourage him in living for the Lord. It is passing on correct teaching about Christian living to the next generation. Unfortunately there is no set timing when the lessons of life are learned.

Today ask Jesus Christ: "Am I spending enough time with the people You have given to me? Help me make a difference in others' lives."

A helping word to one in trouble is often like a switch on a railroad track—but one inch between a wreck and smooth rolling prosperity.
—Henry Ward Beecher

Day 223
THE UNKNOWN GOD

The woman said, "I know that Messiah" (called Christ) "is coming. When he comes, he will explain everything to us." Then Jesus declared, "I who speak to you am he."
John 4:25–26

When the Vandals overwhelmed North Africa in the fifth century, they did everything they could to destroy the Christian faith. The last Vandal king that ruled over North Africa was Thrasamund, who ascended to the throne in A.D. 496. He offered Christians rewards and pardons for criminal offenses if they would convert to Arianism. He did not allow vacancies in the churches to be filled and had over sixty church leaders exiled to Sardinia. Thrasamund finally met his defeat when he led an expedition to Tripoli to conquer the Moors. The Moors soundly defeated the Vandals and Thrasamund was killed in A.D. 523.

The Moorish Khalif who defeated Thrasamund showed all possible reverence for the buildings of the Christian church. He said, "I do not know who the God of the Christians is but if he is as powerful as he is represented, he will take vengeance on those who insult him and help those who do him honor."

For many today, church buildings represent an unknown god. Their only contact with Jesus Christ is your daily testimony. Is there someone in your life who doesn't know Jesus Christ? Today in prayer ask the Lord who you can befriend this week. Ask this person to join you in church this Sunday.

> As an introductory theme, linking the setting to the sermon, the Unknown God provides an effective strategy for introducing Christian preaching without offending pagan sensibilities.
>
> —Carl R. Holladay

Day 224
THE ENCOURAGEMENT OF FRIENDS

Only Luke is with me. Get Mark and bring him with you, because he is helpful to me in my ministry.
2 Timothy 4:11

Nathaniel Hawthorne graduated from Bowdoin Col-lege in 1825. His friends were Henry Wadsworth Longfellow, Herman Melville, and Henry David Thoreau. In 1837

Hawthorne published his first book, *Twice-Told Tales,* a collection of stories. That year the United States entered an economic depression and Hawthorne lost his job in a publishing house.

The next year he found work at the Customs House in Salem, Massachusetts, and was engaged to marry Sophia Peabody. While working in the Customs House, Hawthorne wrote little because of his responsibilities to family and work.

In June 1849, after working at the Customs House for eleven years, Hawthorne was suddenly fired. The next month his mother died. Because of these sudden changes Hawthorne became depressed and listless. But his wife Sophia continually encouraged him to finish a book he had begun writing. So he worked on the manuscript.

A few months later James T. Fields, an aggressive and capable publisher, visited Hawthorne looking for manuscripts to publish. Hawthorne didn't think people would want to read anything by the "most unpopular author in America." But Fields was persistent. Reluctantly Hawthorne took out a few pages of the first draft of his manuscript. Fields was elated as he read the draft of *The Scarlet Letter.* In March 1850 *The Scarlet Letter* was published. Literary critics claim it is one of the finest of American novels.

When life's circumstances deal a blow the Lord is ready to build us up in ways we don't expect. One of these ways is through friends. Paul had Luke, Timothy had Mark. When you are down do you call on your friends for encouragement? Today in prayer thank God for friends with whom you enjoy mutual encouragement.

> Better to have one Christian friend than anything the
> world might offer me.
>
> —William Biederwolf

IT IS GREATER STILL
TO DO THE LORD'S WILL

So then, those who suffer according to God's will should commit
themselves to their faithful Creator and continue to do good.
1 Peter 4:19

William and Catherine Booth were the founders of the Salvation Army. They were also the parents of eight children: William, who served as General of the Army; Ballington, who was the U.S. National Commander; Catherine, who was a missionary in France and Switzerland; Emma, who was Co-Commander in the U.S.; Herbert, who was Commandant in Canada and the U.S.; Evangeline, who served as General of the Army; Lucy, who was a Commander in France, Switzerland, Norway, and South America; and Marian, who was limited by physical infirmities and was a Staff Captain.

Marian Booth had a brilliant mind and sweet disposition. She contracted smallpox as a child and was a semi-invalid most of her life. She was the only introvert in a family of extroverts and the only one never to marry. A friend once told her "Marian, it is a pity that a woman of your capabilities should be hindered by sickness from doing the Lord's work." Marian replied, "It's wonderful to do the Lord's work, but it's greater still to do the Lord's will!"

The Lord's will is the best choice you can make in your life. It is not always fun, and it sometimes involves pain. But God's will displays the glory and love of Jesus Christ. Today give thanks that Christ is faithful and commit yourself to God's will.

No healthy saint ever chooses suffering; he chooses God's will, as Jesus did, whether it means suffering or not.

—Oswald Sanders

A TRUSTWORTHY SAYING

Here is a trustworthy saying that deserves full acceptance:
Christ Jesus came into the world to save sinners—
of whom I am the worst.
1 Timothy 1:15

Hugh Latimer was a gifted orator. He was zealous and passionate. But Thomas Bilney realized that there was something missing in Latimer's life—Jesus Christ. Bilney saw a world of God's gifts in Latimer and wanted to share Christ with him. One day he asked Latimer if he could confess his soul to him. Bilney fell on his knees and allowed his pent-up soul to share with Latimer a verse that had changed his life: "This is a faithful saying, and worthy of all acceptation, that Christ Jesus came into the world to save sinners; of whom I am chief" (1 Timothy 1:15 KJV). Latimer was overwhelmed. He knelt with Thomas Bilney that day and together they reread 1 Timothy 1:15.

Hugh Latimer went on to confront wrong wherever he saw it. He was called "the honestest man in England." His forthright speech caused much discomfort in the monarchy. Finally Latimer was martyred—burned at the stake in 1555. The verse he treasured most throughout his life was 1 Timothy 1:15.

We all come to hard times in our lives when we need to return to faith's foundations. Today give thanks to Christ that He came into the world to save sinners. This is powerful assurance.

> All my theology is reduced now to this narrow compass: "This is a faithful saying, and worthy of all acceptation, that Christ Jesus came into the world to save sinners."
>
> —Dr. Archibald Alexander

*I went in response to a revelation and set before them
the gospel that I preach among the Gentiles.
But I did this privately to those who seemed to be leaders,
for fear that I was running or had run my race in vain.*
Galatians 2:2

When Herb Elliott was sixteen he had run the mile in four minutes, twenty-two seconds. Coach Percy Cerutty saw Elliott run and told him he could help him to knock off a half a minute. "Son," Cerutty said, "do you know what it takes to run a mile under four minutes? Do you know what it is to run until you can hardly stand up, to suck in hot air until you're almost unconscious? Do you know what it is to run that kind of race?"

Elliott responded, "I don't care what it takes; I want to run the mile under four minutes."

In less than eighteen months of training, Herb Elliott ran his first sub-four-minute mile and in the same year he set a new world record for the mile and the 1,500 meters. In a period of twelve days in 1958 Elliott ran three 1,500-meter races and two sub-four-minute miles.

It is 1960; Rome, Italy; the Olympic Games; the 1,500 meter race: Elliott falls in behind the leaders. At 1,000 meters he moves easily in front of the pack. At the backstretch, Elliott sees Cerutty in the stands waving a white towel. This is the signal that Elliot is on course for a new world record. Elliott responds with a burst of speed and finishes with a world record of 3:35.6.

Do you respond to Christ as you run the race of faith? Today in prayer give thanks that Christ Jesus gives you the grace to run your course and finish the race.

The gospel preached by Paul in the early years was
the gospel still being preached by him years later.
—James Montgomery Boice

IT IS NO LONGER I

So I say, live by the Spirit, and you will not gratify
the desires of the sinful nature.
Galatians 5:16

Augustine was born to a Christian mother and a pagan father in North Africa. He turned his back on his mother's faith and by age eighteen he was keeping a mistress. He became a professor of rhetoric and taught in Carthage, Rome, and later in Milan.

There Augustine started searching for truth. His mother Monica came to Milan. She prayed for him and told him about Christ. The preaching of Ambrose also influenced the young man. It was while reading Paul's epistle to the Romans in a quiet garden that Augustine made Christ Lord of his life.

He went on to become the leader of the church in Hippo, Africa. His autobiography *Confessions* is known as one of the best autobiographies of all time. His book *The City of God* has remained a favorite through the centuries.

Soon after his profession of faith Augustine was walking down the street in Milan. There he was accosted by a prostitute whom he had known most intimately. She called but he would not answer her call. He kept right on walking.

"Augustine," she shouted. "It is I!"

He replied, "Yes, but it is no longer I."

We can never satisfy our sinful nature. This pursuit carries us further and further away from Christ. But we can put on Christ and walk in the Spirit. Today thank Christ that He has provided the Holy Spirit so you may overcome your sinful nature.

Though every believer has the Holy Spirit, the Holy Spirit does not have every believer.

—A.W. Tozer

ALL GLORY, LAUD AND HONOR

I will praise God's name in song and
glorify him with thanksgiving.
Psalm 69:30

Theodulf was a Spanish theologian who served in the court of Charlemagne. He was appointed Bishop of Orleans and made it his priority to raise the academic standards of those who were in ministry. Theodulf was also known as a skilled poet, author, and a patron of the arts.

After Charlemagne died a rumor circulated that Theodulf was plotting against Louis I, Charlemagne's son. So in A.D. 818 Theodulf was imprisoned. During this time in prison he wrote the hymn "All Glory, Laud and Honor."

In A.D. 821 Theodulf was singing this hymn and worshipping the Lord in his prison cell. Louis was visiting nearby and overheard Theodulf's worship. Louis was so moved that he pardoned Theodulf.

Here are the words which Theodulf sang so many years ago:

> *All glory, laud and honor to thee, Redeemer, King,*
> *To whom the lips of children made sweet hosannas ring:*
> *Thou art the King of Israel, thou David's royal Son,*
> *Who in the Lord's name comest, the King and*
> *Blessed One!*

Sometimes only through song can we express our gratitude and thanks to Christ. Today give thanks to God and glorify Him in song.

Joyful, joyful, we adore Thee, God of Glory, Lord of love; Hearts unfold like flowers before Thee, Opening

to the sun above. Melt the clouds of sin and sadness,
Drive the dark of doubt away; Giver of immortal
gladness, fill us with the light of day.

—Henry Van Dyke

Day 230
FLEE LUST

Flee from sexual immorality.
All other sins a man commits are outside his body,
but he who sins sexually sins against his own body.
1 Corinthians 6:18

Dr. C. Everett Koop was Surgeon General of the
United States from 1981 to 1989. In the *Report on AIDS from
the Surgeon General,* Koop writes: "The AIDS virus attacks a
person's immune system and damages his/her ability to fight
other disease. Without a functioning immune system to ward
off other germs, he/she now becomes vulnerable to becoming
infected by bacteria, protozoa, fungi, and other viruses and
malignancies, which may cause life-threatening illness. . . ."
Dr. Koop stresses that to control the spread of AIDS, "People
must be responsible about their sexual behavior."

Dr. Koop also wrote an article titled "God's Sovereignty
Remains My Greatest Comfort." Though he does not directly
address the area of sexual conduct Koop says this about the
Christian's reliance on God's will: "But in a time of adversity
or trouble, the Christian has the opportunity to know God in
a special and personal way. Indeed, it necessitates acknowledg-
ing our own inability to cope. It is then that we learn we must
rely completely on the grace and mercy of a loving God. And
how wonderful to know we have a Lord who knows the end
from the beginning!"

The sovereign God created sex and sexual desire but He

has placed restrictions on it for our own benefit. Sexual immorality is not something to toy with. Are you tempted to engage in sex outside of marriage? Today in prayer ask for the grace and mercy of Jesus Christ to flee from sexual immorality.

> There's a word for those folks who linger and try to reason with lust: victim.
>
> —Charles Swindoll

Day 231
HIS KINGDOM FIRST

But seek his kingdom,
and these things will be given to you as well.
Luke 12:31

John Wanamaker began working at age thirteen as an errand boy. He soon switched to selling men's clothing. In 1857 Wanamaker became the secretary for the Young Men's Christian Association (YMCA) in the Philadelphia area. In 1858 he began the Bethany Sunday School—the most active Sunday school system in the world. By 1861 Wanamaker started his own men's clothing business. Within ten years this company, Oak Hall, was the largest retail store in the country.

In 1877 Wanamaker opened "Grand Depot" the first department store in Philadelphia. In March 1889 President Harrison asked him to become the Postmaster General of the United States. Wanamaker remained in this position until 1893. As Postmaster General he instituted technical advances which streamlined mail handling and he pushed for delivery of parcel post.

When someone once asked him how he could do so much at once Wanamaker answered, "Early in life I read, 'Seek ye first the kingdom of God, and his righteousness, and all these things shall be added unto you.' The Sunday school is my business, all the rest are the things." Wanamaker sought the kingdom of God in a specially constructed soundproof room in his store. There he spent thirty minutes every day reading his Bible and praying.

The Lord wants His kingdom to be the first and foremost priority in your heart. Then your life will be rich and full. Today in prayer put God's kingdom first and allow Him to be faithful in adding all the rest.

> So Jesus says, "Bend all your life to obeying God's will and rest content with that."
>
> —William Barclay

Day 232
THE DISEASE OF SIN

What shall we conclude then? Are we any better? Not at all!
We have already made the charge that Jews and
Gentiles alike are all under sin. As it is written:
"There is no one righteous, not even one."
Romans 3:9–10

In 1906 six members of William Henry Warren's household contracted typhoid. This was considered a poor man's disease caused by bad water, bad milk, or bad oysters. But the Warrens were a wealthy banking family who vacationed on Long Island's fashionable north shore.

George Soper, a sanitary engineer for the State of New York, investigated the cause of the Warrens' case. The state wanted to prevent public hysteria since the mortality rate for typhoid fever was ten percent.

Soper reviewed the Warrens' habits. Their cook, Mary Mallon, an Irish immigrant who had previously cooked for wealthy families in New York, did not display any signs of typhoid. But whenever Mallon began a new job members of the household displayed symptoms of typhoid in three weeks. Early in 1907 health officials removed her from the Park Avenue home where she was working. The press called her

"Typhoid Mary"—the first person to be identified as a healthy carrier of typhoid fever.

Mallon vehemently denied that she had spread the disease to twenty-two people but was confined to a bungalow on North Brother Island in the East River. In 1910 she was released. In 1915 Mallon was returned to custody after a second typhoid outbreak was attributed to her. Fifty-one infections and three deaths were directly attributed to Mary Mallon.

Everyone has contracted sin. Each of us is a carrier. Sin is the disease that separates us from God. Today thank Christ that only He can heal us from the deadly effects of sin.

> Our sins are not to be numbered by the conscious violations of duty; they are as numerous as the moments of our existence.
>
> —Charles Hodge

Day 233
THE FIRST RESORT

Be joyful in hope, patient in affliction, faithful in prayer.
Romans 12:12

According to historian David Barrett over 160,000 Christians were martyred for their faith in 1996. There have been more Christian martyrs in the twentieth century than in all other centuries combined. Christians are most persecuted and intolerance is highest in Saudi Arabia, Southern Sudan, Somalia, Iran, Northern Sudan, China, Yemen, North Korea, Morocco, and Comoro Islands. In Saudi Arabia Christianity is illegal. There two Filipino missionaries were executed in 1997 for sharing their faith.

Terry Madison of the missions organization Open Doors has said: "May I suggest that we do first what we so often do last when all else fails—pray! If the Church doesn't pray, who will? If Christians living in freedom don't call upon the name of the Lord for those in pain for their faith in restricted societies, who will?"

The hope for all Christians is Jesus Christ. Some believers are under persecution for that hope. Are we praying as the first resort to ease their suffering? Today thank Christ that He is our hope and faithfully pray for a persecuting country or Christian missionary.

Much prayer, much power.

—Peter Deyneka

Day 234
GREAT EXPECTATIONS

Then Peter said, "Silver or gold I do not have, but what I have
I give you. In the name of Jesus Christ of Nazareth, walk."
Taking him by the right hand, he helped him up, and
instantly the man's feet and ankles became strong. He jumped
to his feet and began to walk. Then he went with them into
the temple courts, walking and jumping, and praising God.
Acts 3:6–8

In Charles Dickens' *Great Expectations* the central character is Pip—an orphan apprentice at a blacksmith shop under the care of Joe Gargery. Pip has dreams of one day becoming a rich gentleman.

One day an attorney appears at the blacksmith shop and says, " 'Now, I return to this young fellow. And the communication I have got to make is, that he has Great Expectations.' Joe and I gasped, and looked at one another. My dream was out. . . . "

Pip goes to live with a Miss Halversham and becomes rich. His benefactor remains anonymous for most of the book. As Pip grows older he says, "As I had grown accustomed to my expectations, I had insensibly begun to notice their effect upon myself, and those around me. Their influence on my own character. . .I knew very well was. . .not all good." Pip had snubbed Joe and the friends that he had in his youth. He was too busy chasing his dream of riches and happiness.

Pip expected money to bring happiness. At the end of the book, after being arrested for indebtedness, he discovers that happiness has nothing to do with money.

Happiness only comes from the author of life—Jesus Christ. No amount of money can heal the emptiness we have without Him. Are you unhappy; looking for money to turn your life around? Today in prayer give thanks that Christ cares for you and that your greatest expectations are fulfilled in Him.

> We grow rich by depositing the Word of God in our hearts.
>
> —Wilbur Smith

Day 235
BLESSED BY GIVING

The disciples, each according to his ability, decided to provide help for the brothers living in Judea. This they did, sending their gift to the elders by Barnabas and Saul.
Acts 11:29–30

*C*yrus Hamlin was born in Waterford, Maine, and went on to graduate from Bowdoin College and Bangor Theological Seminary. In 1839, he arrived in Turkey and founded a school for Armenian students. Much of Cyrus Hamlin's life is chronicled in his parents' diaries. In one account they tell how young Cyrus stretched his faith in giving and gained a heart for world missions.

When he was ten years old, his mother gave him seven cents to celebrate the Christmas holiday. The money could be spent any way he wished. Thoughts of gingerbread and candy canes filled the young boy's head. "Perhaps, Cyrus, you will put a cent or two into the missionary box at church," said his mother.

As he trudged along to church the boy questioned himself: "Shall I give one cent or two? I wish she had not said one cent or two. I shall do the greater and give two." But after a bit more walking his conscience said: "What, five cents for your stomach and two for the lost! Five cents for gingerbread and two for souls! So I decided four cents for gingerbread and three cents for souls." But presently Hamlin felt it must be three cents for gingerbread and four for souls. When he finally arrived at the missions box young Cyrus dropped in the entire seven cents.

When people give, both the giver and the receiver of the gift are blessed by the Lord. Today ask Christ which ministry at your church needs your extra gift.

> Money-giving is a good criterion of a person's mental
> health. Generous people are rarely mentally ill people.
> —Karl Menninger

Day 236
THE DESTRUCTIVENESS OF GREED

I have written you in my letter not to associate with sexually
immoral people—not at all meaning the people of this
world who are immoral, or the greedy and swindlers,
or idolaters. In that case you would have to leave this world.
But now I am writing you that you must not associate with
anyone who calls himself a brother but is sexually immoral or
greedy, an idolater or a slanderer, a drunkard or a swindler.
With such a man do not even eat.
1 Corinthians 5:9–11

In the popular film *Wall Street* the character portrayed by Michael Douglas declares to a company's shareholders:

"Greed is good." He thinks that greed is a great motivation for productivity.

The nature of greed is better described in Aesop's Fable "The Goose With the Golden Eggs":

"One day a countryman going to the nest of his goose found there an egg all yellow and glittering. When he took it up it was as heavy as lead and he was going to throw it away because he thought a trick had been played upon him. But he took it home on second thought and soon found to his delight that it was an egg of pure gold. Every morning the same thing occurred and he soon became rich by selling his eggs. As he grew rich he grew greedy; and thinking to get at once all the gold the goose could give, he killed it and opened it only to find nothing. Greed often over reaches itself."

A little bit more. If this is your view of money you may have a problem with greed. Contentment is not found in money. It is found only in Christ. Today in prayer ask Christ to reveal your needs and expose your desires. He will take care of your needs.

> One of the weaknesses of our age is our apparent inability to distinguish our needs from our greeds.
> —Don Robinson

Day 237
THE TRUTH OF GOD'S LOVE

Love does not delight in evil but rejoices with the truth. It always protects, always trusts, always hopes, always perseveres.
1 Corinthians 13:6–7

Most people look at Genesis chapter five as a boring list of "begats." But if you look at the meaning of each name from Adam to Noah it is hard not to be touched by God's love:

Hebrew	English
Adam	Man
Seth	Appointed
Enosh	Mortal
Kenan	Sorrow
Mahalalel	The Blessed God
Jared	Shall come down
Enoch	Teaching
Methuselah	His death shall bring
Lemech	The despairing
Noah	Comfort

Read down the list of English meanings to the Hebrew names: "Man (is) appointed mortal sorrow; (but) the Blessed God shall come down, teaching (that) His death shall bring the despairing comfort (or rest)."

This is the gospel in a nutshell as spelled out by God from the beginning. The message of 1 Corinthians 13:6–7 is evident throughout the Bible. Christ has always been protecting, trusting, hoping, and persevering. Today give thanks to Jesus for his love and ask Him to give you the same overflowing love for those who do not know His salvation.

God's love is not a conditional love, it is an open-hearted, generous self-giving which God offers to men.

—J. B. Phillips

OUR ONLY COMFORT

David took these words to heart and was very much afraid
of Achish king of Gath. So he pretended to be insane in their
presence; and while he was in their hands he acted like a
madman, making marks on the doors of the gate and
letting saliva run down his beard.
1 Samuel 21:12–13

A certain madness and sadness occurs when we lose our trust in Christ. David Hume was a popular philosopher in the eighteenth century. His works on the natural history of religion look at different cultures and argue that the belief in many gods was the first religion. He saw belief in one God as an evolutionary development. He asserted that fear was the true cause for religion and neither belief in one God nor many gods really mattered.

But David Hume's philosophical world took a tumble when his mother fell gravely ill. She was a Christian yet foolishly followed her son's teachings. On her deathbed she wrote, "Dear son, my health has forsaken me. I am failing rapidly; I cannot live much longer. My philosophy affords me no comfort in my distress. I have lost the hope and comfort of religion and am sinking in despair. You can offer me something that will replace the hope of religion that I have lost. Hurry home, I beseech you, to comfort me, or at least write me what consolation you can afford in the hour of death." Hume hurried home, but he did not have any philosophical speculations to comfort his dying mother.

Our only comfort in stressful times is Jesus Christ. Are you trusting Him with your whole life? In prayer thank the Lord that He is faithful when you are not. Thank Him that He comforts when there is no other comfort.

A great many men say, "Oh, I have profound reverence and respect for God." Yes, profound respect, but not faith. Why, it is a downright insult.

—D. L. Moody

Day 239
BODY BUILDING

It was he who gave some to be apostles, some to be prophets, some to be evangelists, and some to be pastors and teachers, to prepare God's people for works of service, so that the body of Christ may be built up until we all reach unity in the faith and in the knowledge of the Son of God and become mature, attaining to the whole measure of the fullness of Christ.
Ephesians 4:11–13

Once there were four men named Everybody, Somebody, Anybody, and Nobody. They all met together to form a church. Everybody was excited. Somebody yelled, "Praise the Lord!" "Anybody can do this!" they all shouted in agreement. Nobody kept still.

Everybody was to bring Somebody to church. Everybody was to welcome Anybody. And Everybody would leave Nobody to himself.

Somebody was to preach the morning message. Somebody was to sing a heartfelt solo. Somebody was to acknowledge Anybody who needed prayer or to announce upcoming events of interest.

Anybody could give prayer requests. Anybody could give announcements of interest. Anybody could bring a covered dish and help with the children's Sunday school. Anybody could be an usher and greeter. Nobody would be excluded.

The next Sunday came. Everybody overslept and forgot to bring Somebody to church. Embarrassed for not bringing Somebody and missing church, Everybody couldn't face Anybody

273

and stayed away. Somebody could have called Anybody but was too proud that he would be dependent on Anybody. And that Sunday you couldn't find Anybody. Only Nobody showed up.

The Lord has given each of us gifts so we may minister to the church. When we use our gifts the body of Christ is built up. Do you know what gifts Christ has given to you? Are you using your gifts? Today thank God for your gifts and ask Him how you can best use them.

> Ministry itself is a gift and not a work looking toward a reward. It is a cumulative, building up of the body of Christ.
>
> —Theodore O. Wedel

Day 240
THE SOURCE OF STRENGTH

David was greatly distressed because the men were talking of stoning him; each one was bitter in spirit because of his sons and daughters. But David found strength in the LORD his God.
1 Samuel 30:6

Under Pakistani law a person found guilty of blasphemy against Islam can be put to death. There, it is blasphemy to say that Jesus Christ is the Son of God. Even if a court does not convict a person of blasphemy, an angry mob may gather and try to kill someone accused of this. Since 1993 four Christians have died by the hands of such mobs. Arif Iqbal Bhatti, a Muslim judge, was assassinated for acquitting two Christians of blasphemy.

On November 6, 1997, Ayub Masih along with his parents and three brothers faced blasphemy charges. Ayub, a Christian, knew that speaking about his faith put his life in danger. He and his family were in chains at the Sahiwal Courthouse when a guard pointed at him and said loudly,

"Oh, so you are Ayub Masih!" Seconds later, a shot was fired at Masih. Eyewitnesses said the bullet passed under Masih's arm and did not injure anyone. The gunman was a former neighbor who brought charges against Masih. Police have refused to take action against the gunman. Masih's trial was delayed until his safety could be assured.

There is only one place to find true comfort and strength. It is in Jesus Christ. Are you distressed because others hate you because of your faith? Today in prayer give thanks to the Lord who protects you, strengthens you, and comforts you in times of trouble.

> If we have God in our hearts, we have enough for courage and for strength.
>
> —Alexander MacLaren

Day 241
GOOD SHEPHERDS

Be shepherds of God's flock that is under your care, serving as overseers—not because you must, but because you are willing, as God wants you to be; not greedy for money, but eager to serve; not lording it over those entrusted to you, but being examples to the flock.
1 Peter 5:2–3

H. R. P. Dickson, author of the book *The Arab of the Desert,* once witnessed a Bedouin shepherd call, one by one, the fifty-one ewes in his flock. He then restored each of them to their mothers to suckle.

Shepherds know their sheep because each one has a particular flaw—crossed eyes, bowed legs, droopy ears, etc. But despite their faults shepherds go to great lengths to care for their sheep. They live with patience and vigilant care for the benefit and protection of their sheep.

D. L. Moody said, "I would like to know if there is a man or woman on earth who doesn't need the care of a shepherd. Haven't we all got failings? If you really want to know what your failings are, you can find someone who can point them out. God would never have sent Christ into the world if we didn't need his care. We are as weak and foolish as sheep."

Serving God's people requires self-sacrifice and a deep knowledge and care for people. Today in prayer, give thanks to the Lord for the minister, pastor, or elder who cares for you. Ask that Christ would continue to be their shepherd.

> It pays to serve the Lord; but don't serve the Lord because it pays; for if you serve the Lord because it pays, it then may not pay.
> —Robert G. LeTourneau

Day 242
THE STAIN REMOVER

You are already clean because of the word I have spoken to you.
John 15:3

Shakespeare's *MacBeth* is a classic tragedy. As the story goes, MacBeth's cousin Duncan is the Scottish king. But Lady MacBeth is pushing her husband to become king of Scotland. So she helps plan the murder of Duncan. One night MacBeth drugs Duncan's bodyguards and stabs the sleeping king.

The next morning MacBeth feigns fury and grief over the death, blames Duncan's bodyguards, and puts the "treasonous" bodyguards to death. But Duncan's loyal general Banquo suspects foul play. So MacBeth has Banquo and others murdered. Such murders continue until a bloody civil war ensues.

Lady MacBeth, who sparked this conflict, becomes increasingly fearful and remorseful. The trauma of the bloodshed causes her to sleepwalk. One evening Lady MacBeth's lady-in-waiting summons a physician to observe her distressed behavior. The sleepwalking Lady MacBeth approaches a washbasin, and proceeds to obsessively wash her hands, shouting "Out, damned spot! Out, I say!" The physician concludes, "More needs she the divine than the physician. God, God forgives us all!"

We all need a fresh start when the guilt of sin overcomes us. Are you troubled by past sins? Today confess your sins to Christ, turn away from them. God forgives us for the sake of Jesus Christ!

> My case is bad, Lord, be my advocate, my sin is red;
> I'm under God's arrest.
>
> —Edward Taylor

Day 243
WORDS TO LIVE BY

The man who saw it has given testimony,
and his testimony is true.
He knows that he tells the truth,
and he testifies so that you also may believe.
John 19:35

Dr. E. V. Rieu was a distinguished British scholar educated at Oxford. He was an editor at Penguin Books from 1944 to 1964. He was President of the Virgil Society and Vice-President of the Royal Society in Literature. Among his works were translations of Homer's *Iliad* and *Odyssey*, Virgil's *Pastoral Poems* and *The Voyage of the Argo* by Apollonius of Rhodes. Rieu had an excellent command of the Greek language and his translations were characterized by elegance and clarity.

One day the senior editor at Penguin Classics asked Rieu to consider translating the Gospels. At the age of sixty the life-long agnostic agreed to try it. At that time his son said, "It will be interesting to see what Father makes of the four Gospels. It will be even more interesting to see what the four Gospels make of Father."

Within a year Dr. Rieu was converted to Christianity. His finished work, *The Four Gospels,* is a popular book. Rieu observed the following: "I got the deepest feeling that the whole material was extraordinarily alive. My work changed me. I came to the conclusion that these words bear the seal of the Son of Man and God."

The Bible is the Word of God. It breathes life into the human soul. When you read your Bible, are you impressed that the words are God's Word? Today thank God for the Bible.

> I read in the Scriptures that God would send a perfect sacrifice to atone for my sins, one called the Messiah. I knew that only one person in all of history could seriously be considered Yeshua—known to the Gentiles as Jesus! And this Jewish boy, not being very religious, in the privacy of my own room, prayed "Messiah, if you're there, come into my heart and life and cleanse me with your precious blood of atonement."
> —Manny Brotman

Day 244
NO MIDDLE GROUND IN THE FAITH

Then Agrippa said to Paul, "Do you think that in such a short time you can persuade me to be a Christian?" Paul replied, "Short time or long—I pray God that not only you but all who are listening to me today may become what I am, except for these chains."
Acts 26:28–29

Everyone expected Aaron Burr to become a preacher. His grandfather was Jonathan Edwards the great preacher of

America's Great Awakening. His father was a preacher too. But Burr never made a profession of faith in Christ.

While attending Princeton University, Burr went to an evangelistic meeting. He was moved by the sermon and started to make his way forward during the altar call. "Look, there is Aaron Burr. He's going forward," someone whispered. Embarrassed, Burr returned to his pew.

Burr pursued a career in law, went on to be elected to the New York State Assembly, and then vice president of the United States. In September, 1836, at the age of eighty, Burr was told that he was about to die. "Doctor, I can't die," he said. "My grandfather, father, and mother were all pious people and they prayed for my conversion a thousand times. It is impossible that a child of so many prayers would be lost." Pastor VanPelt was with Burr at his deathbed and asked him, "Do you have good hope, through grace, that all your sins will be pardoned for the sake of our Lord Jesus Christ?" Burr replied moments before his death, "On that subject I am coy."

There is no middle ground—you either believe in Jesus Christ or you do not. This requires a personal decision. Do you know someone who is sitting on salvation's fence? Today pray that they would come over to the side of Christ, taste His love, and follow Him.

> Agrippa was not minded even to appear to lend support to Paul's case. What would Festus think if he expressed or even seemed to express agreement with the man whose great learning had turned his head? Therefore he could not admit that he did believe the prophets; on the other hand, he could not say that he did not believe them, for his reputation for orthodoxy and his influence with the Jews would be gone if he did.
>
> —F. F. Bruce

Day 245
DEVELOP AN ATTITUDE OF GRATITUDE

For although they knew God, they neither glorified him as God nor gave thanks to him, but their thinking became futile and their foolish hearts were darkened.
Romans 1:21

At the beginning of Shakespeare's *King Lear,* Lear is an old man. His daughters, Regan and Goneril, have flattered their father to the extent that he has relinquished much of his power and possessions to them. Instead of honoring their father and showing him kindness in his old age, the daughters have become "tigers, not daughters." Stripped of his authority and ignored by the palace staff, King Lear laments: "Ingratitude, thou marble-hearted fiend, More hideous when thou show'st thee in a child than in the sea-monster!" The king continues by describing the anguish of seeing his own children become so ungrateful. Lear tells Goneril of the pain of ingratitude, "that she may feel how sharper than a serpent's tooth it is to have a thankless child!"

Ingratitude can break a parent's heart. God too is dismayed by a thankless attitude. In Luke 17 Christ shows his displeasure with ingratitude when only one of ten lepers returns to thank Him. "Were not all ten cleansed? Where are the other nine? Was no one found to return and give praise to God except this foreigner?" (vv. 17–18). Are you developing an attitude of gratitude toward the Lord and others? Starting today resolve to say, "Thank You," to Christ.

> Thankfulness is the opposite of selfishness. The selfish person says, "I deserve what comes to me! Other people ought to make me happy." But the mature Christian realizes that life is a gift from God, and that blessings of life come only from his bountiful hand.
> —Warren W. Wiersbe

THANKSGIVING EVAPORATES WORRIES

Let the peace of Christ rule in your hearts, since as members
of one body you were called to peace. And be thankful.
Colossians 3:15

The Oregon Trail stretched from Independence, Missouri, two thousand miles to the Oregon Country. Here is one traveler's record: "It is so hot now that if we wear our bonnets we drip with sweat. But if we don't, we're burned by the sun. It's a dilemma. We just crossed a dry lake with the surface cracked like a broken platter. We're sure glad we stayed an extra month in Salt Lake City. If it was any hotter than this, we don't know how we could travel. . . . We are supposed to reach Salt Springs tomorrow. Our water is low and we are very thirsty, so we're anxious to get there."

Another party of pioneers suffered greatly from a scarcity of water. Broken wagons caused delays in the stifling heat. Optimism and cheer were gone. One night they gathered to air their complaints. At the campfire, one of them arose and said, "Before we do anything else, I think we should first thank God that we have come this far with no loss of life, with no serious trouble from the Indians, and that we have enough strength left to finish our journey." After the prayer, there was silence. No one had any grievances which they felt were important enough to voice.

Does an uncertain future make you anxious and overshadow God's blessings in your life? Trade your worries for peace. Christ gives peace. We need only give Him our anxiety. Today, thank Jesus Christ for the blessings in your life. His peace will take over from your worry.

When thou hast thanked thy God for every blessing sent, what time will then remain for murmurs or lament?

—Richard Chenevix Trench

TREAT GOD LIKE A KING

And I do whatever you ask in my name,
so that the Son may bring glory to the Father.
John 14:13

*J*ohn Newton went to sea as a boy and eventually commanded a slave ship. But he surrendered his life to Jesus Christ and became a preacher in Great Britain. Today he is best known for writing the hymn "Amazing Grace." He often told this story:

A man was bargaining with Alexander the Great—the man wanted a huge sum of money in exchange for his daughter's hand in marriage. The ruler consented and told him to request of his treasurer whatever he wanted. So he asked the treasurer for an enormous amount. The keeper of the funds was startled and said he couldn't give him that much without a direct order. Going to Alexander, the treasurer argued that even a small fraction of the money requested would more than serve the purpose.

"No," replied Alexander, "let him have it all. I like that fellow. He does me honor. He treats me like a king and proves by what he asks that he believes me to be both rich and generous." Newton would conclude his story saying, "In the same way, we should go to the throne of God's grace and present petitions that express honorable views of the love, riches, and bounty of our king!"

The chief end of prayer is not the answers to prayer. Prayer is meant to bring glory to God. When you lay aside your own will and ask Christ to receive glory in a situation you are truly praying in Jesus' name. Today in prayer put aside your will. Allow God to answer prayer only to glorify His name.

Jesus, we love you, we worship and adore you.
Glorify thy name in all the earth. Glorify thy name,
glorify thy name, glorify thy name in all the earth.
—Donna Adkins

Day 248
IN GOD WE TRUST

Whoever loves money never has money enough; whoever loves
wealth is never satisfied with his income. This too is meaningless.
Ecclesiastes 5:10

In 1911 the American Tobacco Company controlled ninety-two percent of the world's tobacco business. The fortune of the company's owner, James Buchanan Duke, grew by more than one million dollars a day. A year before his death Duke established "The Duke Endowment" which contributed vast sums of money to churches and universities. Though he was a churchgoer most of his life, Duke had made money his god. This is evidenced by his last words to his daughter Doris.

"Promise me that you will keep our fortune safe until I return in another life and lay claim to it once again. Always obey the rules that I'm about to tell you and no one will ever take our fortune, or any part of it, away from us.

"Trust no one. Never trust anyone—even if you want to do otherwise with your whole heart; even if you feel certain that someone may deserve your trust—don't do it. That is life's first rule. Follow it and you will never be disappointed. . . . Live by your own will. Never live by the will of another, not even of the man you marry. Follow these rules. Make me proud of you."

Money was never meant to take preeminence in our lives. That place is reserved for Jesus Christ. Do you put too much trust in the currency which states "In God We Trust"? Money is a tool to use not to love. Today in prayer thank Christ that only in Him can you wisely place your trust.

> Building one's life on a foundation of gold is just like
> building a house on foundations of sand.
> —Henrik Ibsen

THE FRONT ROW OF WARRIORS

*Moreover, at Daniel's request the king appointed Shadrach,
Meshach and Abednego administrators over the province of
Babylon, while Daniel himself remained at the royal court.*
Daniel 2:49

One of the great city-states of ancient Greece was Sparta.
It had a smaller population than the other city-states and so was
devoted to military readiness. All of Sparta was expected to
place service to their city-state above personal concerns for the
sake of the city's survival. Sparta was aggressive and its warriors
were among the best. The city was easily defended because it
was nestled on a small plain between rugged mountains. Early
visitors to the city expected to see elaborate defenses and were
surprised to find nothing of the kind.

Plutarch wrote that someone once asked Archidamidas, a
resident of Sparta: "What number there might be of the
Spartans?" He answered: "Enough, sir, to keep out wicked
men." In a poem idealizing the Spartan ideal, Tyrtaeus writes:
"Know that it is good for the city and the whole people when
a man takes his place in the front row of warriors and stands
his ground without flinching."

Daniel, Shadrach, Meshach, and Abednego realized service may sometimes mean being the only believer in a certain
place. Are you one of the few Christians at your work or in
your neighborhood? Congratulations, you are in the front row!
Praise Jesus Christ that you can be His ambassador to people
who may never have been in a church. Today in prayer ask the
Lord how you can serve Him where He has placed you.

If the world is cold, make it your business to build
fires.

—Horace Traubel

LINING UP WITH GOD'S WILL

"For I know the plans I have for you," declares the Lord,
"plans to prosper you and not to harm you, plans to give you
hope and a future. Then you will call upon me and come
and pray to me, and I will listen to you. You will seek me
and find me when you seek me with all your heart."
Jeremiah 29:11–13

Born in London and educated at Brighton College, F. B. Meyer made the most of his life in Christ and traveled throughout the world to preach the good news.

Once, while he was crossing the Irish Channel on a dark night, Meyer stood on the deck of the ship, turned to the captain and asked, "How do you know Holyhead Harbor on so dark a night as this?" The captain pointed out three lights on the horizon. "Do you see those three lights? Those three lights must line up behind each other as one, and when we see them so united we know the exact position of the harbor's mouth."

Meyer applied this to the Christian life: "When we want to know the will of God there are three things which always occur; the inward impulse, the Word of God, and the trend of circumstances! God in the heart, impelling you forward; God in his book corroborating whatever he says in the heart; and God in circumstances, which are always indicative of his will. Never start until these three things agree."

As Christians, we often miss God's will because we neglect His Word, ignore His prompting of our heart, or try to plow through circumstances. Are you charting your life's course according to God's will? Today in prayer give thanks that Christ reveals enough of His will so that you can live your life for Him.

As to the will of God, it falls under a twofold consideration of his secret and revealed will. The distinction is found in that Scripture: "The secret things belong unto the Lord our God: but these things which are revealed belong unto us" (Deuteronomy 29:29 KJV). The first is the rule of his own actions: the latter of ours.

—John Flavel

Day 251
HE STILL CAN HEAL

Then will the eyes of the blind be opened and the ears of the deaf unstopped. Then will the lame leap like a deer, and the mute tongue shout for joy.
Isaiah 35:5–6

Watson Spoelstra knows about the healing power of Jesus Christ. In 1957, "Waddy" was a hard-charging, successful sports writer for the *Detroit Free News.* He came home one evening to find his daughter lying on the floor with a brain hemorrhage. While waiting in the hospital Waddy visited the chapel and prayed, "Look God, I think you're in this room because my mother thought so much of you. I'll make a deal with you. You do something about Ann and I'll let you do something about me." Later Waddy said, "With that little feeble half-step that I took the Lord reached out and touched me and I knew at that moment that somehow my life was going to be different, and it was." Ann was healed and Waddy started serving the Lord by using his sports writing to highlight Christian athletes.

In 1994 Waddy again saw the Lord's healing power. His wife Jean suffered with congestive heart failure for almost three years. One day, after a medical checkup, a doctor reported to Jean, "Your heart and lungs are clear." Waddy's response was, "Praise the Lord!"

The Lord can heal although often he does not. We may never know why divine healing is given or withheld, but we do know the Great Physician Jesus Christ. Today pray to God that the world will be healed through Jesus Christ from its spiritual hemorrhaging.

> Physical healing is a living process, and as such it is an inner mystery, in the end known only to the cells themselves which are involved and the one who created them.
>
> —Morton T. Kelsey

Day 252
THE DOCTOR'S TOOLS

We know that the law is good if one uses it properly. We also know that law is made not for the righteous but for lawbreakers and rebels, the ungodly and sinful, the unholy and irreligious; for those who kill their fathers or mothers, for murderers.
1 Timothy 1:8–9

The Law of God is like an x-ray machine that scans a person's head. The resulting x-ray can reveal deadly lesions or tumors. But the x-ray machine cannot remove any abnormalities. It can detect if something is wrong but it cannot provide a remedy.

The Law is also like a sphygmomanometer which measures blood pressure. A nurse attaches the cuff and inflates it to check the systolic and diastolic pressure of a patient. If the blood pressure is too high or too low the sphygmomanometer is useless to correct it. Instead a doctor may prescribe diet and exercise to correct the problem.

The Law of God reveals that humans fall short of God's standard. But the Law is not the remedy to this sickness. The Great Physician has made the diagnosis of sin and also prescribed the remedy in Christ. Thankfully we are acceptable to God through the grace of Christ. Today, give thanks to Christ

287

for the Law. Without it we would not know how much we need grace!

> No man may put off the Law of God. The Way of
> God is no ill Way. My joy is in God all the Day.
> —Thomas Dilworth

Day 253
YOU CAN LEARN A LOT FROM A GOOSE

> *If any woman who is a believer has widows in her family,*
> *she should help them and not let the church be*
> *burdened with them, so that the church can help*
> *those widows who are really in need.*
> 1 Timothy 5:16

Milton Olson has studied Canada geese and compiled these lessons:

1. Geese fly in a V formation for greater range of the entire flock. As each bird flaps its wings, it creates an uplift for the bird following. This adds seventy-one percent to their flying range than if one bird was flying alone. Lesson: People who share a sense of common direction and community get where they are going quicker and easier.

2. When a goose falls out of formation it feels the resistance of flying alone and quickly gets back into formation. Lesson: Stay in the company with those headed in the direction you want to go.

3. When the lead goose gets tired another goose takes the point position. Lesson: It pays to take turns doing hard tasks and sharing leadership.

4. The geese in formation honk to encourage the lead goose. Lesson: Be sure your honking is helpful.

5. When a goose gets sick or wounded two geese fall out of formation and follow it to the ground and protect it. They stay until their companion dies or is able to fly again and then launch out to catch up with the flock. Lesson: Stand by each other in difficult times.

Who needs help in your family or church? Remember the kindness and care you have received in the past and ask Christ what kindness you can provide for them.

There is no better exercise for the heart than reaching down and lifting people up.
—John Andrew Holmer

Day 254
THE LIVING RELAY

*And the things you have heard me say in the presence
of many witnesses entrust to reliable men who
will also be qualified to teach others.*
2 Timothy 2:2

When James Taylor was growing up John Wesley was often a guest in his parent's home in Yorkshire, England. By 1830 Taylor was a successful evangelist in England but he often prayed for China. His son, J. Hudson Taylor became a missionary and founded the China Inland Mission.

Meanwhile, in the winter of 1882, Dixon Hoste attended one of D. L. Moody's gospel meetings and surrendered his life to Christ. Soon afterward Hoste read a booklet written by J. Hudson Taylor which convinced him that he was to be a missionary to China.

Hoste was faithful in prayer and in 1903 succeeded Taylor as the Director of the China Inland Mission. He continued in the mission field until 1945. One of the Chinese pastors whom Hoste raised up in the faith was named Hsi. Hoste called Hsi a pacesetter in the faith because he gave his life fully to Christ.

When the communists took over mainland China many people feared that few Christians would endure there. But by the 1980s there were an estimated sixty million Christians in China thanks to the labor of believers like Hsi.

Our legacy is passed down from Christ Himself by way of a living relay. Today give thanks for the faithful men and women who have helped you grow in the faith and ask Christ to give you an opportunity to pass on the baton of faith.

O fill me with Thy fullness, Lord, until my very heart o'erflow, in kindling thought and glowing word, thy love to tell, thy praise to show.

—Frances Ridley Havergal

Day 255
THE GUARDIAN OF OUR WAY

At my first defense, no one came to my support, but everyone deserted me. May it not be held against them. But the Lord stood at my side and gave me strength, so that through me the message might be fully proclaimed and all the Gentiles might hear it. And I was delivered from the lion's mouth.
2 Timothy 4:16–17

Ira Sankey was the music director and soloist for the nineteenth-century evangelist D. L. Moody. Once while traveling Sankey was recognized and asked to sing. He suggested that everyone join him in singing the hymn by William Bradbury, "Savior Like a Shepherd Lead Us." One of the verses of this hymn begins, "We are thine—do thou befriend us, be the guardian of our way."

When the singing finished a man stepped out of the crowd and asked, "Were you in the army, Mr. Sankey?"

"Yes, I joined up in 1860."

"Did you ever do guard duty at night in Maryland about 1862?"

"Yes, I did."

"Well, I was in the Confederate Army," said the man, "and I saw you one night at Sharpsburg. You were wearing your blue uniform and I had you in my gunsight as you stood there in the light of the full moon. Then just as I was about to pull the trigger, you began to sing." Sankey was stunned.

"It was the same hymn you sang tonight," continued the man. "My mother often sang it but I never expected to hear it sung at midnight by a soldier on guard duty. I realized you were a Christian and I couldn't shoot you." Sankey lovingly embraced his former enemy.

The Lord is faithful to protect us even when we are unaware of danger. When you face danger Christ is at your side. Today in prayer give thanks that Christ is the guardian of your way.

> We are thine; do thou befriend us; Be the guardian of our way; Keep thy flock; from sin defend us; Seek us when we go astray.
>
> —William Bradbury

Day 256
TAKE PAINS TO DO WHAT IS RIGHT

For we are taking pains to do what is right,
not only in the eyes of the Lord but also in the eyes of men.
2 Corinthians 8:21

On September 13, 1995, an Amish woman named Mary Lambright was killed when a truck driven by Curtis

Peterson hit her horse-drawn buggy. She left her husband Mahlon and eleven children. Peterson's insurance company offered Mahlon Lambright a wrongful death settlement totaling $212,418. But Lambright went before Wisconsin's Dunn County Circuit Court and asked the judge to drop the petition of wrongful death settlement against Peterson.

"I admire him," said David Richie, guardian ad litem for nine of the family's eleven children. Mahlon doesn't want the settlement "for the simple fact that he felt the money would cause more problems than it would solve."

Lambright feared his children would not appreciate Amish traditions if he took the money. He pointed out to the court the Amish community helped them by providing food and clothing and holding an auction. Emanuel Miller, a spokesman for the Amish community, said "It shows that he's not seeking revenge or he would have accepted the money. Our Bible says revenge is not for us."

Doing what is right brings joy to both God and man. Today thank Christ that He receives glory when we do what is right in His name.

> I prefer to do right and get no thanks rather than to
> do wrong and get no punishment.
>
> —Marcus Cato

Day 257
THE POWER OF LOVE

How great is the love the Father has lavished on us, that we should be called children of God! And that is what we are! The reason the world does not know us is that it did not know him.
1 John 3:1

In 1876 Annie Sullivan's mother died and her father abandoned her. She was eight years old, slightly blind in one eye, and very introverted. She was placed in the Massachusetts State Infirmary in Tewksbury near Boston. But she was unresponsive to help and isolated in the basement where the truly troubled were confined.

Then a new staff member came to the asylum—Maggie Carroll. She was a Christian and took it upon herself to show Annie God's love. Maggie would talk to Annie, read her stories, and talk about God. She spent her lunch hour with Annie and prayed for her. But she saw no change in the girl's behavior. One day Maggie brought a plate of brownies to Annie and to her delight when she returned a brownie was gone.

Eventually Maggie broke through. At age fourteen Annie entered Boston's Perkins Institute for the Blind. She could not read or write when she entered Perkins, but Ann Sullivan went on to become one of the greatest teachers of all time. For it was Ann Sullivan who taught Helen Keller—another little blind girl labeled hopeless. Helen Keller became great because of Ann Sullivan. Ann Sullivan accomplished great things because of Maggie Carroll who was not afraid to share God's love.

Has God's love changed your life? Today, ask Christ how you can love others that they may may be born again as a child of God.

We are apt to forget that children watch examples better than they listen to preaching.

—Roy L. Smith

YOURS FOR THE ASKING

Know that a man is not justified by observing the law,
but by faith in Jesus Christ. So we, too, have put
our faith in Christ Jesus that we may be justified
by faith in Christ and not by observing the law,
because by observing the law no one will be justified.
Galatians 2:16

When the Spanish-American War broke out Clara Barton, the founder of the American Red Cross, was prepared to offer relief. A Red Cross team of doctors and nurses, and fourteen hundred tons of supplies arrived in Santiago, Cuba, as the fighting began. The American and Cuban field hospitals were located side by side and their conditions were deplorable. The American military surgeons refused the Red Cross's offers of help so Barton and her team gave aid to the Cubans.

The Americans soon realized that the Cuban wounded were better taken care of than the American casualties. Under pressure, the American chief surgeon asked Barton for Red Cross help.

Soon after the Battle of San Juan Hill, Colonel Theodore Roosevelt (the future president of the United States) came to Barton and offered to buy food and medicine for the sick and wounded Rough Riders. Barton refused. Roosevelt could not understand. He cared about his men and was willing to pay for the supplies out of his own funds. So Roosevelt went to the surgeon in charge who told him, "Colonel, just ask for it!"

Roosevelt smiled—now he understood—the provisions were not for sale. "I will ask for it," he said. He did so and received the supplies at once.

The work of Jesus Christ is graciously given as a gift. We only need ask. Have you placed your faith in Christ? Today in prayer thank God that through faith in Jesus Christ you are healed from sin.

He has taken our place and died in our stead; He has met the descending stroke of justice, which would have fallen on our own heads if He had not interposed.

—Albert Barnes

Day 259
A FRUITFUL LIFE

But the fruit of the Spirit is love, joy, peace, patience, kindness, goodness, faithfulness, gentleness and self-control. Against such things there is no law.
Galatians 5:22–23

In 1787 representatives from each state of the newly formed United States met in Philadelphia to draft a constitution to govern the nation. These representatives met in the East Room of the State House; the same room where the Declaration of Independence had been signed eleven years earlier.

How should each state be represented? Should Congress have members proportional to the population they served or should each state have equal representation? Months of debate ensued. Then the venerable Benjamin Franklin addressed the Congress.

Franklin had helped frame the Declaration of Independence, negotiated with the French to back the Revolution, and successfully negotiated the treaty ending the war. He noted that prior to the Revolutionary War similar debates had occurred. At that time the Continental Congress decided to open each session with prayer asking the Lord for guiding wisdom. That Congress wrote the Declaration of Independence and fought the War of Independence. Franklin proposed opening each session of the Constitutional Congress with prayer. Without the Lord's help, he said, "We shall be divided by our little partial local interests; our projects will be confounded, and we ourselves shall become a reproach and bye-word to future ages."

By nature all men are self-centered. But through the Holy Spirit we exhibit love. Today thank Jesus Christ that through Him you can live a life of love, joy, peace, patience, kindness, goodness, faithfulness, gentleness, and self-control.

> There are nine graces spoken of, and of these nine Paul puts love at the head of the list; love is the first thing, the first in that precious cluster of fruit.
> —D. L. Moody

Day 260
IN SEASON AND OUT OF SEASON

In the presence of God and of Christ Jesus,
who will judge the living and the dead,
and in view of his appearing and his kingdom,
I give you this charge: Preach the Word;
be prepared in season and out of season;
correct, rebuke and encourage—
with great patience and careful instruction.
2 Timothy 4:1–2

It was the seventh and final game of the 1962 World Series. The New York Yankees took a 1–0 lead over the San Francisco Giants into the bottom of the ninth inning. Matty Alou led off the inning with a single. Yankee pitcher Ralph Terry struck out the next two batters. Then Willie Mays hit a double to right field.

Alou was on third and Mays on second. Yankee manager Ralph Houk walked to the mound and asked Terry if he could get Willie McCovey out and end the game. During this pause Yankee second baseman Bobby Richardson approached Willie Mays and asked him if he knew Jesus Christ as his Savior. The next pitch was a line drive. Richardson fielded it on the fly and the game was over.

On September 17, 1966, the Yankees held "Bobby Richardson Day" to honor the player who had won five Gold Gloves for fielding and had been the World Series MVP of 1960. Richardson wrote a letter about the gospel and had it distributed to every fan in attendance.

Richardson retired from baseball at age thirty-one. He wasn't injured or tired of the game. Rather he was called to devote more time to serving the Lord.

You may never be the World Series MVP but you can learn how to share your faith in Christ with others. Today ask the Lord to prepare someone's heart so you can tell them how you became a Christian.

> The season does not refer to the time but to us. We are to "be ready in season and out of season" whether we feel like it or not.
>
> —Oswald Chambers

Day 261
HEARTILY REJOICE

Praise him for his acts of power; praise him
for his surpassing greatness.
Psalm 150:2

Benjamin Britten, born in Lowestoft, England, was a celebrated composer and pianist. Though he is primarily known for his operas based on Shakespeare, Melville, and Maupassant, Britten composed three works to be performed in church: "Curlew River," "The Burning Fiery Furnace," and "The Prodigal Son."

He also composed "Venite, Exultemus Domino" based on Psalms 95 and 96:

O come, let us sing unto the LORD; let us heartily rejoice in the strength of our salvation.

Let us come before his presence with thanksgiving; and show ourselves glad in him with psalms.

For the LORD is a great God; and a great King above all gods.

In his hand are all the corners of the earth; and the strength of the hills is his also.

The sea is his, and he made it; and his hands prepared the dry land.

O come, let us worship and fall down, and kneel before the LORD our Maker.

For he is the Lord our God; and we are the people of his pasture, and the sheep of his hand.

O worship the LORD in the beauty of holiness; let the whole earth stand in awe of him.

For he cometh, for he cometh to judge the earth; and with righteousness to judge the world, and the peoples with his truth.

Glory be.

There is none greater than God. Praise the Lord for his awesome power!

The power of God is released when the believer begins to praise, for this says to the Lord, "I approve of what you are doing and am relying on your strength."
—Charles Stanley

Day 262
OUR LOVING GOD

Look to the LORD and his strength; seek his face always.
Remember the wonders he has done, his miracles,
and the judgments he pronounced.
1 Chronicles 16:11–12

David Allen is a missionary to Thailand. In early 1997, shortly after arriving back in the United States on a routine furlough, Allen became gravely ill. Within two months, his weight dropped from 172 to 139 pounds. He was unable to eat and was afflicted with severe stomach pain and diarrhea. Doctors in Los Angeles were baffled at the cause of his illness. He was flown to Dallas where tests found two types of microscopic intestinal parasites, but it took several additional weeks of testing before positive identification was made.

During this time Allen was the object of worldwide prayer. His teammates began to pray and E-mail friends who began to pray. Allen received more than seven thousand E-mail messages of encouragement from people in seventy different countries. Entire congregations and Christian organizations prayed for his recovery. The U.S. Senate Chaplain wrote him and said that Christian senators were regularly praying for him.

David Allen had much of his intestinal lining destroyed by the infection, but he recovered and was expecting to return to Thailand in 1998. He gratefully said, "I believe God has called me to preach the gospel and plant new churches in Thailand. My heart is still there and it is my desire to return."

The Lord is an active God. He continually gives strength and performs miracles. Do you think that God sits passively by, watching over the world? Today thank Christ that in Him you see God's strength and active hand.

The enjoyment of God's favor depends upon devotion to him.

—J. G. McConville

*Now when a man works, his wages are not credited to him
as a gift, but as an obligation. However, to the man who
does not work but trusts God who justifies the wicked,
his faith is credited as righteousness.*
Romans 4:4–5

George Needham was a gifted teacher, pastor, evangelist, and author in the middle nineteenth century. He explained the typology in Scripture in a simple, logical manner; particularly the Tabernacle as symbolic of Christ's work of redemption.

One day, Needham visited a very rich, important gentleman and asked, "Are you saved?"

"No, but I am trying to be a Christian."

"How long have you been trying?" Needham pressed.

"For twelve years," said the man.

"Permit me to say that you have been very foolish."

The man was perplexed by the pastor's remark, "What do you mean by that?"

"Well," said Needham, "you have been trying for so many years, yet you haven't succeeded. If I were you, I would give up trying and start trusting."

When he left the man's home Needham wondered if the brief meeting would amount to anything. That evening the rich man sat in Needham's congregation. The pastor spotted the man in the pew with a peaceful, glow on his face. After the service the rich man told Needham, "I have been foolish indeed, wasting twelve precious years of life vainly trying when salvation could have been mine by simply trusting."

God's economy is not based on works—it is based on faith. We receive good credit from God when we place our faith in Christ's finished work. How is your credit rating with the Lord? Today in prayer ask God to give you the wisdom to live by faith.

But how to get faith strengthened? Not by striving after faith, but by resting on the faithful one.

—J. Hudson Taylor

Day 264
PAID UP

Give everyone what you owe him:
If you owe taxes, pay taxes; if revenue, then revenue;
if respect, then respect; if honor, then honor.
Let no debt remain outstanding, except the
continuing debt to love one another,
for he who loves his fellowman has fulfilled the law.
Romans 13:7–8

In May 1833, at age twenty-four, Abraham Lincoln was postmaster in New Salem, Illinois. The annual pay was only fifty dollars a year but it afforded Lincoln time to pursue his studies in law. Lincoln trusted the people in New Salem. He was criticized by outsiders for leaving the post office unlocked, but the citizens of the small town were glad to be able to pick up their mail at any time.

On May 30, 1836, Lincoln sorted the mail for the last time in New Salem. The population had moved away and the office was no longer needed.

Several years after the post office had closed Lincoln was serving in the Illinois legislature. A postal agent visited New Salem to settle the accounts with the expostmaster. The agent informed Lincoln that seventeen dollars was due to the federal government. Lincoln opened an old trunk and took out a yellow cotton rag bound with a string. Untying it he spread out the cloth and there was the seventeen dollars. He had been holding it untouched for years. "I never use any man's money but my own," he said.

People often judge others by their ability to handle money. Are you trustworthy in paying taxes and debts? Today ask the Lord to help you to be a good steward of the money He has entrusted to you.

Neither a borrower nor a lender be.
—William Shakespeare

Day 265
THE PRIORITY OF PRAYER

So Peter was kept in prison, but the church was
earnestly praying to God for him.
Acts 12:5

David Cho was born in Pusan, Korea, and raised in a traditional Buddhist household. At age eighteen David came to know the Lord through the witness of a high school girl. Ostracized by his family, Cho studied at the Full Gospel Bible Institute in Seoul and founded the Full Gospel Central Church —the largest congregation in the world with over 500,000 members.

Ralph Neighbour tells about meeting with pastor Cho: They talked for some time. Then, "his secretary entered the room to inform him it was time for his next appointment. I dismissed myself and sat in the waiting room for a friend who was coming to meet me. Curious about who Cho's next visitor would be, I observed his office door to see who would follow me. Fifteen minutes later no one had entered that door. Tactfully I said to his secretary, 'Has Dr. Cho's next appointment been delayed?'

"She smiled and said, 'Oh, no. They are together now. You see, each day he uses this time to talk to the Lord.' "

Prayer—do it standing, sitting, or kneeling; do it with your eyes closed or open; looking downward or heavenward. The position of your body is not nearly as important as the position of your heart. Are you regularly spending time in prayer? Today seek the Lord that He would give you a heart for prayer.

> A person who is not praying is a person who is straying.
>
> —George Verwer

Day 266
THE SURGEON OF LIGHT

Do you not know that the wicked will not inherit the kingdom of God? Do not be deceived: Neither the sexually immoral nor idolaters nor adulterers nor male prostitutes nor homosexual offenders nor thieves nor the greedy nor drunkards nor slanderers nor swindlers will inherit the kingdom of God. And that is what some of you were. But you were washed, you were sanctified, you were justified in the name of the Lord Jesus Christ and by the Spirit of our God.
1 Corinthians 6:9–11

Light Amplification by Stimulated Emission of Radiation (LASER) has been used medically since the 1960s. It has become the instrument of choice when treating a variety of maladies. Laser surgery for skin disfigurements is particularly effective. Pulsed Dye Lasers are able to treat port-wine stains, warts, spider veins, stretch marks, and broken blood vessels. Ruby lasers are used to remove tattoos, freckles, and moles. CO_2 lasers remove acne scarring and other raised scarring.

The benefits of laser surgery include less scarring and reduced infection. Lasers act in a variety of ways to destroy the targeted skin cells such as a focused pulse or a continuous blast of light. Most often patients report little or no pain from the surgery because the laser seals off the small arteries, veins, and nerve endings in the area. Under the hand of a skillful surgeon the marks which disfigure the skin can be permanently removed by light.

Jesus Christ is the light of the world. He has permanently removed the stain of sin from your soul. By His death you are justified, spotless, without disfigurement. When you look at your life do you still see the stain of sin? Today give thanks that you are justified in the name of the Lord Jesus Christ and by the Spirit of our God.

You are free. Prove that you are by successfully resisting sin.

—George Stoeckhardt

Day 267
CALLED, HELD, AND KEPT

"Where, O death, is your victory?
Where, O death, is your sting?"
The sting of death is sin, and the power of sin is the law.
But thanks be to God!
He gives us the victory through our Lord Jesus Christ.
1 Corinthians 15:55–57

Frances Ridley Havergal started reading the Bible on her own at age four. At seven she began to write her thoughts in verse. She received the best of training in music and the arts, was fluent in several languages, and read the Bible in the original Greek and Hebrew. Havergal authored such famous hymns as "I Gave My Life For Thee," "I Am Trusting Thee, Lord Jesus," and "Take My Life And Let It Be."

For most of her life Frances Havergal endured various illnesses and at age forty-three she learned she would soon die. Havergal said, "If I am really going it is too good to be true." She placed her favorite Scripture verse where she could easily see it: "The blood of Jesus Christ his Son cleanseth us from all sin." Moments before she died, Havergal asked a friend to read Isaiah 42. Verse 6 reads, "I, the LORD, have called you in righteousness; I will take hold of your hand. I will keep you. . . ." Then Miss Havergal stopped her. "Called, held, kept," she whispered. "That's enough. I'll just go home to glory on those words!" A few minutes later she entered the presence of the Lord. Although Isaiah 42:6 refers to Christ, Frances Havergal applied it to her own life thus demonstrating her confidence that the Lord could keep her safe until the very end.

Do you sometimes feel mournful about death? Death has been defeated! Remember, a Christian's death is an entrance into eternity with God.

Take my love—my God; I pour at thy feet its treasure store; Take myself—and I will be ever, only, all for thee; ever, only, all for thee.
—Frances Ridley Havergal

Day 268
THE STRAIGHT PATH

And lead us not into temptation, but deliver us from the evil one.
Matthew 6:13

C. S. Lewis, in his book *Prayer,* writes about the phrase "lead us not into temptation." "I was never worried myself by the words 'lead us not into temptation,' but a great many of my correspondents are. The words suggest to them what someone has called a fiend-like concept of God, as one who first forbids us from certain fruits and then lures us to taste them. But the Greek word means trial, a trying circumstances of every sort; a far larger word than the English temptation. So that the petition essentially is, 'Make straight our paths.' Spare us, where possible, from all crises, whether of temptation or affliction."

The shortest distance between two points is a straight line. The surest way to talk and to walk with God is never to leave Him. After forty days of fasting Christ was tempted three times to leave the Father. He endured all temptation and did not sin. But let us pray to not even come close to temptation—"Keep it far from me so that I may stay on a straight path with Christ."

An amusing bumper sticker says, "Do not lead me to temptation, I can find it for myself." This is true. We all know our own weaknesses and where to find temptations. But today may your heart's prayer be "Lord Jesus, I want to enjoy this entire day with You. Make my path straight."

> There is a silly idea about that good people don't know what temptation means.
>
> —C. S. Lewis

Day 269
WHEN ANGER CONSUMES

"In your anger do not sin": Do not let the sun go down while you are still angry, and do not give the devil a foothold.
Ephesians 4:26–27

The great feud of American folk history was between the McCoys of Pike County, Kentucky, and the Hatfields of Mingo County, West Virginia. Their lands were separated by the Tug Fork of the Big Sandy River.

The reason for the feud remains unclear. Some say it was because the Hatfields were loyal to the South, while the McCoys were loyal to the North. Also, in 1865, the mysterious murder of Harmon McCoy was never solved. Others say it started when Ole Ran'l McCoy accused Floyd Hatfield of pig stealing, while still others say the cause was the love affair between Roseanna McCoy and Johnse Hatfield.

In January 1888 a series of revenge killings took place on

both sides of the Tug Fork. Before the feud ended in 1891 an estimated twenty men, women, and children had died.

Things took a turn for the better in latter years. In 1911 the leader of the Hatfield family, William "Devil Anse" Hatfield, became a Christian. In 1976 two survivors of the original families, Jim McCoy and Willis Hatfield, shook hands at a public ceremony dedicating a monument to the feuds' victims. Eight years later Jim McCoy passed away at age ninety-nine. His burial service was provided at no charge by the Hatfield Funeral Home.

Are you angry at someone? Today in prayer ask Christ to free you from your anger.

> Anger must not be suffered to break out into violence. It must be kept within the control of conscience and of reason.
>
> —R. W. Dale

Day 270
ALWAYS TEST FOR INTEGRITY

Here is a trustworthy saying: If anyone sets his heart on being an overseer, he desires a noble task. Now the overseer must be above reproach.
1 Timothy 3:1–2

At 7:00 P.M. on September 27, 1994, the 510-foot deep-sea ferry *Estonia* left the port Tallinn, Estonia, en route to Stockholm, Sweden. One hundred sixty-two crew members and 897 passengers were onboard for the overnight voyage. The ferry had been crossing the Baltic Sea for over a decade, the crew was experienced, and nothing indicated that there was any danger to the ship.

At 8:30 P.M. the *Estonia* encountered rough weather. Rain and high seas slowed the ferry and pummeled its hull. At midnight water was observed pouring through the front-loading cargo doors. Pumps were activated immediately but within fifteen minutes the crew was overwhelmed by the water surging in. At 1:24 A.M. the ship sent a distress call. It had started listing and continued to take on water. At 2:00 A.M. the ship went down sixty miles from Stockholm. The sinking of the *Estonia* claimed 921 lives. Only 138 people survived.

Before the *Estonia* sailed two Swedish safety inspectors had spent five hours examining her seaworthiness. They noted damaged and worn rubber seals around the front-loading cargo doors. These problems were written up but the lead inspector did not think they effected the ship's seaworthiness.

Ships, like leaders, must have integrity. The *Estonia* failed the integrity test. Our church leaders must also have integrity. It is incumbent that we select our leaders not on their social status but by the measure of their integrity. This week pray that the church will select leaders of integrity.

> Ministers, in order that they be shining lights, should walk closely with God and keep near to Christ. They should spend much time with him in prayer.
> —Jonathan Edwards

Day 271
THE STRONGEST FORCE

The weapons we fight with are not the weapons of the world. On the contrary, they have divine power to demolish strongholds.
2 Corinthians 10:4

On October 25, 1854, in the midst of the Battle of Balaclava during the Crimean War, the British were in a position to retake an important hill outside the city. The Russian Army had overrun the British artillery situated there but were forced to retreat by a British counterattack. Lord Raglan, commander of the British forces, saw a chance to seal the victory and ordered his cavalry division commander, Lord Lucan, to dash to the deserted artillery and retake it for the British. Unfortunately Lord Lucan mistakenly ordered his men to take the wrong hill. His light brigade charged up a hill fortified by Russian artillery and entrenched troops. Lucan's brigade was equipped only to fight against foot soldiers and other horseback troops. As the British cavalry galloped in formation toward the Russian line they were mowed down by enemy fire. Of the 673 soldiers of Lucan's Light Brigade only 195 returned. It is said that no cavalry attack was ever executed with more precision, discipline, and bravery. Yet they did not have the power to demolish the stronghold.

In Christ we have the power of the Holy Spirit. There is no stronger force. Do you rely on prayer or do you ride bravely ahead on your own? Today in prayer thank Christ that through Him strongholds are demolished.

> A successful campaign can be waged in the spiritual realm only as worldly weapons are abandoned and total reliance is placed on the spiritual weaponry.
> —Murray J. Harris

Day 272
ORDINARY PEOPLE

"Salvation is found in no one else, for there is no other name under heaven given to men by which we must be saved." When they saw the courage of Peter and John and realized that they were unschooled, ordinary men, they were astonished and they took note that these men had been with Jesus.
Acts 4:12–13

Thousands of Russian Jews immigrated to the United States around the turn of the century. Among them were

David Bronstein and Esther Peltz who met and married in Baltimore. David took free English lessons at a Baptist church. It was not long before he and Esther found the Messiah. Esther described their new faith: "We are still Jews. We keep a kosher home and believe just as all Jews except we know that Jesus is the Messiah."

David sensed God calling him to be a missionary to their people. The Bronsteins moved to Chicago where David graduated from Moody Bible Institute and McCormick Theological Seminary.

David held open community forums for Jews on Chicago's North Side to discuss subjects of the day. Esther organized summer school and camp for the children and mothers' groups and free medical service for the women. She urged the women to seek help in a relationship with the Messiah. The Bronsteins welcomed acquaintances to their table for kosher meals, Yiddish conversation, and gospel appetizers.

This couple brought many Jews to Christ through their love and gentle persuasion. In 1934 David founded the First Hebrew Christian Church of Chicago, known today as Adat Katikvah Congregation of Hope.

When we submit ourselves to Christ, His Spirit empowers us to do the extraordinary. Share your faith where the Lord has placed you—in your family, neighborhood, and workplace. Today thank Jesus for saving you. Ask Him to use you to advance His kingdom.

> The world has yet to see what God can do with and for and through and in a man who is fully and wholly consecrated to him.
>
> —Henry Varley

Day 273
GET RID OF THE DIRT

*Therefore, get rid of all moral filth and the evil that
is so prevalent and humbly accept the word planted in you,
which can save you.*
James 1:21

William Farel was an early French-Swiss Reformer who studied in Paris and later was forced to move to Switzerland. He was a fiery orator who imposed strict discipline. He mentored John Calvin who defined much of Reformation theology. For twenty-seven years Farel preached in the cathedral in Neuchatel, Switzerland. There he was often in conflict with those who placed tradition before the Word of God. Once, preaching an evangelistic message in the cemetery of a Roman Catholic parish, the monks began to ring the church bells to drown out his message.

Farel died peacefully when he was seventy-six years old. Those close to him were impressed that even up to his death, he remained zealous in placing the authority of Scripture above all.

Three hundred years after his death a statue of Farel was erected to commemorate his mark on the Reformation. It is a statue of the man holding the Bible aloft. It is a tribute that *Sola Scriptura,* the Bible and the Bible alone, is the authority for humanity. This is what made all the difference to the Reformers. Icons, statues, rituals, and traditions were stripped away so that the Word of God would grow.

Why are there so many sins in this world? Because God's Word has been neglected. Is *Sola Scriptura* your motto for life? Today in prayer ask God to examine your heart; confess your sins and let the Word of God live in you.

I beg you, my dearest brother, to live among these
sacred books, to meditate on them, to know nothing

311

else, to seek nothing else. Does not this seem to you to be a little bit of heaven on earth?

—Jerome

Day 274
GOD'S GRACE IS TRULY AMAZING

And God is able to make all grace abound to you,
so that in all things at all times, having all that you need,
you will abound in every good work.
2 Corinthians 9:8

The son of an English sea captain, John Newton went to sea at the age of eleven. He nearly lost his life several times during a storm which almost sunk his ship and Newton cried out to God for salvation. Later this new Christian was promoted to captain of a slave ship. The inhumanity of the business caused Newton to finally leave the sea. Then, while working as a tide surveyor, Newton studied for the ministry and for the last forty-three years of his life preached the gospel in Olney and London.

At eighty-two Newton said, "My memory is nearly gone, but I remember two things, that I am a great sinner, and that Christ is a great savior." John Newton's tombstone reads, "John Newton, Clerk, once an infidel and libertine, a servant of slaves in Africa, was, by the rich mercy of our Lord and Savior Jesus Christ, preserved, restored, pardoned, and appointed to preach the faith he had long labored to destroy." Newton is best known for writing the hymn "Amazing Grace," a personal testimony to God's unmerited favor.

The Lord's grace is not dependent on our actions but on Christ's unchanging character. God lavishes grace upon us, His children. Today in prayer thank Jesus Christ that His grace does not depend on you. Praise Him that your works need only be in response to His love and grace.

'Twas grace that taught my heart to fear, and grace
my fears relieved; How precious did that grace
appear the hour I first believed!

—John Newton

Day 275
GIVE THANKS TO THE LORD IN SONG

I had the leaders of Judah go up on top of the wall.
I also assigned two large choirs to give thanks.
Nehemiah 12:31

Martin Rinkart was born in 1586 in Eilenberg,
Saxony, Germany. When he was a boy, Martin was a choirboy
in the famous St. Thomas Church of Leipzig, Germany, where
J. S. Bach later became musical director. Rinkart attended
the University of Leipzig and was ordained a minister of the
Lutheran Church. At age thirty-one he was called back to
Eilenberg to pastor a church.

Soon after arriving there, the Thirty Years' War erupted in
Europe. Refugees streamed into the city. Disease followed and a
deadly plague broke out. Soon Martin Rinkart was the only pastor in Eilenberg and performing up to fifty funerals a day.
When the plague subsided over five thousand people were dead.
The Peace of Westphalia ended the Thirty Years' War and the
Elector of Saxony ordered thanksgiving services throughout
the land. With this renewal of hope Martin Rinkart wrote the
words to the song "Now Thank We All Our God" even though
his heart was breaking from the loss of friends and family.

Singing to the Lord can lift your heart. This Sunday in
church concentrate on the words you sing, and sing out! Don't
worry if you may be a little off-key because Jesus is only listening to your heart's song.

Now thank we all our God, with hearts and hands and voices, who wondrous things hath done, in whom his world rejoices, who from our mother's arms hath blessed us on our way with countless gifts of love, and still is ours today.

—Martin Rinkart

Day 276
THE ETERNAL PURPOSE OF LIFE

"Meaningless! Meaningless!" says the Teacher.
"Utterly meaningless! Everything is meaningless."
What does man gain from all his labor
at which he toils under the sun?
Ecclesiastes 1:2–3

Nathan Stubblefield lived his entire life in Murray, Kentucky, where the town erected a monument to the man they call the father of radio. Stubblefield has also been called a mystic, a mendicant, and a martyr to his invention. In 1892 he developed a crude "wireless telephone." Stubblefield received a patent and soon formed The Wireless Telephone Company of America. But he was convinced everyone wanted to steal his patent from him. Unfortunately he was right and met up with unscrupulous business partners. Stubblefield was crushed by these "animals from the city" and became a recluse. He lived out his life in a tin shack built between four trees where he occupied his mind with visions of greater inventions.

Two weeks before his death Stubblefield visited with his neighbor Mrs. L. E. Owens. He asked her to write his story. She wrote, "I lived fifty years before my time. The past is nothing. I have perfected now the greatest invention the world has ever known. I've taken light from the air and the earth as I did with sound. I want you to know about making a whole hillside blossom with light." Nathan Stubblefield died of starvation at age seventy. He had many visions but never knew success.

A relationship with Jesus Christ lends meaning to the human life. Has your life become one of chasing after material things or elusive success? Today in prayer give thanks to Christ for the eternal purpose of human life.

> Our greatest danger in life is permitting the urgent
> things to crowd out the important.
> —Charles E. Humel

Day 277
IN THE BOSOM OF JESUS CHRIST

Then Daniel (also called Belteshazzar) was greatly perplexed for a time, and his thoughts terrified him. So the king said, "Belteshazzar, do not let the dream or its meaning alarm you." Belteshazzar answered, "My lord, if only the dream applied to your enemies and its meaning to your adversaries!"
Daniel 4:19

Charles Wesley was one of the best and most prolific hymn writers to ever serve the church. He wrote over sixty-five hundred hymns including favorites such as "Christ the Lord Has Risen Today," "Hark! The Herald Angels Sing," and "O for a Thousand Tongues to Sing." In his hymns he tried to provide Christian teaching and words to use as public praise to bring glory to Jesus Christ. In the fall of 1736 Wesley was returning to England following a disappointing trip to America. The ship he was traveling on entered a storm. Wesley sat depressed in his stateroom. He was startled by a small bird that fluttered into the room. It darted against his chest and crept inside his coat. He gently put his hand over the trembling creature. Its tiny heart was palpitating against his own. Wesley reflected on how helpless this small bird was. He saw in its frantic flight a picture of his own search for refuge in God. So he wrote the words to "Jesus, Lover of My Soul." These lyrics echo in the hearts of many believers who have been distressed at living in this world.

How do you handle frightful times? Even a godly man such as Daniel experienced thoughts that terrified him· In the most dreadful moments of life Jesus Christ is your hiding place. Today thank the Lord He is your shelter in times of terror.

> Jesus, lover of my soul, let me to thy bosom fly, while the nearer waters roll, while the tempest still is high! Hide me, O my Savior, hide—till the storm of life is past; safe into the haven guide; O receive my soul at last!
>
> —Charles Wesley

Day 278
BLESSED ARE THOSE WHO MOURN

Blessed are those who mourn, for they will be comforted.
Matthew 5:4

*R*obert Murray McCheyne was born in Edinburgh, studied arts and divinity at the University of Edinburgh and in 1836 became minister of St. Peter's Church, Dundee. He lived to be only thirty years old, dying of typhus in 1843. He pastored only seven years and was often stricken with illness. Yet in his short life he made a great impact upon his church, his town, his country, and the world.

Shortly after his death a young pastor visited St. Peter's, McCheyne's former church. He wanted to know why McCheyne had such a great influence in his life. The old maintenance man of St. Peter's led the preacher into the rectory and showed him some of McCheyne's books lying on a table. Then he motioned to the chair he had used, and said, "Sit down and put your elbows on the table." The young pastor sat. "Now put your head in your hands." He placed his head in his hands. "Now let the tears flow; that's what McCheyne did!" Next the old man led him into the church and said, "Put your elbows on the pulpit." The visitor did. "Now put your face in your hands." He complied. "Now let the tears flow; that's what McCheyne used to do!"

Are you grieved by the condition of this world? Today in prayer take heart and come to the One who will turn your mourning into joy, Jesus Christ.

> Man's inhumanity to man/Makes countless thousands mourn!
>
> —Robert Burns

Day 279
THANKS BE TO GOD

But as for me, I will always have hope;
I will praise you more and more.
Psalm 71:14

Felix was born in Cantalice, Italy, son of a peasant farmer. He worked as a shepherd boy and as a farm laborer but would spend much of his free time in prayer either in church or in a solitary place. He cultivated a spirit of thankfulness and by the time he was twenty entered a monastery. Felix solicited food and funds for his monastic order. When given anything he replied, "Thanks be to God." This constant praise to Christ was continually on his lips.

Whenever he appeared on the streets of Rome, Felix encouraged people to stop sinning and live a life pleasing to Christ. He once came across two men engaged in a duel. Rushing between them he grasped both swords crying, "Thanks be to God." Taken aback, both men repeated, "Thanks be to God."

317

"Now, the battle is done," said Felix. He then listened to the men's grievances. They prayed together and were reconciled.

Felix was known as "Brother Thanks be to God." Little children would chant "Thanks be to God" whenever he walked by, and often he would take the opportunity to teach them a spiritual truth by making up a song. It is said that theologians would come to Felix for advice on how to live the Christian life and for Bible teaching. His humility and simplicity was based on thanking the Lord and praising Christ for His goodness towards humanity.

You can never thank Christ enough. When was the last time you said "Thanks be to God" outside of a church service? Today in prayer give thanks in your heart to Christ and seek to praise Him more and more every day.

> O help us to appreciate all that we have, to be content with it, to be grateful for it, to be proud of it—not in an arrogant pride that boasts, but in a grateful pride that strives to be more worthy. In Thy name, to whose bounty we owe these blessings spread before us, to Thee we give our gratitude. Amen.
>
> —Peter Marshall

Day 280
THE HEROIC TRAITOR

See that what you have heard from the beginning remains in you. If it does, you also will remain in the Son and in the Father. And this is what he promised us—even eternal life.
1 John 2:24

During the American Revolutionary War, British General John Burgoyne commanded six thousand regulars and was pushing from Canada south to Albany, New York. There was only a disorganized force of revolutionists between Burgoyne and Washington's army. But these repeled and defeated Burgoyne on the farmlands of Saratoga, New York.

There is a curious monument at the Saratoga National Historical Park. The inscription reads: "In memory of the most brilliant soldier of the Continental Army, who was desperately wounded on this spot, the sally port of Burgoyne's great redoubt, 7th October, 1777, winning for his countrymen the decisive battle of the American Revolution, and for himself the rank of major general." Nowhere on the monument is the man's name. At the time of the battle he was considered second only to Washington as an American hero. He fought valiantly at Saratoga. But then something went terribly wrong. The man deserted the cause for which he fought so bravely.

Benedict Arnold was the hero of Saratoga. Later in the war he tried to give the British the plan for the defenses of West Point, fled from America, and lived out the remaining years of his life in disgrace in England. A sad epilogue: Arnold's last request was to be buried in his American uniform.

It is important to grow in the grace and knowledge of Jesus Christ. Christ is the vine, we are the branches. Our everlasting monument is the gift of eternal life. Resolve today not to wander from the God of grace.

In the passion of Christ, our life is everlasting.
—Julian of Norwich

THE GIFT OF HOPE

*For everything that was written in the past was written to
teach us, so that through endurance and the encouragement
of the Scriptures we might have hope.*
Romans 15:4

On October 8, 1997, Hurricane Pauline ripped into
the southwest coast of Mexico. It was the worst hurricane to
hit Mexico in over twenty years. Its 115-mph winds ravaged
the city of Acapulco and the surrounding area. Over 230 people were killed and thousands were left homeless. After the
storm subsided food, water, and clothing poured in to the area.

Three weeks after the storm subsided the Bible Society of
Mexico, assisted by the United Bible Societies (UBS), distributed over one million Bibles to the people affected by the hurricane. Why bring Bibles to storm victims? Steven Downey of
UBS explains: "God speaks to people in crisis, and in crisis
people turn to God. They need spiritual, not just material
support. That is why we are here."

Luis Romero was one of those who gained encouragement from the Scriptures during this time. The seventy-one-
year-old man was forced from his flooded home. At a Red
Cross shelter he eagerly read the Bible. He had lost most of his
personal possessions but found hope in the Word of God.

Difficult times will come to everyone. The Bible teaches
that through such times we may come to know God. Are you
spending enough time reading your Bible? Today thank Christ
that he has provided the Bible to comfort and give you hope.

Read the Scripture, not as an attorney may read a
will, merely to know the sense, but as the heir reads
it, as a description and proof of his interest.
—John Newton

A Good Soldier of Jesus Christ

Endure hardship with us like a good soldier of Christ Jesus.
No one serving as a soldier gets involved in civilian affairs—
he wants to please his commanding officer.
2 Timothy 2:3–4

In 1771 Francis Asbury set sail from England for America in response to John Wesley's call for volunteer evangelists to the colonies. When the American Revolution broke out five years later many missionaries returned to England. But not Asbury.

Once the war was over the passion to evangelize America caused Asbury to travel countless miles. In his diary he wrote that he often felt "strangely outdone for want of sleep, having greatly been deprived of it in my journey through the wilderness; which is like being at sea, in some respects, and in others worse. Our way is over mountains, steep hills, deep rivers, and muddy creeks; a thick growth of reeds for miles together; and no inhabitants but wild beasts and savage men. . .we ate no regular meal; our bread grew short, and I was much spent."

For over forty years Asbury preached an average of two sermons a day and traveled more than a quarter million miles planting the seed of the gospel. When Francis Asbury started his ministry there were no more than a thousand Christians in the Methodist Church in America. When he died more than 200,000 had been brought under the sway of his ministry.

When our heart is set on serving Christ, His love and grace overcome any hardship. Today spend some time to thank Christ for His love toward you. Ask Him to strengthen and sharpen your view of Him.

Men fail through lack of purpose rather than through lack of talent.

—Billy Sunday

THE IMPERISHABLE LIFE

Praise be to the God and Father of our Lord Jesus Christ!
In his great mercy he has given us new birth into a living
hope through the resurrection of Jesus Christ from the dead,
and into an inheritance that can never perish, spoil or fade—
kept in heaven for you, who through faith are shielded
by God's power until the coming of the salvation that is
ready to be revealed in the last time.

1 Peter 1:3–5

When the famous chemist Sir Humphry Davy was asked what he considered his greatest discovery he answered, "Michael Faraday."

Michael Faraday was born in 1791 and completed his formal schooling at age thirteen. He apprenticed in a bookbinding shop and read everything he could get his hands on. After hearing a series of lectures by Davy, he decided on a life of science and became an assistant under Davy. Faraday eventually became Professor of Chemistry at the Royal Institution and assumed Davy's chair of chemistry. Faraday is best remembered for his work in electromagnetism. He developed the first electric generator, the first electric transformer, and the first electric motor.

He also made several noteworthy contributions in the field of chemistry. One day Faraday's assistant accidentally knocked a little silver cup into a beaker of very strong acid. In almost no time the silver cup dissolved. The assistant ran to get the great scientist. Faraday quickly put an alkaline material into the beaker and the silver precipitated out of the solution to the bottom of the beaker. Faraday sent the shapeless mass of silver to a silversmith who recreated the silver cup.

When you see life perishing, spoiling, or fading away, does your heart die a little? It is sad to see life passing. But be encouraged! In resurrection death is forever conquered. Today in prayer praise the Lord that by His resurrection He has given us eternal life.

> I'm resting on certainties. I know that my Redeemer lives; and because he lives, I shall live also.
> —Michael Faraday

Day 284
HOW FEAR EVAPORATES

There is no fear in love. But perfect love drives out fear,
because fear has to do with punishment.
The one who fears is not made perfect in love.
1 John 4:18

Abraham Lincoln's life in the White House was filled with anguish, fear, and heartache. The American Civil War erupted in April 1861. It cost over 500,000 casualties. Lincoln's son Willie died in 1862 at the age of three. But Lincoln's biggest test was the battle of Gettysburg.

This three-day battle caused over fifty thousand casualties. Lincoln confided to an Army general how he stayed confident when others were in fear. "When everyone seemed panic-stricken I went to my room and got down on my knees before Almighty God and prayed. Soon a sweet comfort crept into my soul that God Almighty had taken the whole business into his own hands."

A second testimony of Lincoln's dependence on the Lord is found in his own Bible. The words to Psalm 34:4 are almost smudged out because Lincoln's fingers had touched them many times. This verse says, "I sought the LORD, and he answered me; he delivered me from all my fears."

In the love of Jesus Christ your fears melt away. The God of love has taken away the worst human fear—death. The next time fear takes hold of you focus on the resurrection of Jesus

Christ. Soon your fears will evaporate in the light of God's love.

Love and fear cannot exist together.

—Machiavelli

Day 285
YOU DIED WITH CHRIST

I have been crucified with Christ and I no longer live, but
Christ lives in me. The life I live in the body, I live by faith in
the Son of God, who loved me and gave himself for me.
Galatians 2:20

Robert Greene (R. G.) Lee was born in 1886 on a South Carolina farm to poor but religious parents. He sensed God's call to be a preacher early in his life and in spite of many obstacles heeded the call. He was ordained at his boyhood church in 1910 and went on to receive his Ph.D. in International Law in 1919.

Dr. Lee became a legend during sixty-plus years of ministry. He preached more than eight thousand sermons, including 1,275 presentations of his historic message, "Payday Someday." During his pastorate at Bellevue Baptist Church in Memphis from 1927–1960 over twenty-four thousand people joined the church. He authored more than fifty books of sermons and served several terms as president of both the Tennessee and Southern Baptist Conventions. Lee died at the age of ninety-two.

Once during a trip to Israel Dr. Lee visited the site where many believe Jesus Christ was crucified. He told his Arab guide that he wanted to walk to the top of the hill but the guide tried to discourage him. The preacher was determined to climb the hill so the guide accompanied him. When they reached the crest Dr. Lee removed his hat and bowed his head, deeply moved. The guide asked him, "Sir, have you been here before?" Dr. Lee replied, "Yes! Two thousand years ago."

Christ lives His life in us today because we died and rose with Him two thousand years ago. Today thank Jesus that His death gave you new life.

> And can it be that I should gain an interest in the Savior's blood! Died He for me who caused His pain? For me who Him to death pursued? Amazing love! How can it be that Thou, my God, should'st die for me?
>
> —Charles Wesley

Day 286
KEEP IN STEP

Those who belong to Christ Jesus have crucified
the sinful nature with its passions and desires.
Since we live by the Spirit, Let us keep in step with the Spirit.
Let us not become conceited, provoking and envying each other.
Galatians 5:24–26

In the third century a young man from a well-to-do home heard the Gospel of Matthew read. He took Matthew 19:21 literally: "If you want to be perfect, go, sell your possessions and give to the poor, and you will have treasure in heaven. Then come, follow me."

At age twenty Antony gave away his possessions. For the next thirty-five years he lived as a hermit in the Egyptian desert. Antony was surprised that in his life of solitude he was constantly tempted to sin. In *The Life Of Antony,* Athanasius writes that the hermit was tempted to return to his life of wealth and ease. He learned that it wasn't his external environment that tempted him to sin, it was his own nature. He also learned that to combat the sin nature you must read and study the Bible and trust God fully.

Antony broke his life of solitude when others came to him to learn how to be godly. He taught the benefits of prayer, meditation, and fasting. He visited prisoners and preached in areas where the Word had not been heard. In the last forty-five years of his life Antony was involved in the lives of people. He had learned to walk in the Spirit without withdrawing from those who needed the love of Christ.

We cannot escape our sinful nature without fixing our eyes upon Christ. Do you erect exterior barriers to keep you away from your innermost sin? Today thank Christ that our sin nature is crucified when we walk in the Spirit.

> God calls very few to be monks in a monastery. We can't live or do business in this world without rubbing shoulders with those driven by the world's desires. So we must make a practical decision not to be conformed while we are in the system, and at the same time, a radical decision to give God the green light to transform our mind.
>
> —Charles Swindoll

Day 287
THANK HIM FOR BEING NEAR

We give thanks to you, O God, we give thanks,
for your Name is near; men tell of your wonderful deeds.
Psalm 75:1

During World War I Franklin Delano Roosevelt was a member at St. Thomas Episcopal Church in Washington, D.C. Once elected president he rarely attended church, though at St. Thomas pews were reserved for him with red velvet cord. Roosevelt preferred to worship in the White House.

Though he was a public figure faith was a private matter to Roosevelt. He once remarked, "I can do almost anything in the 'goldfish bowl' of the President's life but I'll be hanged if I can say my prayers in it. By the time I have gotten into that pew and settled down with everyone looking at me I don't feel like saying my prayers."

One Christmas Eve the telephone rang in the rector's office at St. Thomas Church. "Tell me, Reverend," the caller asked, "are you holding a Christmas Eve service tonight?" The minister reported that there would certainly be a service that evening. The caller then asked, "And do you expect President Roosevelt to attend your church tonight?"

The rector realized that the caller was interested in seeing the president. He replied: "That, I can't promise. I'm not sure about the president's plans for this evening. But I can say that we fully expect God to be in our church tonight and we feel secure in the knowledge that His attendance will attract a reasonably large congregation."

Christ is always in attendance to our prayers. Today thank Christ and praise Him that He is near and hears your voice.

> Gratitude to God makes even a temporal blessing a taste of heaven.
>
> —William Romaine

Day 288
THE JOY IN PRAISING THE LORD

Let everything that has breath praise the LORD.
Praise the LORD.
Psalm 150:6

C. S. Lewis was professor of medieval and Renaissance literature at Oxford and Cambridge universities. He was once cynical about Christianity. But he came to know Jesus Christ and became one of the best-loved defenders of the faith.

Lewis had difficulty grasping why God wants praise. "We

all despise the man who demands continued reassurance of his own virtue, intelligence or delightfulness," Lewis wrote. To him, praising seemed like bartering, if you praise the Lord then He will grant your prayer request. Then Lewis hit upon the real meaning of praise to God: "I never noticed that all enjoyment spontaneously overflows into praise unless (sometimes even if) shyness or the fear of boring others is deliberately brought in to check it."

By praising God we express our love for Him. In praise comes pure and undefiled joy. It is a perfect expression of love toward God. As Lewis writes, "The Scotch catechism says that man's chief end is 'to glorify God and enjoy him forever.' But we shall then know that these are the same thing. Fully to enjoy is to glorify. In commanding us to glorify him, God is inviting us to enjoy him."

Do you enjoy the Lord? Then praise Him! Praise Him out of your love for Him. Today praise the Lord with all your heart. Praise Him for no other reason than that you love Him. Enjoy praise!

> All good gifts around us are sent from Heaven above,
> Then thank the Lord, O thank the Lord, For all his love.
>
> —James Montgomery Campbell

Day 289
HOWDY, JOHN. THANK YOU, JOHN!

I tell you that in the same way there will be more rejoicing in heaven over one sinner who repents than over ninety-nine righteous persons who do not need to repent.
Luke 15:7

John Broadus grew up on a farm in Culpeper, Virginia. He went on to become one of the most respected preachers in the world. He had depth of understanding, balance in delivery, and insight which few preachers attain. His book *A Treatise on the Preparation and Delivery of Sermons* is a classic. During the Civil War Broadus served as a chaplain in the Confederacy and was a favorite of General Robert E. Lee.

John Broadus became a Christian as a little boy. Soon he was instrumental in bringing Sandy Jones, his red-haired schoolmate, to Christ. When this happened Sandy said to his friend, "Thank you, John! Thank you!"

Dr. Broadus later left Culpeper and became president of the Southern Baptist Theological Seminary. Every summer when he returned to his hometown, an awkward, red-haired farmer in plain clothes would stick out his thin, bony hand and say, "Howdy, John. Thank you, John! Thank you for telling me about Jesus!" His friends tell that when Dr. Broadus lay dying and his family was gathered around him, he said, "The sweetest sound I expect to hear in heaven, next to the welcoming voice of him whom, having not seen, I have tried to love and serve, will be the welcome voice of Sandy Jones, saying, 'Howdy, John, and thank you, John!' "

When you hear the testimony of someone who has come to Christ, do you get excited? Today thank God for your salvation. Ask Him for an opportunity to bring someone to salvation through faith in Christ.

Our Lord Jesus Christ has always been interested in sinners. He came down from the glory of his Father's house to save sinners.

—H. A. Ironside

Day 290
OUR VOLUNTEER SUBSTITUTE

But God demonstrates his own love for us in this:
While we were still sinners, Christ died for us. Since we have
now been justified by his blood, how much more shall we be
saved from God's wrath through him!
Romans 5:8–9

America's first military draft came during the Civil War. The Conscription Act of 1863 provided for men from the northern states to serve in the military for up to two years. Anyone drafted could furnish a substitute, however, or pay $300 an exemption. Of those drafted, 46,347 chose to serve themselves. Over 100,000 men had a substitute serve for them.

But there was a scandal: Substitutes would collect a bounty to serve for someone (up to $777) and desert the ranks only to show up in another part of the country to collect another bounty to enlist for someone else. One enterprising man "served" as a substitute for thirty-six men before he was arrested for desertion and imprisoned.

Not all substitutes were dishonest. Cornelius Hulsapple was a private in the 97th Pennsylvania Infantry Regiment from October 1864 to the war's end. He served in North Carolina and saw combat at Fort Fisher. He substituted for W. R. Ridgway and wrote Ridgway twice during the war. Hulsapple made the following remark in one of his letters: "You will never have it said that you put in a man in your place that was afraid to meet the enemy at any time or place."

Jesus Christ volunteered to be our substitute. He took our place, faced death, and won! Do you ever forget that Christ conquered death for you? Today give thanks that while you were still a sinner Christ died for you. Through His substitution you are justified before God.

God's love is seen in Christ's laying down his life for those who were neither just nor good, but ungodly sinners.

—F. F. Bruce

Day 291
IT IS FAITH THAT SAVES

But the man who has doubts is condemned if he eats,
because his eating is not from faith;
and everything that does not come from faith is sin.
Romans 14:23

Israel's Religious Affairs Ministry is an official government agency headed by a Chief Rabbinate. The Ministry provides religious services to the population of Israel and deals with all matters related to the provision of religious services. This includes the appointment of religious councils, providing Torah education, providing financial assistance for the building of synagogues, and fostering tradition of the Jewish religious way of life. It oversees the religious courts which carry the same authority as civil courts. It also has exclusive jurisdiction over Jewish marriage and divorce and makes judgment on alimony, child support, custody, and inheritance.

This agency monitors restaurants who advertise that they serve kosher food. Dubbed the "Cheeseburger Police," the agency has a twenty-four hour hotline to receive reports of violations of Jewish dietary laws where kosher food is served. Rabbinate official Rafi Yochai reports that the response has been tremendous since the hotline was opened. His office levies fines ranging from $290 to $580.

Jewish law forbids pork and certain other foods, requires special slaughtering and preparation techniques for animal products, and forbids mixing milk products with meat—such as cheeseburgers. These Jewish dietary laws have their roots in the Old Testament books of Leviticus and Deuteronomy.

Only faith in Christ saves us from sin. Do you have faith in customs, habits, or traditions? Are these replacing Christ in your heart? Today in prayer thank the Lord that you are saved only through faith in Him.

> The doing of anything, such as eating non-kosher food, is sinful if it does not proceed from the conviction that "all things are clean" since such a man is doing what he is still inwardly convinced is wrong.
> —Matthew Black

Day 292
WHEN GOD CALLS

While they were worshipping the Lord and fasting, the Holy Spirit said, "Set apart for me Barnabas and Saul for the work to which I have called them." So after they had fasted and prayed, they placed their hands on them and sent them off.
Acts 13:2–3

William Carey completed his formal education by age twelve, became an apprentice shoemaker at age fourteen, and a Christian at age eighteen. He realized he had gifts for preaching and for languages and soon felt the Lord calling him to the mission field.

From 1790 until June 1793 he faced numerous obstacles to his following the Lord's call. For example, the directors of the East India Company opposed his missionary work: "The sending out of missionaries into one Eastern possession is the maddest, most extravagant, most costly, most indefensible project which has ever been suggested by a moonstruck fanatic." But in June, 1793, Carey and his family set sail to India. In the first years Carey's son died of dysentery, his wife suffered a nervous breakdown, and a close friend squandered the mission's money. Through all this Carey never doubted that the Lord had called him to the mission field. His response to hardship was, "He is all-sufficient."

Today Carey is known as the father of modern missions. His work and that of others made the Bible available in forty-four languages. Through his efforts the Bible was distributed to 300,000,000 people. Carey's missionary and translation work inspired the founding of the London Missionary Society, the American Mission Board, and the American Baptist Missionary Union.

Christ calls each of us to serve Him. Do you know what the Lord desires for your life? Today in prayer worship Christ as Lord and let Him confirm in you the plan for your life.

> If you do not feel the consecrated glow, I beseech you return to your homes and serve God in your proper spheres; but if assuredly the coals of juniper blaze within, do not stifle them, unless, indeed other considerations of great moment should prove to you that the desire is not a fire of heavenly origin.
> —Charles Spurgeon

Day 293
PERMISSIBLE VS. BENEFICIAL

"Everything is permissible for me"—but not everything is beneficial. "Everything is permissible for me"—but I will not be mastered by anything. "Food for the stomach and the stomach for food"—but God will destroy them both. The body is not meant for sexual immorality, but for the Lord, and the Lord for the body.
1 Corinthians 6:12–13

In the eastern part of Australia lies an area similar to the Florida everglades. It is the Nardoo River Catchment—a sensitive ecological zone where the water is filtered by water lilies and a fern called the nardoo plant. Growing in 10 centimeters or less of water, the nardoo filters the surrounding water by removing brackishness from seasonal ponds. The spores of the nardoo plant (*Marsilea drummondi*) can be collected in the dry season. Broken on grindstones, these spores are separated from their outer cases and then made into a bread or a porridge. But the spores of the nardoo fern do not contain any calories, proteins, carbohydrates, vitamins, or minerals. Without these it is a worthless food.

The British explorers Burke and Wills explored the Cooper's Creek area of Australia. They tried to survive on a diet of nardoo alone when their own food supplies ran out. The spores swelled in their stomachs when reconstituted in water but provided no benefits as a food. Their stomachs were full but members of the exploration party died of starvation. The nardoo was not harmful; neither was it beneficial.

Many things in modern life are permissible to us—they are not harmful—but are they beneficial? Today in prayer give thanks that you do not live by bread alone, but by every word which proceeds from the mouth of God.

> Christians should barely consider what is in itself lawful to be done, but what is fit for them to do.
> —Matthew Henry

Day 294
STAND FIRM IN THE FAITH

Be on your guard; stand firm in the faith;
be men of courage; be strong. Do everything in love.
1 Corinthians 16:13–14

When Nero was the emperor of Rome the soldiers assigned to guard him were known as the "Emperor's

Wrestlers." These champions would often chant: "We, the wrestlers, wrestling for thee, O Emperor, to win for thee the victory and from thee, the victor's crown."

The emperor's wrestlers were once fighting in far away Gaul under the centurion Vespasian. Many of these soldiers were becoming Christians. So Nero issued an order to all of the Roman army—everyone must renounce their faith in Christ or die.

The news reached Vespasian in midwinter. He ordered any Christians among his men to step forward. Forty out of one hundred did so. Vespasian paused—so many select soldiers! "The decree of the emperor must be obeyed but I am not willing that your comrades should shed your blood. March out upon the lake of ice. I shall leave you there to the elements."

Stripped, they marched toward the center of the ice chanting: "Forty wrestlers, wrestling for thee, O Christ, to win for thee the victory and from thee, the victor's crown!" Through the night Vespasian heard the faint chant. Dawn came; One man crept back toward the fire; The chanting changed; "Thirty-nine wrestlers. . ."

Vespasian knew he had to take a stand—either he was for or against Jesus Christ. He stripped and joined his men on the ice chanting: "Forty wrestlers, wrestling for thee, O Christ, to win for thee the victory and from thee, the victor's crown!"

Are you ever tempted to leave Christ in difficult circumstances? Today tell God the trials you face and let Christ fill you with strength and love so you may endure.

> Soldiers of Christ, arise, and put your armor on,
> strong in the strength which God supplies through
> his eternal son; Strong in the Lord of hosts, and in
> his mighty power: who in the strength of Jesus trusts,
> is more than conqueror.
>
> —Charles Wesley

Day 295
RICH BEYOND IMAGINATION

Praise be to the God and Father of our Lord Jesus Christ,
who has blessed us in the heavenly realms with every
spiritual blessing in Christ.
Ephesians 1:3

At the beginning of the twentieth century William Randolph Hearst was one of the wealthiest men in America. He was a powerful newspaper publisher, twice a member of the U.S. House of Representatives. He produced over 100 Hollywood movies and was an insatiable art collector.

Hearst's collection included approximately ten thousand items—paintings, sculpture, tapestries, and furniture. He owned fine collections of armor, stained glass, Gothic mantels, Egyptian mummies, choir stalls, religious icons, Navajo rugs, antique silver, and Mexican saddles. He once had a Spanish castle disassembled, each part numbered, and stored in a warehouse. He housed his collections in eight mansions including San Simeon in California. Known today as the Hearst Castle, the acreage of this estate would cover half of Rhode Island. He owned an entire city block of warehouses in New York City where his collections were stored.

Once he instructed an agent to obtain a certain artistic masterpiece. Price was no object. After many months of researching the agent reported that Hearst already owned the masterpiece. It had been stored in one of his warehouses for years.

We are blessed in Christ far more than we can imagine. Every spiritual blessing is ours. Today give thanks to the Lord that you are spiritually rich beyond measure.

Those blessings are sweetest that are won with prayer
and worn with thanks.

—Thomas Goodwin

Little Silver Boxes with Bows on Top

Do not let any unwholesome talk come out of your mouths,
but only what is helpful for building others up according to
their needs, that it may benefit those who listen.
Ephesians 4:29

Florence Littauer is a popular conference speaker and author. When she and her husband Fred were raising their two children they taught that the family's conversation had to meet the test of Ephesians 4:29. That is, their words had to be positive, build up the family, and favor the hearer.

Once Florence attended a Sunday worship service. The pastor noticed her in the congregation and called upon her to give the children's sermon. Totally unprepared, Littauer asked the Lord for help. Immediately Ephesians 4:29 came to her mind.

She stood before the youngsters and told them she was going to teach them a verse she had taught her own children. She discussed the words and phrases of the verse with them and then summarized their findings. "We are not to say bad words but good words that will build each other up. Our words should minister grace—do a favor, give a present to each other."

"The idea of presents brightened them all up," she later wrote, "and then one precious little girl stood up, stepped into the aisle, and said loudly to the whole congregation, as if serving as my interpreter, 'What she means is that our words should be like little silver boxes with bows on top.'"

God wants our words to be verbal presents to encourage others. Do you know people who need to be encouraged? In prayer ask Jesus to make your words like little silver boxes with bows on top.

We all need encouragement. We can live without it just as a young tree can live without fertilizer, but unless we receive that warm nurturing, we never reach our full potential, and like the tree left to itself, we seldom bear fruit.

—Florence Littauer

Day 297
THE PREDATOR

*And no wonder, for Satan himself
masquerades as an angel of light.*
2 Corinthians 11:14

The polar bear is the largest member of the bear family. Males weigh as much as two thousand pounds. They walk an average of 100,000 miles during their lifetime and are able to swim sixty miles without resting. Their white coats are extremely well suited for the arctic environment. Biologists cannot use traditional aerial photography to estimate populations because polar bear fur blends so well with the snow and ice. These bears are primarily carnivores. Their favorite diet consists of seals.

A hunting polar bear will sometimes lie motionless for fourteen hours near a hole in the ice waiting for a seal to surface for a breath of air. If a seal is resting on top of the ice a polar bear will swim under the ice to the seal's exact location. Below the surface the bear makes a tiny scratching sound imitating a fish. The seal hears this, dives in the water for a quick meal, only to be entrapped in the deadly embrace of its predator.

Satan appeals to us to please God by our good behavior. This is the trick of a predator. Only faith in Jesus Christ satisfies God. Today ask the Lord to teach you the truth of the gospel and so protect you from the evil one.

False teachers cannot comfort or make happy a timid conscience; they only make hearts confused, sad, and melancholy so that people are gloomy and act sad.

—Martin Luther

TELLING IT LIKE IT IS

As Jesus was getting into the boat, the man who had been
demon-possessed begged to go with him. Jesus did not let him,
but said, "Go home to your family and tell them how much the
Lord has done for you, and how he has had mercy on you." So
the man went away and began to tell in the Decapolis how
much Jesus had done for him. And all the people were amazed.
Mark 5:18–20

The American industrialist Henry John Heinz gave his testimony of faith in Jesus Christ in his will. "Looking forward to the time when my earthly career shall end, I desire to set forth at the very beginning of this will, as the most important item in it, a confession of my faith in Jesus Christ as my Savior.

"I also desire to bear witness to the fact that throughout my life in which there were the usual joys and sorrows, I have been wonderfully sustained by my faith in God through Jesus Christ. This legacy was left to me by my sacred mother, who was a woman of strong faith, and to it I attribute any success I may have attained during my life."

It can be intimidating to tell your family of your new life in Christ because they knew you before your decision for Him. But Christ is faithful. He is with you. Your family and friends may not understand but they will be watching. And if you let Christ shine forth in your life eventually they will acknowledge that He has done things for you and they will be amazed. The power of a personal testimony should never be underestimated. Continue to let Christ be the center of your life in all that you do and let people know that He is making a difference in you.

Your story, your life, is a testimony to God's goodness, his grace, his forgiveness. So share who you are with people. Let them know you have struggles but that Jesus has made a difference.

—Rebecca Manley Pippert

Day 299
THE SUBSTITUTE

God presented him as a sacrifice of atonement, through faith in his blood. He did this to demonstrate his justice, because in his forbearance he had left the sins committed beforehand unpunished—he did it to demonstrate his justice at the present time, so as to be just and the one who justifies those who have faith in Jesus.
Romans 3:25–26

During World War II, Rudolf Hess was the commandant of the most heinous Nazi concentration camp—Auschwitz. Hess' father wanted his son to become a missionary but Rudolf balked at the idea. As a young man Hess found that his prayers had dissolved into distressed stammering and he consciously turned his back on God. It was a decision which plagued him the rest of his life.

In 1941 Hess was put in charge of the newly opened Auschwitz. Those who were first confined there were political prisoners. One was Maximilian Kolbe, a Franciscan priest. Kolbe shared his meager food with his fellow prisoners, prayed for his captors, and encouraged those who were despondent.

If someone escaped ten other prisoners were tortured until they died. After one such escape ten names were announced. The last was that of Franciszek Gajowniczek who sobbed "My wife and my children." Then, an eleventh man made his way to the front of the formation. It was Kolbe. The German soldiers raised their rifles. Kolbe approached Hess.

"Herr Commandant, I wish to make a request, please. I want to die in the place of this prisoner." Kolbe pointed at the weeping Gajowniczek. Everyone was stunned. Hess stood motionless for several moments, then ordered, "Request granted."

Jesus Christ substituted His life for yours so that you may live. Do you sometimes take this for granted? Today thank Christ that although justice punishes sin, in God's mercy Christ bore that punishment.

> Grace and life were given you, but meant bitter work
> for him. It cost him much.
>
> —Martin Luther

Day 300
SEEK GOD FIRST

Moreover, when God gives any man wealth and possessions, and enables him to enjoy them, to accept his lot and be happy in his work—this is a gift of God. He seldom reflects on the days of his life, because God keeps him occupied with gladness of heart.
Ecclesiastes 5:19–20

Robert LeTourneau never intended to be wealthy. He only wanted to live his life for the Lord. He was a farmer and mechanic who designed heavy-duty earthmoving equipment and offshore drilling platforms. His company's equipment was used to build the vast interstate highway system and countless other projects.

Bob LeTourneau was first and foremost a Christian. He gave away almost ninety percent of what he earned. He understood his responsibility to the Lord and invested millions of dollars in missionary development projects in Liberia, West Africa, and Peru. These brought the gospel, education, and medical aid to thousands of people. LeTourneau's lifetime motto was "Not how much of my money do I give to God, but how much of God's money do I keep for myself."

During much of his adult life LeTourneau traveled across

the U.S. and throughout the world to share his testimony about the joy of serving Christ. Each time he spoke he began by saying, "I'm just a mechanic that God has blessed, and it seems he wants me to go around telling how He will bless you too."

Do you worship the gift or the One who has given the gift to you? Today in prayer, thank Christ for life, the work He has given to you, and the money He has provided for you to enjoy this life.

His alms were money put to interest in the other world.

—Robert Southey

Day 301
HALLEY AND NEWTON

Young men, in the same way be submissive to those who are older. All of you, clothe yourselves with humility toward one another, because, "God opposes the proud but gives grace to the humble." Humble yourselves, therefore, under God's mighty hand, that he may lift you up in due time.
1 Peter 5:5–6

*E*dmond Halley is remembered for the discovery of the comet which bears his name. He was a brilliant mathematician and astronomer who developed the first magnetic charts of the Atlantic Ocean and invented a diving helmet for salvaging shipwrecks. But Halley's major contribution to science was his encouragement and support of Isaac Newton.

Newton was a mild, retiring gentleman who brilliantly calculated a new type of mathematics. But Newton had laid his equations aside and done nothing to bring them to the attention of the scientific world. Halley understood the importance of Newton's work and urged him to write a book. So Newton perfected the new mathematics, now known as

"Differential and Integral Calculus." He also put forth four theorems of planetary orbits.

Halley put aside his own work in astronomy to correct Newton's 550-page thesis. He supervised its publication and financed its printing. The resultant work, *Mathematical Principles of Natural Philosophy,* made Newton famous. Historians today call Halley's action one of the most selfless acts of modern science.

In the body of Christ there is only one head—Jesus Christ. The rest of us are simply members of equal standing. Do you wrestle with pride? Today in prayer thank God that He made Christ to be head over all things to the church. Seek ways to serve and strengthen the members of Christ's body.

> When God intends to fill a soul he first makes it empty; when he intends to enrich a soul he first makes it poor; when he intends to exalt a soul, he first makes it sensible of its own miseries, wants and nothingness.
>
> —John Flavel

Day 302
START WITH PRAYER

On their release, Peter and John went back to their own people and reported all that the chief priests and elders had said to them. When they heard this, they raised their voices together in prayer to God. "Sovereign Lord," they said, "you made the heaven and the earth and the sea, and everything in them."
Acts 4:23–24

The controversial reformer John Knox came to know Jesus Christ as his Savior in about 1545. He immediately began preaching the gospel and spoke out boldly against sin. In 1547, Knox was imprisoned by the French. He was forced to be a galley slave aboard ship for nineteen months. While imprisoned he ministered in letters to other captives held by the French. Edward VI of England helped secure Knox's release and with renewed energy Knox began a twenty-three-year public ministry. He was the founder of the Presbyterian Church in Scotland.

On his deathbed, Knox called to his wife and said, "Read me that Scripture where I first cast my anchor." After he listened to the beautiful prayer of Jesus Christ in John 17, Knox summoned one last burst of energy and prayed, interceding for humanity. He prayed for the lost who had not received the gospel. He prayed for those who had recently trusted Christ. And he prayed for protection for the Lord's servants, many of whom were facing persecution. As Knox prayed, his spirit departed to be with the Lord.

Queen Mary once said, "I fear [Knox's] prayers more than I do the armies of my enemies." And Knox prayed until the moment of death.

Great ministries don't just happen. They are the Lord's answer to the prayers of His people. Do you want Christ to work in a magnificent way? Remember, God's work starts with prayer and continues in prayer.

Men may make defiant gestures against God; in the end God must prevail.

—William Barclay

Day 303
Sweet Words to the Ear

*Consequently, faith comes from hearing the message, and the
message is heard through the word of Christ.*
Romans 10:17

In 1815 Robert Moffat was reluctantly accepted as a
missionary to South Africa. Moffat was a poor student but
truly loved Christ. Two years later in South Africa he married
Mary Smith, his employer's daughter. Mary quickly discovered
a problem in sharing the gospel with the South Africans. She
wrote to her husband: "The gospel has not yet been preached
to them in their own tongue in which they were born. They
have heard it only through interpreters. . .who have themselves
no just understanding, no real love of the truth. We must not
expect the blessing till you are able, from your own lips and in
their language, to bring it through their ears into their hearts."

In the next fifty years the Moffats had a profound effect in
South Africa. Under arduous conditions they translated the
entire New Testament, many hymns, and *The Pilgrim's Progress*
into the Bechuana language. Many people were won to Christ
because they had the Word in their own language. The Moffat's
faith and action were an inspiration to their son-in-law David
Livingstone who later took the gospel to the African interior.

The spoken Word of God is powerful. When you share
your faith with others, do you quote Scripture? Today thank
Christ for His Word and its power to convey the faith.

> The greatest missionary is the Bible in the mother
> tongue. It never takes a furlough, is never considered
> a foreigner.
>
> —William Cameron Townsend

Day 304
TAKING THE WORD TO HEART

How can a young man keep his way pure?
By living according to your word. I seek you with all my heart;
do not let me stray from your commands.
I have hidden your word in my heart
that I might not sin against you.
Psalm 119:9–11

*S*ome years ago, the respected Christian leader D. J. De Pree of Zeeland, Michigan, addressed the annual Gideon convention in Washington, D.C. In his message he pointed out the top ten spiritual activities we must fully engage in in order to fully realize the revitalizing power of the Word of God. They are:

Read it (1 Timothy 4:13);

Eat it—that is, take it into our very being (Job 23:12; Jeremiah 15:16);

Bathe in it for spiritual cleansing (John 15:3);

Look into it as a mirror to see our true self (James 1:23–25);

Meditate on it (Psalm 1:2; 1 Timothy 4:15);

Memorize it (Deuteronomy 11:18; Psalm 119:11);

Study it (2 Timothy 2:15; Hebrews 5:12–14);

Teach it to others (Deuteronomy 11:19; Colossians 3:16);

Talk about it (Joshua 1:8);

Sow its seeds of truth in the field of the world (Matthew 13:3–9; Luke 8:11).

Are you taking the Word of God to heart? Are you passing its joy on to the children in your life? Today in prayer thank Christ for His Word. Remember that the final resting place for the Word of God is not the head but the heart.

The Bible will keep you from sin, or sin will keep you
from the Bible.

—D. L. Moody

Day 305
KNOW THAT HE DIED FOR YOU

The LORD lives! Praise be to my Rock!
Exalted be God my Savior!
Psalm 18:46

On November 1, 1947, President Harry Truman was
preparing to speak at an outdoor ceremony. He was living in
Blair House in Washington, D.C. while the White House was
being renovated.

That day two young Puerto Rican men approached Blair
House from opposite directions. They were Oscar Collazo
and Griselio Torresola—activists for Puerto Rican independence. They drew their pistols and fired on the Secret Service
agents and White House Police officers who were on guard.
Two minutes later the shoot-out was over. Torresola and
White House Officer Leslie Coffelt were killed. Collazo and
two other White House policemen were wounded. Neither
assailant reached the entrance to the building.

Officer Leslie Coffelt left behind a wife and step-daughter.
President Truman was saddened by the loss of his guard and
became concerned for the safety of those assigned to guard
him. Several weeks after the young policeman's death there was
a benefit dinner to raise support for the Coffelt family.
President Truman spoke with great emotion: "You can't understand just how a man feels when somebody else dies for him."

Jesus Christ died for you. And because He rose from the

dead you have new life in Him. Today praise Jesus Christ that not only did He die for you, but He lives for you as well!

> A true Christian is a man who never for a moment forgets what God has done for him in Christ, and whose whole comportment and whole activity have their root in the sentiment of gratitude.
>
> —John Baillie

Day 306
TRUST THE LORD

"Where is your faith?" he asked his disciples. In fear and amazement they asked one another, "Who is this? He commands even the winds and the water, and they obey him."
Luke 8:25

In November, 1857, a serious leak developed in the heating system at George Müller's orphanage. Winter was near and the boiler had to be repaired or replaced. Action was required but Müller did not know how to proceed. He prayed. It was best to see if the boiler could be repaired instead of replacing it with a new one.

Five days prior to the day repairs were to begin a cold north wind blew into London. Without the boiler the children could become dangerously cold. Müller prayed for two things, that the weather would become milder and that the repairs would go swiftly and smoothly.

On the day of the repairs an uncommon southerly wind blew. Temperatures rose and no indoor heating was needed. The workers found the leak immediately and insisted on staying through the night to finish the job. The heating system was repaired in thirty hours.

We have difficulty forecasting the weather, never mind

controlling it. But for the Lord the weather is simply another part of creation. Today thank Christ that you can trust Him with things you cannot understand or control.

> There is something better than understanding God, and that is trusting God.
>
> —G. L. Knight

Day 307
WHERE THERE IS MEANING

I have seen all the things that are done under the sun; all of them are meaningless, a chasing after the wind.
Ecclesiastes 1:14

J. Robert Oppenheimer was born in New York City in 1904. He graduated from Harvard University, went to Britain to do research at Cambridge University, received his doctorate from Gottingen University in Germany, and soon became a professor of physics at the University of California at Berkeley and California Institute of Technology. In 1943 Oppenheimer was selected to lead the Manhattan Project for the development of the atomic bomb. In 1947, he was selected as head of the Institute for Advanced Study at Princeton University, chaired the General Advisory Committee of the Atomic Energy Commission, and was the nation's top advisor on nuclear policy. While chairman of this committee Oppenheimer opposed the development of the hydrogen bomb. This stance was seen as soft on communism. In 1954, he was forced to resign this position. Oppenheimer's security clearance was eventually reinstated by President Lyndon Johnson in 1963. In his last years, he developed ideas on the relationship of science and society. In 1966, a year before he died, he said, "I am a complete failure!" When asked about his achievements he replied, "They leave on the tongue only the taste of ashes."

Degrees, honors, positions and awards in themselves have no meaning. But in Christ everything that we possess has meaning because it can bring glory to Him. In your pursuits ask this question: "Who is going to get the glory?" Today in prayer ask Christ to be glorified in all that you do.

> Learning will not alter men's natural tempers, nor cure them of their sinful distempers; nor will it change the constitution of things in this world; a vale of tears it is and so it will be when all is done.
>
> —Matthew Henry

Day 308
FOOLISH THINKING

It is better to heed a wise man's rebuke
than to listen to the song of fools.
Ecclesiastes 7:5

On April 26, 1986, the worst nuclear accident in history occurred at Chernobyl in the former Soviet Union. Thirty-one people died immediately and over 135,000 people were evacuated from the surrounding area. Over ten thousand people are expected to die from cancer and other diseases because of their exposure to the radiation from this accident. How could this have happened?

There were two engineers in the control room that night. They wanted to see if a coasting turbine would be able to provide enough energy to sufficiently run pumps to keep the reactor core cool. The reactor was lowered to very unstable lower ranges. One by one computers issued warnings, "Stop! Dangerous! Go no further!" Rather than shutting off the experiment these engineers shut off the alarms and kept going. To safely control the stability of the reactor, a minimum of twenty-six control rods are needed to regulate the flow of energy. It is estimated that there were only eight control rods at the time the unauthorized test was started. Forty seconds later the reactor's power reached a hundred times the design value. Seconds later two explosions emptied eight tons of radioactive fuel into the atmosphere.

It is not easy to receive a rebuke. Do you put up a wall when hearing a wise rebuke? Today in prayer ask the Lord to give you a ready ear for wisdom.

Talk sense to a fool and he calls you foolish.
—Euripides

Day 309
DON'T LET SIN ESCAPE

Therefore, O king, be pleased to accept my advice:
Renounce your sins by doing what is right,
and your wickedness by being kind to the oppressed.
It may be that then your prosperity will continue.
Daniel 4:27

In 1869, Frenchman Leopold Trouvelot was living in Medford, Massachusetts. An astronomer by trade, Trouvelot had an interest in insects and was trying to raise a silk moth that was resistant to disease. He believed if he was able to breed such a moth, that it would revolutionize the silk industry.

One evening, to his horror, Trouvelot discovered that a few of the gypsy moths he had imported from Europe had escaped. He notified his neighbors and begged them to help him kill or capture the gypsy moths. But they thought, "Why be alarmed because of a few stray moths?"

In 1889 Medford had an outbreak of gypsy moths which defoliated its deciduous trees. The moth is capable of feeding on over 300 species of trees and shrubs. Through the years it has spread an average of twelve miles a year. In 1992 Virginia reported over 800,000 acres infested with gypsy moth. In 1995 Ohio reported over thirty-five thousand acres were defoliated. Each year in the United States and Canada over two million acres of trees are infested with this little moth. It could have all been avoided if some people at the beginning understood the seriousness of a few escaped moths.

Do you ever tell others about the seriousness of sin? It is not a desirable task, but don't let it slide. Like little moths feeding on trees, sin can consume human life. You can disagree with sin without being disagreeable. Today in prayer ask Christ for wisdom and tact when speaking about sin.

It does not spoil your happiness to confess your sin.
The unhappiness is not making the confession.
—Charles Spurgeon

Day 310
WE TWO SHALL WIN

Then he continued, "Do not be afraid, Daniel. Since the first day that you set your mind to gain understanding and to humble yourself before your God, your words were heard, and I have come in response to them."
Daniel 10:12

Daniel Crawford served as a missionary to Angola and Zaire for twenty-two years. He had the difficult task of following in the steps of David Livingstone. Crawford didn't have the imposing personality of his famous predecessor, so at first he had trouble winning the loyalty of the tribal people. Even the people in his church back home weren't sure he could carry on the work. However, the Lord worked through him and Crawford learned to present the gospel and teach Christian truth by using illustrations from the native culture. When he died a well-worn copy of the New Testament was found in his pocket. A poem evidently his own, handwritten on the inside cover, revealed the secret of his success:

I cannot do it alone! The waves dash fast and high;
The fog comes chilling around, And the light goes out in
   the sky.
But I know that we two shall win in the end—
Jesus and I.
Coward, and wayward, and weak, I change with the
   changing sky,
Today so strong and brave, Tomorrow too weak to fly;
But he never gives in! So we two shall win—
Jesus and I!

We win when we humble ourselves before the Lord and rely on Christ's strength. On whose strength do you rely? Today thank Christ that He hears your words and He is able to overcome all obstacles.

God is quick to answer prayer and to come to the help of those who truly seek him.

—D.S. Russell

Day 311
MARVELOUS IN OUR EYES

*The stone the builders rejected has become the capstone;
the LORD has done this, and it is marvelous in our eyes.*
Psalm 118:22–23

Nicolaus Copernicus was nineteen years old when Christopher Columbus followed the stars to the West Indies.

Copernicus constructed a new system of astronomy which consisted of a solar system with the sun and not the earth as the center. His theories were rejected by both the Catholic and the emerging Protestant churches. Copernicus's book, *Revolutions,* was published during the last year of his life and drew criticism from two sources. Philosophers held onto Aristotle's theory that the earth was the fixed center of the universe. Churchmen accused Copernicus of contradicting the Bible. Many opposed him on both counts.

Nearly a century later Galileo was charged with heresy and warned not to defend the Copernican theory. In 1632, at nearly seventy years of age, the invalid Galileo published a book which held to the Copernican theory. He was immediately summoned to trial and remained under house arrest until his death in 1642.

Isaac Newton's success with theoretical physics finally brought the Copernican theory triumph and Copernicus is now considered the founder of modern astronomy.

Jesus was rejected because he did not match the Pharisees' concept of a messiah. Who is the center of your universe? Have you molded Jesus to become who you think He should be? Or is he the Lord of all? Take time now to contemplate the size of your God—the God who created the universe. Worship His awesome greatness and His marvelous love.

> What, but God? Inspiring God! Who boundless Spirit all, and unremitting energy, pervades, adjusts, sustains, and agitates the whole.
>
> —James Thomson

Day 312
THE ONE TRUE GOD

Now to the King eternal, immortal, invisible, the only God,
be honor and glory for ever and ever. Amen.
1 Timothy 1:17

One is struck by the limitations of the Greek gods. The mighty Zeus was considered the most powerful of the gods. But Zeus was not eternal; he was born. In Greek mythology some of the gods died. The scope of their power was limited. Zeus was lord of the sky and was the rain god, but he did not exercise power at sea. That realm was under his brother Poseidon's power. Another god, Apollo, was forced into servitude. Morally the Greek gods lacked integrity. Zeus had many affairs and other gods committed murder, adultery, and displayed treachery.

Hermes, the illegitimate son of Zeus, was a cattle thief. He was a messenger god and had the appearance of either an old man or a young man. Hermes was limited because he was invisible only when wearing a special helmet.

The God of our Lord Jesus Christ is unlimited—eternal, immortal, invisible, with no contradiction. Jesus Christ is the rock when all else fails. In Christ we have the one true God. Today in prayer praise the Lord who is like no other.

> We impoverish God's ministry to us the moment we forget he is Almighty; the impoverishment is in us, not in him.
>
> —Oswald Chambers

Day 313
FIGHT THE GOOD FIGHT

Fight the good fight of the faith. Take hold of the eternal life to which you were called when you made your good confession in the presence of many witnesses.
1 Timothy 6:12

He was a twenty-to-one long shot—on November 9, 1996, Evander Holyfield shocked the boxing world by retaining the WBA heavyweight boxing title against the favored challenger, Mike Tyson. How did he do it? Holyfield credits Jesus Christ and hard work.

Holyfield knew a match against Tyson would be the fight of his life. He chose Gary Bell to be his sparring partner. Bell has the physical makeup and punching resemblance of Tyson. For thirteen weeks Bell beat up on Holyfield. Holyfield was barely able to go three or four rounds with Bell. With only three weeks before the fight, Holyfield was finally able to beat Bell. "To be a winner you have to go through what's necessary for the prize. And Gary Bell was only the first step. So I prayed, I prayed a lot."

On November 9, Holyfield entered the ring. Philippians 4:13 was embroidered on the lapel of his robe. But Holyfield didn't leave Christ in his corner. During the fight he was praying. At one point Holyfield came back to his corner talking. His trainer said, "Evander, what did you say?" "I wasn't talking to you," he responded—he was praying. In the eleventh round the fight was stopped. Holyfield was declared the winner with a technical knockout over Tyson.

How to fight the good fight: Pray; train hard; walk closely with Christ; don't let setbacks discourage you; pray.

I'm gonna give him the glory and that glory is gonna touch a lot of people's lives and help people overcome a lot of obstacles in their life.

—Evander Holyfield

HE ENDURED TO THE END

Here is a trustworthy saying:
If we died with him, we will also live with him; if we endure,
we will also reign with him. If we disown him,
he will also disown us; if we are faithless,
he will remain faithful, for he cannot disown himself.
2 Timothy 2:11–13

John Bradford was chaplain to King Edward VI and was one of the most highly regarded preachers in Britain. In his three-year public ministry Bradford dedicated himself to preaching, reading, and praying. He slept four hours a night and ate one meal a day.

Queen Mary ascended to the throne in 1553 and Bradford was imprisoned. He kept busy writing letters of encouragement. Once he wrote, "It is an amazing thing that ever since I have been in this prison, and have had other trials to bear, I have had no touch of my rheumatism or my depression of spirit."

Bradford knew that soon the guards would make that long walk to his cell and he would be martyred. When that day came he looked to heaven and exclaimed, "I thank God for it; I have looked forward to this and now suddenly it is time. May the Lord make me worthy." John Bradford prayed and was led out to be burned at the stake. With Bradford was another believer, John Leaf. Just before he died, Bradford said to Leaf, "Be of good comfort, brother; for this evening we shall have a merry supper with the Lord."

Christ is faithful to provide strength and comfort when you think you cannot take another step. Today ask Christ to strengthen you so that you can endure to the end.

Jesus died to be true to the will of God; and the Christian must follow that same will, whatever light may shine or shadow fall.

—William Barclay

SET YOUR HOPE ON CHRIST

Therefore, prepare your minds for action; be self-controlled;
set your hope fully on the grace to be given you
when Jesus Christ is revealed.
1 Peter 1:13

The marksman Gary Anderson, a two-time Olympic gold medal winner, says that the best time to fire a shot from a rifle is right after an exhale. Body movement caused by breathing can be best controlled at this point. But there is only a ten to twelve second period after an exhale that you can shoot before your eyes begin to blur and the lungs strain to resume breathing.

Lanny Bassham, the 1976 Olympic gold medalist in shooting agrees with Anderson: "Our sport is controlled nonmovement. We are shooting from fifty meters—over half a football field—at a bull's-eye three-quarters the size of a dime. If the angle of error at the point of the barrel is more than .005 of a millimeter, you drop into the next circle and lose a point. So we have to learn how to make everything stop. I stop my breathing. I stop my digestion by not eating for twelve hours before the competition. I train by running to keep my pulse around sixty beats per minute so I have a full second between beats. You do all of this and you have the technical control. . . . Then you have the other eighty percent of the problem—the mind!"

The cares of the day can blur our hope in Christ. Have you stood still recently to fix your mind on Christ? Today take time to decompress from work, family, and urgent tasks. Focus on your eternal hope—Jesus Christ.

> For Christians, the consummation of this grace occurs at the unveiling of Jesus the Messiah at the second coming.
>
> —Edwin A. Blum

WHERE ARE YOUR WORRIES?

Cast all your anxiety on him because he cares for you.
1 Peter 5:7

In 1874 Mary Slessor left Scotland as a missionary to Calabar, West Africa, a region ruled by witchcraft and superstition. She wrote home: "My one great consolation and rest is in prayer."

When Mary traveled on the Calabar River on the mission's steam launch she would bury her head in her hands and cry out in fear to the Lord if any strange sound came from its engines. Despite her natural fears, she never let them prevent her from doing what the Lord desired. Instead she cast all her anxiety on him.

After a particularly draining day of traveling Slessor was trying to sleep in a crude hut. She wrote: "I am not very particular about the bed these days, but as I lay on a few dirty sticks laid across and covered with a litter of dirty corn shells, with plenty of rats and insects, three women and an infant three days old alongside, and over a dozen sheep and goats outside, you don't wonder that I slept little. But I had such a comfortable quiet night in my own heart."

There is only one place for your worries—Christ's heart. What cares are weighing on you? There is nothing so great or so small that the Lord cannot handle it. In prayer give all your cares to Christ because He cares for you.

> Oh, how great peace and quietness would he possess who should cut off all vain anxiety and place all his confidence in God.
>
> —Thomas à Kempis

Day 317
GIVE TO GOD WHAT IS GOD'S

He saw through their duplicity and said to them,
"Show me a denarius. Whose portrait and inscription are on
it?" "Caesar's," they replied. He said to them, "Then give to
Caesar what is Caesar's, and to God what is God's."
Luke 20:23–25

On November 13, 1861, Reverend M. R. Watkinson wrote the Secretary of the Treasury, Salmon P. Chase. Watkinson was concerned that the coinage of the country did not recognize God. He closed his letter: "From my heart I have felt our national shame in disowning God as not the least of our present national disasters."

A week later Chase wrote to the director of the Mint:

"Dear Sir: No nation can be strong except in the strength of God or safe except in his defense. The trust of our people in God should be declared on our national coins. You will cause a device to be prepared without necessary delay with a motto expressing in the fewest and tersest words possible this national recognition. Yours truly, S. P. Chase."

An act of Congress was passed on April 22, 1864, changing the composition of the one-cent coin and authorizing the minting of a two-cent coin. Both were inscribed with the motto, "In God We Trust." The Coinage Act of 1873 provided for inscribing "In God We Trust" on all coins. The act was subsequently strengthened in a 1955 Act of Congress mandating that the motto "In God We Trust" appear on all coins of the United States.

Money comes and it goes—it does not deserve our trust. But the Lord is always present and trustworthy. Do you sometimes think, "If only I had a little more money"? Today in prayer give thanks that Christ will meet all of your needs.

My whole trust is in God, and I am ready for whatever he may ordain.

—Robert E. Lee

Day 318
THE TIME HAS COME

"The time has come," he said. "The kingdom of God is near.
Repent and believe the good news!"
Mark 1:15

*G*eorge Whitefield was an itinerant preacher in the 1700s
and a leading figure in the American revival known as the
Great Awakening. Born and raised in England, he preached
the gospel in Britain, Wales, Ireland, Scotland, and in the
American colonies. He aggressively preached in public halls,
barns, open fields, and wherever an opportunity arose. George
Whitefield mentioned in his journal that during his first voyage to Georgia, the ship's cook had a bad drinking problem.
When the cook was reproved for it and other sins, he boasted
that he would be wicked until the last two years of his life, and
then he would reform. Whitefield added that within six hours
of the time the cook made that boastful statement, he died of
an illness related to his drinking.

We don't choose when we are born and we don't choose
when we die. But we can choose how we shall live. Eternal life
starts the moment you ask Jesus Christ into your life. He will
save you from eternal separation from God. But putting off
Christ is not a good idea. It is also not a good idea for
Christians to be involved in sin. The time has come for all of
us to repent and get serious with God.

Of all of the acts of man, repentance is the most divine.
The greatest of all faults is to be conscious of none.

—Thomas Carlyle

Day 319
HE REDEEMED US

*Christ redeemed us from the curse of the law by becoming a
curse for us, for it is written: "Cursed is everyone who is hung
on a tree." He redeemed us in order that the blessing given to
Abraham might come to the Gentiles through Christ Jesus, so
that by faith we might receive the promise of the Spirit.*
Galatians 3:13–14

John Pierpoint (J. P.) Morgan was a millionaire
banker. He helped reorganize the New York Central Railroad,
the Southern Railroad, the Erie Railroad, and other major rail-
ways to keep them financially solvent. He backed the formation of General Electric, U.S. Steel, and International
Harvester. He collected art, rare books, and antiques and left
many of these collections to the Metropolitan Museum of Art
and other institutions. Morgan was an extrovert, a risk taker,
and a controversial public figure. But J. P. Morgan knew that
the most important part of life is Jesus Christ the Savior. Below
is a section of his will which describes his faith in Christ:

"I commit my soul in the hands of my Savior, full of confidence, that, having redeemed me and washed me with His
most precious blood, He will present me faultless before the
throne of my heavenly Father.

"I entreat my children to maintain and defend, at all haz-
ard and at any cost of personal sacrifice, the blessed doctrine of
complete atonement of sins through the blood of Jesus Christ
once offered, and through that alone."

Faith in Jesus Christ. Nothing else will do. Do you have
the confidence that you are a child of God through Christ's
finished work? Today in prayer give thanks that Christ paid the
price for you and through Him you are saved.

I went very unwillingly to a society in Aldersgate
Street, where one was reading Luther's preface to the

Epistle to the Romans. While he was describing the change God makes in the heart through Jesus Christ, Christ alone for salvation, an assurance was given me that He had taken away my sins, even mine, and saved me from the law of sin and death.

—John Wesley

Day 320
A DEADLY TRAP

Brothers, if someone is caught in a sin,
you who are spiritual should restore him gently.
But watch yourself, or you also may be tempted.
Galatians 6:1

In early 1980 in the Arabian Sea, Commander Walt Williams was taxiing his A-6 aircraft toward the U.S.S. *Kitty Hawk's* catapult. But instead of being catapulted off the end of the deck at 100 miles per hour the aircraft rolled off at thirty-five miles per hour. Williams pulled the ejection handle and his seat shot into the air giving him one swing in his parachute before landing in the water. Then disaster struck. The parachute, which moments earlier had saved his life, dragged him underwater. The shroud lines tangled around his arms and legs. Every movement worsened the situation. A diver frantically cut the lines away from the downed pilot.

Commander Williams drowned. His parachute enabled him to survive the crash of his aircraft but was the cause of his death.

The U.S. Navy gives all of its aviators survival training. They are hooked up to a parachute and dropped into a swimming pool. If a shroud line wraps itself around an arm or leg they are taught to patiently lift each individual shroud line and back away from it. The only way to avoid a deadly situation is to patiently remove each line.

Sin can entwine a life. Do you know someone caught up in sin? Today in prayer ask the Lord how you can gently restore them to the life He intended for them.

The enemy will wait forty years, if necessary, to set a trap for you.

—Joe Aldrich

Day 321
GOD WILL NOT DESERT US

The apostles left the Sanhedrin, rejoicing because they had been counted worthy of suffering disgrace for the Name. Day after day, in the temple courts and from house to house, they never stopped teaching and proclaiming the good news that Jesus is the Christ.
Acts 5:41–42

Jonathan Goforth trusted Christ as his Savior when he was eighteen years old in Ontario, Canada. Goforth and his wife were called to missionary service and sailed to China in 1887 to minister in the Honan Province. In the next forty-six years Goforth evangelized and trained two generations of Christian leaders. At age seventy he opened Manchuria for Christ.

During their ministry in China the Goforths experienced great suffering. Five of their eleven children died in childhood. Jonathan suffered from typhoid fever, malaria, jaundice, pneumonia, and carbuncles. He was scarred from sword wounds inflicted during the Boxer Rebellion. Three times he and his family lost all their possessions to fire, flood, and war. Once Jonathan helped dry his wife's tears and said, "Well, my dear, after all, they were just material things; and the Word says that we should take joyfully the spoiling of our goods! Cheer up, we'll get along somehow. God will not desert us!"

At age seventy-one Jonathan became blind but remained

on the mission field for three more years. He returned to Canada at age seventy-four and spoke at 481 meetings during the eighteen months prior to his death. The verse that kept him going was Zechariah 4:6, " 'Not by might nor by power, but by my Spirit,' says the LORD Almighty."

Are you tired? Opposed? Are you feeling the heartache of a loss? Today claim Zechariah 4:6, " 'Not by might nor by power, but by my Spirit,' says the LORD Almighty." Share the Spirit with Jonathan Goforth.

> They found cause for joy in the thought that God had counted them worthy to suffer this disgrace for the sake of Jesus' name. It was insignificant, to be sure, when compared with the shame and anguish that he had endured; but, as far as it went, it was participation in his sufferings, such as he had warned them to expect.
>
> —F. F. Bruce

Day 322
THANKS IN THE MORNING

It is good to praise the LORD and make music to your name,
O Most High, to proclaim your love in the morning
and your faithfulness at night, to the music of
the ten-stringed lyre and the melody of the harp.
Psalm 92:1–3

Andrew Murray was a South African minister, pastor, and author. He served in farming communities where the population was dispersed over a wide area. The Lord used Murray's writings to build up these congregations. Many of Murray's 240 publications have become classics because of their thoughtful devotional instruction. Below is a portion of his teaching on the importance of morning prayer:

"Alone with God—that is the secret of true prayer, of true power in prayer, of real, face-to-face fellowship with God, and of power for service. There is no true, deep conversion, no true, deep holiness, no clothing with the Holy Spirit and with power, no abiding peace or joy, without being daily alone with God. There is no path to holiness, but in being much and long alone with God.

"What an inestimable privilege is the institution of daily secret prayer to begin every morning. Let it be the one thing our hearts are set on—seeking, and finding, and meeting God."

Nutritionists tell us that the most important meal of the day is breakfast. Scripture tells us that it is good to start each morning proclaiming praise and love for the Lord. Are you taking time to spend a few moments each morning praising Christ? Today thank Christ for His love toward you and His faithfulness each day.

> For each new morning with its light, Father, we thank thee. For rest and shelter of the night, Father, we thank thee.
>
> —Ralph Waldo Emerson

Day 323
FULL SURRENDER

"I am the Lord's servant," Mary answered.
"May it be to me as you have said." Then the angel left her.
Luke 1:38

One night in 1865 William Booth took a walk through the slums of London's East End. When he returned home he told his wife, "Catherine, I seemed to hear a voice sounding in my ears, 'Where can you go and find such heathen as these, and where is there so great a need for your labors?' Darling, I have found my destiny!" That year William and Catherine Booth opened the Christian Mission in the London slums.

In 1878 the Mission changed its name to the Salvation Army, designed uniforms for men and women officers, and adopted a semimilitary system of leadership to combat evil. Today the organization provides spiritual, social, medical, educational, and other community services to the poor and needy in more than 100 countries.

Someone once asked William Booth the secret of his success: His eyes filled with tears. After a few moments he said, "There have been men with greater brains or opportunities than I, but I made up my mind that God would have all of William Booth there was." Years later when one of his daughters heard about his comment regarding his full surrender to God she said, "That wasn't really his secret. His secret was that he never took it back."

Has God called you to a task? What keeps you from absolute surrender to Him? Today in prayer offer yourself completely to the Lord for the work He has prepared for you.

> When it comes to accomplishing things for God, you will find that high aspirations, enthusiastic feelings, careful planning, and being able to express yourself well are not worth very much. The important thing is absolute surrender to God. You can do anything he wants you to do if you are walking in the light of full surrender.
>
> —Francois Fenelon

Day 324
THE NOBLE EXPRESSION

I will sacrifice a thank offering to you and call on the name
of the LORD. I will fulfill my vows to the LORD in the presence
of all his people, in the courts of the house of the LORD—
in your midst, O Jerusalem. Praise the LORD.
Psalm 116:17–19

Sarah Josepha Hale was author of the children's poem "Mary's Lamb" and editor of the magazine *Lady's Book*. She helped to establish the Fatherless and Widows Society of Boston, the Merchant Marine Library Association, the Bunker Hill Monument, and worked tirelessly for thirty-six years for the establishment of Thanksgiving as a national holiday.

In 1789, George Washington first set the last Thursday of November as a national day of thanksgiving. But the holiday soon slipped into obscurity. In 1827 Sara Hale sought to re-establish Thanksgiving as a national holiday. She individually contacted each state's governor and by 1852 twenty-nine states and all the territories observed the holiday. But Presidents Taylor, Fillmore, Pierce, and Buchanan all ignored her pleas.

In 1863 the United States was engulfed in the Civil War. Hale wrote Secretary of State William Seward. He responded, "I have received your interesting letter—and have commended the same to the consideration of the President." Four days later President Lincoln issued his Thanksgiving Day proclamation and America has since had a national day of Thanksgiving.

You need not wait until the fourth Thursday of November to thank the Lord. You can show your appreciation every day by living your life for Him. Today in prayer ask God what you can do to give thanks.

Thanksgiving is the noblest expression of the noblest of the heart. It is gratitude flowing through the lips.

It is gratitude looking up with all its generous and swelling emotions and giving out those fragrant sacrifices to God, the author of all good, by fitting acts, and by a fitting service.

—E. M. Bounds

Day 325
CONTINUALLY PRAISE THE LORD

I will exalt you, my God the King;
I will praise your name for ever and ever.
Every day I will praise you and
extol your name for ever and ever.
Psalm 145:1–2

Thomas "Stonewall" Jackson, one of the South's most beloved and effective generals in the Civil War, had a deep religious conviction and a fierce fighting spirit. Before the war Jackson developed the habit of prayer when he served as a professor at Virginia Military Academy:

"I have so fixed the habit in my own mind that I never raise a glass of water to my lips without lifting my heart to God in thanks and prayer for the water of life. Then, when we take our meals there is grace. Whenever I drop a letter in the post office I send a petition along with it for God's blessing upon its mission and the person to whom it is sent. When I break the seal of a letter I have just received I stop to ask God to prepare me for its contents and make it a messenger of good. When I go to the classroom and await the arrangement of the cadets in their places that is the time to intercede with God for them. And so in every act of the day I have made the practice habitual."

Prayer is a discipline that leaves the heart glad and grateful. Have you developed the habit of thanksgiving and prayer? Today give thanks and praise—Jesus Christ is Lord!

Thanksgiving was never meant to be shut up in a single day.

—Robert Caspar Lintner

Day 326
THE LIGHT OF THE FATHER'S HOUSE

Always giving thanks to God the Father for everything,
in the name of the Lord Jesus Christ.
Ephesians 5:20

In her book, *Mama's Way,* Thyra F. Bjorn tells of the evening when she was a girl and accompanied her father to the shack of a poverty-stricken old man. "He was crippled with age and pain, yet he offered what hospitality he could, and when they prayed together, the old man's face came alive as the agony of his present life gave way to radiant joy. Rather than asking anything of God, the man thanked him in detail for his shack, his warm bed, his visitors, for everything that was a part of his seemingly cramped and limited existence. When he had finished, he looked as happy and contented as though he had no discomfort at all."

On the way home through the dark cold fall air, Thyra's father sighted the lamp being lit in their parsonage in the valley below and called his daughter's attention to it. Then the thought struck the young girl that this too was what the old man in the cabin had seen: He had seen his Father's house and knew that he soon would be home. There would be no more sickness or pain or loneliness there, and no more sorrow. And the light of prayer would lead him home.

How often do we take the gifts of God for granted, failing to give thanks to Christ in all things? Thank God for all you have. It won't be too long until all of us see the light of our Father's house leading us home.

370

O Lord, that lends me life, lend me a heart replete
with thankfulness.

—William Shakespeare

Day 327
THE SOIL OF THANKSGIVING

*I will extol the LORD at all times; his praise will always
be on my lips. My soul will boast in the LORD; let the
afflicted hear and rejoice. Glorify the LORD with me;
let us exalt his name together.*

Psalm 34:1–3

With steadfast and unwavering faith, with hard and
patient toil,

The Pilgrims wrung their harvest from a strange and ster-
ile soil.

And when the leaves turned red and gold beneath the
autumn sun,

They knelt beside the scanty sheaves their laboring hands
had won,

And each grave elder, in his turn, with bowed and reverent
head,

Gave thanks to bounteous Heaven for the miracle of bread.

And so was born Thanksgiving Day. That little dauntless
band,

Beset by deadly perils in a wild and alien land,

With hearts that·held no fear of death, with stern,
unbending wills,

And faith as firmly founded as the grim New England hills,

Though pitiful the yield that sprang from that unfruitful sod,

Remembered in their harvest time the goodly grace of
God.

God grant us to look on this, our glorious native land,

As but another princely gift from his Almighty hand.
May we prove worthy of his trust and keep its every shore
Protected from the murderous hordes that bear the torch
of war,
And be the future bright or dark God grant we never may
Forget the reverent spirit of that first Thanksgiving Day.
"Thanksgiving Day"—J. J. Montague.

Thanksgiving can blossom during difficult times. The best way to get through tough times is to praise the Lord. Today in prayer thank Jesus Christ for your life.

Pride slays thanksgiving, but a humble mind is the soil out of which thanks naturally grows.

—Henry Ward Beecher

Day 328
THANKS FOR HIS UNFAILING LOVE

Let them give thanks to the LORD for his unfailing love
and his wonderful deeds for men.
Let them sacrifice thank offerings
and tell of his works with songs of joy.
Psalm 107:21–22

In early 1863 the Union's Army of the Potomac engaged a smaller Confederate force at the Battle of Fredericksburg. Superior to the Confederates in equipment and numbers, the Union took terrible losses. For President Lincoln the loss at this crucial battle, so close to Washington D.C., was a spiritual wake-up call. Just prior to the conclusion of the battle the President issued a Proclamation for a National Day of Fasting, Humiliation and Prayer:

"We have been the recipients of the choicest bounties of heaven. We have been preserved, these many years, in peace and prosperity. We have grown in numbers, wealth and power, as no other nation has ever grown. But we have forgotten God. We have forgotten the gracious hand which preserved us in peace and multiplied and enriched and strengthened us; and we have vainly imagined, in the deceitfulness of our hearts that all these blessings were produced by some superior wisdom and virtue of our own.

"Intoxicated with unbroken success, we have become too self-sufficient to feel the necessity of redeeming and preserving grace, too proud to pray to God that made us! It behooves us, then to humble ourselves before the offended Power, to confess our national sins, and to pray for clemency and forgiveness."

Christ is not fickle. His love is unfailing and He blesses us even when we forget His goodness. Are you taking the Lord's wonderful deeds for granted? Today in prayer give thanks to Christ that His love never fails.

> When it comes to life, the critical thing is whether you take things for granted or take them with gratitude.
> —G. K. Chesterton

Day 329
PRAISE HIM IN THE SANCTUARY

Praise the LORD. Praise God in his sanctuary;
praise him in his mighty heavens.
Psalm 150:1

Albert Benjamin (A. B.) Simpson was a pastor in Canada, Kentucky, and New York City. He founded the Christian Missionary Alliance. This excellent preacher once said, "Our highest form of service is the ministry of prayer."

Simpson authored some seventy books, many hymns, and was an accomplished poet. Many of his hymns and poems sprang from prayer. Here is his poem for Thanksgiving Day:

As we gather round our firesides
On a new Thanksgiving Day,
Time would fail to count the blessings
That have followed all our way—
Grace sufficient, help, and healing,
Prayer, oft answered at our call,
And the best of all our blessing:
Christ Himself, our all in all!
While we love to count the blessings,
Grateful for the year that's gone,
Faith would sweep a wider vision,
Hope would gaze yet farther on,
For the signals all around us
Seem with one accord to say:
Christ is coming soon to bring us
Earth's last, best Thanksgiving Day!

Today give thanks that you are among the chorus that lifts praise to Jesus Christ.

His glory fills the universe; his praise must do no less.
—Derek Kidner

Day 330
GIVE THANKS DAILY

Praise the LORD. Give thanks to the LORD,
for he is good; his love endures forever.
Psalm 106:1

King Alfonso XIII was the king of Spain from his birth in 1886 until his abdication during the Spanish Civil War in 1931. His father died six months prior to his birth and Alfonso had a special desire to be a good ruler to make his father proud. He was generous and open-minded.

One day the king learned that the boys who served in his court did not pray before their meals. So Alfonso gave a banquet and invited them to attend. Midway through the dinner a ragged beggar came in, sat down, and began to eat ravenously. When he was finished, he left the dining hall without saying a word. "That ungrateful wretch ought to be whipped," shouted the boys. "He ate the king's food and never showed gratitude."

Quietly the king rose and silence fell over the boys. "Daily you have taken the rich blessings of life from the hand of your heavenly Father," said the king. "You've enjoyed his sunshine, breathed his air, eaten food he has provided, and you have not bothered to say thank you for any of them. You are more ungrateful than this beggar."

Thanksgiving should not be reserved for one day a year. Thanksgiving should be a daily attitude of your heart. Today look to Jesus Christ in prayer. Let your heart overflow with praise. Give thanks that God's love endures forever.

> Now, therefore, I do recommend and assign Thursday, the twenty-sixth day of November, to be devoted by the people of these States to the service of that great and glorious Being, who is the Beneficent Author of all the good that was, that is, or that will be, that we may then all unite in rendering unto him our sincere and humble thanks for his kind care and protection.
>
> —George Washington

THANK THE LORD IN TOUGH TIMES

*Now when Daniel learned that the decree had been
published, he went home to his upstairs room where
the windows opened toward Jerusalem.
Three times a day he got down on his knees and prayed,
giving thanks to his God, just as he had done before.*
Daniel 6:10

In August, 1620, over 100 people set sail from South-
hampton, England, aboard the *Mayflower* and the *Speedwell*. A
few days out, the *Speedwell* sprung a leak and returned to
England. Twelve of the *Speedwell's* thirty passengers transferred
to the overcrowded *Mayflower*. For nearly fourteen weeks these
people endured conditions most today would consider intolerable. Instead of proceeding to Virginia, their planned destina-
tion, the *Mayflower's* crew dumped them at the first safe harbor.
So in December, 1620, the travelers came ashore at Plymouth,
Massachusetts.

Winter set in on the New England coast. Food supplies ran
low. The people were not skilled or equipped for hunting and
fishing. Many became sick with scurvy or pneumonia and by
winter's end half of them had died. William Brewster, William
Bradford, and Miles Standish were among the survivors. They
overcame their fear of the natives, made friends with a neighboring tribe, and met Samoset and Squanto. These natives spoke
English and taught the settlers to plant corn and other lessons
of survival. The 1621 harvest was bountiful. Ninety Indians
feasted with the pilgrims as they thanked God for bringing them
to the new land and seeing them through the winter.

Don't confuse God with the circumstances of your life!
Perhaps the Lord is using a crisis in your life to draw you close
to Him. The better you know the heart of God the more thankful you will be when a crisis hits. Today in prayer share your
thoughts with Him and listen to His voice in the Scriptures.

I yield thee humble and hearty thanks, that thou hast preserved me from the dangers of the night past and brought me to the light of this day, and the comfort thereof, a day which is consecrated to thine own service and for thine own honor.

—George Washington

Day 332
THE PRIVILEGE

Be imitators of God, therefore, as dearly loved children and live a life of love, just as Christ loved us and gave himself up for us as a fragrant offering and sacrifice to God.
Ephesians 5:1–2

In 1839 David Livingstone heard Robert Moffat speak about missionary opportunities in Africa: "I have sometimes seen, in the morning sun, the smoke of a thousand villages where no missionary has ever been." Livingstone was accepted as a missionary to the African interior.

Livingstone discovered Victoria Falls and was awarded the London Royal Geographical Society's gold medal for crossing the African continent from west to east. But he paid dearly: A lion mauled his left arm and rendered it useless; his wife died while in Africa when he was forty-nine; he lost a son in the Battle of Gettysburg; his daughter died of fever in the jungle; his house was destroyed during the Boer War; and he himself endured rheumatic fever and other illnesses.

Livingstone wrote in his journal: "People talk of the sacrifice I have made. . .Can that be called a sacrifice which is simply paying back a small part of the great debt owing to our God, which we can never repay? Is that a sacrifice which brings its own blest reward in healthful activity, the consciousness of doing good, peace of mind and a bright hope of glorious destiny hereafter? Away with the word in such a view and with such a thought! It is emphatically no sacrifice. Say rather it is a privilege."

Do you desire to imitate Jesus Christ? Today in prayer, thank Christ for the love that He has given you. It is a privilege to live a life of love.

> Circumstances may appear to wreck our lives and God's plans, but God is not helpless among ruins. Our broken lives are not lost or useless. God's love is still working. He comes in and takes the calamity and uses it victoriously, working out his plan of love.
> —Eric Liddell

Day 333
THE DELIVERER

> *He has delivered us from such a deadly peril, and*
> *he will deliver us. On him we have set our hope that*
> *he will continue to deliver us, as you help us by your prayers.*
> *Then many will give thanks on our behalf for the gracious*
> *favor granted us in answer to the prayers of many.*
> *2 Corinthians 1:10–11*

Here are a few Christians whom Jesus Christ has delivered from peril:

Blind her from childhood and you have Fanny Crosby the prolific hymn writer.

Bury him in the snows of Valley Forge and you have George Washington.

Imprison him and you have John Bunyan the author of *The Pilgrim's Progress.*

Make him an orphan and you have David Brainerd the missionary to the American Indians.

Pursue him as an enemy and you have Martin Luther the

premier church reformer.

Make her an invalid and you have Amy Carmichael the missionary to India and author.

Burn his home and you have Jonathan Goforth the opener of the Manchurian mission field.

Send him a stroke and you have George Frideric Handel the composer of the *Messiah*.

Deny him an education and you have Gipsy Smith the popular nineteenth-century preacher.

Give her a poor birth and you have Mary Slessor the missionary to Africa.

Send him to Siberia and you have Georgi Vins the Russian church leader.

There is no circumstance beyond the control of Jesus Christ. Do you allow Christ to operate in every circumstance? Today thank the Lord—He is our hope and deliverer.

You and God make a majority in your neighborhood.
—Bob Jones, Sr.

Day 334
WASHED CLEAN

In him we have redemption through his blood,
the forgiveness of sins, in accordance with the riches
of God's grace that he lavished on us
with all wisdom and understanding.
Ephesians 1:7–8

Dr. Ignaz Semmelweis was an obstetrician at the Vienna General Hospital. There he sought a reason why women were dying from puerperal (childbed) fever. He suspected that doctors were unknowingly infecting patients. Doctors would go directly from dissecting cadavers to examining expectant mothers without pausing to wash their hands. Long before the germ theory was proven by French scientist Louis Pasteur, Dr. Semmelweis suggested the contagious nature of infection.

In 1860 Semmelweis published his findings and instigated a hand-washing procedure that dramatically reduced the mortality rate from puerperal fever. Opponents attacked him fiercely. They argued that doctors and midwives had been delivering babies for thousands of years without washing their hands. They weren't about to begin washing because of an outspoken Hungarian.

Dr. Semmelweis once argued, "Puerperal fever is caused by decomposed material conveyed to a wound. I have shown how it can be prevented. I have proved all that I have said. But while we talk, talk, talk, gentlemen, women are dying. I am not asking anything world shaking. I am asking you only to wash. . . . For God's sake, wash your hands."

The battle took its toll on Semmelweis. He died at the age of forty-seven. In 1865, the year of his death, Dr. Joseph Lister performed his first antiseptic operation. Then it was recognized that Dr. Semmelweis was right.

Do you realize how clean Christ has made you? Today in prayer thank Him for washing away your sins with His blood.

What can wash away my sin? Nothing but the blood of Jesus.

—Robert Lowry

COURAGE AND TESTIMONY

The following night the Lord stood near Paul and said,
"Take courage! As you have testified about me in Jerusalem,
so you must also testify in Rome."
Acts 23:11

*J*ames Haldane was born into a well-to-do home in Dundee, Scotland. Both of his parents died when he was six years old; after studying at Edinburgh University, James joined the Royal Navy. He eventually became the commanding officer of the warship *Melville Castle*. In a fierce engagement with the French, Haldane ordered new recruits to take the place of the experienced sailors who lay dead or wounded on the deck. Angered by the cowardly actions of these recruits, Haldane cursed and told them he hoped they would go to hell. When the battle had been won, one of the recruits, a Christian, said, "Captain, if God had answered your request a little while ago, where would we all be now?" Captain Haldane was struck by the wisdom of the young man's rebuke. In the days to come he gave his life to Jesus Christ.

In 1794 Haldane resigned from the navy and became a preacher. His churches grew because of his reputation as a naval officer and fierce commitment to Christ. Thousands of lives were touched by James Haldane because one young sailor had the courage to share his faith in Christ.

Some people can be intimidating. But all need God's saving grace. Do you know anyone who is intimidating? Do they need to believe the gospel? Today in prayer thank Christ that you can be His witness. Ask Him for the wisdom and strength to share the truth of the gospel.

He can never be at loss for words who has believed
on the Word.

—Jerome

JOHN ADAMS MOVES OUT

"Where, O death, is your victory? Where, O death, is your sting?"
The sting of death is sin, and the power of sin is the law.
But thanks be to God!
He gives us the victory through our Lord Jesus Christ.
1 Corinthians 15:55–57

In a diary entry in 1814 the former president of the United States John Quincy Adams wrote, "My hopes of a future life are all founded upon the gospel of Jesus Christ." In 1846, on the occasion of his seventy-ninth birthday, Adams wrote, "I enter my eightieth year, with thanksgiving to God for all the blessings and mercies which his providence has bestowed upon me throughout a life extended now to the longest term allotted to the life of man."

At that time a friend met Adams on the street, shook his trembling hand, and said, "Good morning, and how is John Quincy Adams today?" Adams replied, "He himself is quite well, sir, quite well. But the house in which he lives at the present is becoming dilapidated. It is tottering upon its foundation. Time and the seasons have almost destroyed it. Its roof is pretty well worn, its walls are much shattered, and it crumbles a little bit more with every wind. The old tenement is becoming almost uninhabitable and I think John Quincy Adams will have to move out of it soon; but he himself is well, sir, quite well." Several weeks later John Quincy Adams suffered a stroke and moved to an imperishable home in heaven.

Christ lives and He has promised everlasting life to all who trust in Him. No matter what happens in this earthly life, we too can give thanks to Him and say that we are well, quite well.

> My storm-swept soul is calm at last. These words of peace God spoke to me: "Thou wilt keep him in perfect peace whose mind is stayed on thee."
>
> —Flora Sorenson

CHRIST AT ROCK BOTTOM

Sacrifice thank offerings to God, fulfill your vows to the
Most High, and call upon me in the day of trouble;
I will deliver you, and you will honor me.
Psalm 50:14–15

Before his arrest and conviction for murder Jeff's life hadn't been easy. In trouble with alcohol and drugs he dropped out of high school and bounced from one hard job to another. He couldn't get his life straightened out. When he was nineteen Jeff's mother died. When he was convicted no one in his family stood by him. They were glad they wouldn't have to worry about him anymore. He would be safe and off the streets.

Time moves slowly in prison. Jeff started to reflect on his life. One weekend volunteers came to the prison from the Residents Encounter Christ ministry. They shared the love of Jesus Christ and told how Christ can change lives. During that weekend in 1993 Jeff gave his life to Jesus Christ. Since his decision for Christ, Jeff has been strengthened by God's love. He is thankful for the new Christian fellowship he has received. He is thankful that God is faithful in fulfilling His promises. And Jeff is thankful his hope is in Jesus Christ. No matter what happens, he is extremely grateful.

Sometimes people need to hit rock bottom before they give thanks to Christ. Today come to Christ in prayer. Thank Him for all the blessings you have received and lay before Him the desires of your heart.

Does your Heavenly Father give you many blessings here below? Then on bended knee before Him, frankly, gladly, tell Him so!

—Geraldine Searfoss

LAUGHTER VS. JOY

*I thought in my heart, "Come now, I will test you with
pleasure to find out what is good." But that also proved to be
meaningless. "Laughter," I said, "is foolish. And what does
pleasure accomplish?" I tried cheering myself with wine,
and embracing folly—my mind still guiding me with wisdom.
I wanted to see what was worthwhile for men to do under
heaven during the few days of their lives.*
Ecclesiastes 2:1–3

In 1835 a troubled man visited a doctor in Florence, Italy. He was filled with anxiety, exhausted from lack of sleep, had difficulty eating, and avoided his friends. The doctor gave him a full examination, found that he was in prime physical condition, and concluded that his patient needed to relax and have a good time. He recommended that the man visit the circus that was in town. Its star performer was a clown named Grimaldi.

Joseph Grimaldi is known as the father of the modern clown. His innovative style brought laughter in new ways to the people of Europe. He was immensely popular and used slapstick, special trick effects, and comic songs to bring humor to his audiences. Night after night he had the people rolling in the aisles. "You must go and see him," the doctor advised. "Grimaldi is the world's funniest man. He'll make you laugh and cure your sadness."

"No," replied the despairing man, "he can't help me. You see, I am Grimaldi."

The sorrows of your heart will not subside through comic relief. Though laughter is enjoyable, only in Jesus Christ do we find joy. Today in prayer thank Christ that though He has given us laughter, He has given us something more important for a joyful life—Himself.

No one is more profoundly sad than he who laughs
too much.

—Jean Paul Richter

Day 339
WITH ALL THY MIGHT

Whatever your hand finds to do, do it with all your might,
for in the grave, where you are going, there is neither
working nor planning nor knowledge nor wisdom.
Ecclesiastes 9:10

Thomas Carlyle was known as one of the best biogra-
phers of the Victorian era. His works asserted the superiority of
the outstanding individual over the masses of humanity and
the right of the strong man to lead. His writings have been
called "an echo of the utterances of the Old Testament
prophets" and he himself called "the vitriolic Jeremiah."

During the early 1850s Roger Stanley, Canon of Canterbury, was walking in Hyde Park with Thomas Carlyle. Stanley
was in a sour mood complaining against the institutions of
Britain. He twice asked Carlyle, "What is the advice which
you would give to a Canon of Canterbury?" Stanley expected
Carlyle to give him a rousing vision. Instead Carlyle replied in
earnest: "Dear Roger, whatsoever your hand findeth to do, do it
with all thy might." Stanley's gifts were not in administration.
He was a gifted preacher and he encouraged his listeners to
make the most of their lives for Christ's glory. He often expressed the thought, "Every position in life, great or small, can
be made almost as great, or as little, as we desire to make it."

People often strive for that which is beyond their reach.
But the Lord wants us to give all of our might to the work at
hand. Have you been halfhearted in the work Christ has given
to you? Today in prayer give thanks for your work and seek the

385

strength to do it with all of your might.

> Men do less than they ought, unless they do all that
> they can.
>
> —Thomas Carlyle

Day 340
GORDON'S GOLD MEDAL

For where your treasure is, there your heart will be also.
Matthew 6:21

During the Crimean War, Charles G. Gordon distinguished himself for bravery. Promoted to captain in 1859, he volunteered for the British forces then fighting in China. He gained the nickname "Chinese Gordon" for successfully defending Shanghai and became a national hero in Britain. Gordon was also a deeply committed Christian. When he returned to England, he remained in the army but gave his spare time to improving the lives of poor youths. When the English government wanted to reward him for his service in China, he declined all money and titles. Finally, after much urging, Gordon accepted a gold medal inscribed with his name and a record of his accomplishments.

Gordon went on to become a major general and was appointed governor of Sudan. He was killed resisting a siege in Khartoum. Following his death the gold medal could not be found. It was learned that Gordon had sent it to Manchester during a famine with the request that it be melted and used for the poor. In his diary for that day he wrote: "The only thing I had in this world that I valued, I have now given to the Lord Jesus." Gordon's love for the Lord caused him to give up all for the gospel's sake.

Think about the most important thing you own. Would

you give it up for God's will? In serving Christ let us look forward to this reward: "Well done, good and faithful servant." Today in prayer give Christ preeminence in your heart.

What you possess in the world will be found at the day of your death to belong to someone else, but what you are will be yours forever.

—Henry Van Dyke

Day 341
IT'S HISTORY NOW

Do not think that I have come to abolish the Law or the Prophets; I have not come to abolish them but to fulfill them.
Matthew 5:17

A colonel in the Turkish army once asked Dr. Cyrus Hamlin, a missionary to Turkey, for proof that the Bible is the Word of God. Knowing that the officer was a well-traveled man, Hamlin asked, "Have you ever visited Babylon?

"Yes," the colonel replied, "and I'll tell you a curious incident about that area. I once hired several Arabs to take me there for a week to hunt. At the end of the first day they insisted on leaving. I protested but they won out. 'It's not safe,' they said. 'None of us dare to remain overnight, for ghosts will come out of the caves to capture us. No Arab will stay to see the sun go down on Babylon!' "

Dr. Hamlin then read to the man from Isaiah 13:19–20, "Babylon, the jewel of kingdoms, the glory of the Babylonians' pride, will be overthrown by God like Sodom and Gomorrah. She will never be inhabited or lived in through all generations; no Arab will pitch his tent there, no shepherd will rest his flocks there."

The colonel was taken back. "That's history you are reading!"

"Yes," replied Hamlin, "but those words were written centuries earlier and the destruction of Babylon only accentuates the truth it declares."

The prophesies regarding the first coming of Jesus Christ look like history today. But at the time they were written, they were future events. As we look back to Christ's first coming may we have the same assurance that the history He made will be fulfilled again in His second coming.

> Jesus places himself in the center of the history of the world's salvation. It is in him that the prophesies are fulfilled, and in his coming that the new order is inaugurated.
>
> —R. T. France

Day 342
THE LIGHT IN DARKNESS

"In that day," declares the Sovereign LORD, "I will make the sun go down at noon and darken the earth in broad daylight."
Amos 8:9

Seasonal Affective Disorder (SAD) was once termed the "winter blues." SAD complaints include depression and fatigue that often occur during the winter months. Articles in the *Journal of the American Medical Association* and a "Task Force Report of the American Psychiatric Association" support the hypothesis that winter depression is the result of delayed circadian rhythms with respect to sleep.

Alfred J. Lewy, M.D., Ph.D., is one of the leading researchers in this field. His findings indicate that people respond positively to the addition of bright light during the hours of darkness between 6 and 9 A.M. and 4 and 7 P.M. When patients are exposed to just an additional one or two hours of bright light their depression subsides.

When Jesus Christ breathed His last upon the cross, the sun was hidden for three hours in the middle of the day. This unnatural darkness was a visible sign that there was something unusually wrong on earth. And yet out of these dark moments of the cross God provided the brightest moment of human history—the resurrection of Jesus Christ. If darkness has overshadowed your life, take heart that Christ has risen and you will see the Light of the world face-to-face one day. Today give thanks to Jesus Christ for lighting the darkness.

> Yet in the dark streets shineth the everlasting light.
> The hopes and fears of all the years are met in thee
> tonight.
>
> —Phillips Brooks

Day 343
CUES FOR PRAYER

I urge, then, first of all, that requests, prayers, intercession
and thanksgiving be made for everyone—
for kings and all those in authority, that we may live
peaceful and quiet lives in all godliness and holiness.
This is good, and pleases God our Savior,
who wants all men to be saved and
to come to a knowledge of the truth.
1 Timothy 2:1–4

In northern Italy in A.D. 610 a pious monk rolled pencil-thin dough and twisted it into figures representing children folding their arms in prayer. The pretzel was a tasty reminder for children to pray.

In the 1800s, Dr. J. H. Jowett asked a servant girl how she prayed for others. She replied that she read the newspaper and first prayed for all the little babies that were listed in the birth announcements column. She prayed that they would be led to the Savior at an early age and become a blessing to their parents. She then prayed for the marriages announced in the wedding section, praying that the couples would have a happy marriage and build their homes centered on Christ. Then she turned to the obituary column and prayed for the loved ones left behind that they would turn to the Lord for their source of comfort.

Here is a handy prayer schedule: Monday—pray for missionaries; Tuesday—tasks that need to be done; Wednesday—workers in the local church; Thursday—thanks to the Lord; Friday—family; Saturday—saints and other Christians' needs; Sunday—salvation for nonbelievers.

No matter what method or practice you choose, prayer is a vital part of every Christian's life. How is your prayer life? Ask the Lord for the grace for daily prayer.

Seven days without prayer makes one weak.
—Allen E. Bartlett

Day 344
LOST IN A STREAM

The sins of some men are obvious, reaching the place of
judgment ahead of them; the sins of others trail behind them.
In the same way, good deeds are obvious,
and even those that are not cannot be hidden.
1 Timothy 5:24–25

In the late thirteenth century some Scots became rebellious toward England. They sought to break away and form their own country. The leader of the Scottish resistance, Robert of Bruce, established defensive lines in the Scottish highlands. King Edward II of England was enraged by the defiance of the Scots and he led his army north to destroy Scottish resistance.

Once Robert of Bruce was hiding in a mountain glen when he suddenly heard the baying of hounds. Though he had gone days without sleep or food, he knew the dogs were on his scent. It would only be a matter of time before they hunted him down. Robert of Bruce ran feverishly as the dogs drew closer and closer. He dived headlong into a mountain stream. Down through the waters he traveled minutes before the dogs' arrival. At the stream's banks the dogs barked excitedly, running in every direction to find Robert of Bruce's scent. The Scotsman was successful in evading Edward's men and later went on to become king of Scotland.

All of our deeds are obvious to the Lord and many are obvious to men. Reputations are built by the lifelong habits we demonstrate. Praise Jesus Christ that He has washed our sins away and that we are able to escape eternal death because He died for us. Today in prayer thank the Lord that our "trail of sin" is lost in the cleansing stream of His blood.

> In each of us there is something growing up which will of itself be hell unless it is nipped in the bud. The matter is serious: Let us put ourselves in his hands at once—this very day, this hour.
>
> —C. S. Lewis

Day 345
ON CHRIST THE SOLID ROCK I STAND

Nevertheless, God's solid foundation stands firm, sealed with this inscription: "The Lord knows those who are his," and, "Everyone who confesses the name of the Lord must turn away from wickedness."
2 Timothy 2:19

Edward Mote was born in 1797 in London. His parents were poor, ungodly innkeepers. Mote spent his Sundays in the streets, "So ignorant was I that I did not know there was a God," he said. The schools he attended did not let the Bible be seen, much less taught.

At the age of sixteen, while an apprentice cabinetmaker, Mote was taken by his master to hear the esteemed preacher John Hyatt, of Tottenham Court Chapel. There he accepted Jesus Christ as his Savior. Mote became a successful cabinetmaker and devout churchman. At age fifty-five he helped finance and build the Horsham Baptist Church and preached there for twenty-one years. Poor health forced him to retire one year before his death in 1874.

Once he was climbing up Holborn Hill in London. Words came to his mind as he planted each foot: "On Christ the solid rock, I stand; All other ground is sinking sand." Mote understood that wealth, health, and popularity all can fade. Only Christ is a sure foundation for life.

In this world of self-centered materialism it is easy to get distracted and, without realizing it, build a life on sand. Today in prayer ask Christ to show you what is solid and what is sinking.

My hope is built on nothing less, Than Jesus blood and righteousness; I dare not trust the sweetest frame, But wholly lean on Jesus' name. On Christ, the solid rock, I stand—All other ground is sinking sand, all other ground is sinking sand.

—Edward Mote

THE ENDURING WORD OF GOD

For you have been born again, not of perishable seed,
but of imperishable, through the living and enduring
word of God. For, "All men are like grass, and all their
glory is like the flowers of the field; the grass withers
and the flowers fall, but the word of the Lord stands forever."
1 Peter 1:23–25

Alexander Duff was born in Moulin, Perthshire, Scotland and studied at St. Andrews University. In October 1829, Duff and his wife sailed on the *Lady Holland* to India for his missionary assignment. His clothes, his prized possessions, and his library of eight hundred volumes were all onboard. On February 13, 1840, while off the southern tip of Africa, the *Lady Holland* ran upon rocks. Everyone was saved but all of their possessions were lost. From the shore a crewman spotted something small floating on the waves. This washed up on the beach. It was Duff's Bible. Of all his possessions, Duff had hoped his Bible would be saved!

In March, 1830, the Duffs continued their trip to India. In May they were nearing the mouth of the Ganges River in India. A monsoon struck and the ship was lodged on a sandbar. The passengers were put ashore on a small island. The next day Alexander Duff used his precious Bible to teach his first missionary class of five boys. A week later the class had grown to 300 listeners.

Throughout history the Word of God has been subjected to more trials then any other book. And it stands today as the best-loved and most enduring book of all time. It is able to change lives into Christ's image. Are you spending enough time in the most precious of all books? Today in prayer thank Jesus Christ that He has given you His Word!

Scripture is clear that new birth is by means of the Word, which the Spirit of God brings to bear upon the heart and conscience.

—H. A. Ironside

Day 347
GROW IN CHRIST

For this very reason, make every effort to add to your faith goodness; and to goodness, knowledge; and to knowledge, self-control; and to self-control, perseverance; and to perseverance, godliness; and to godliness, brotherly kindness; and to brotherly kindness, love. For if you possess these qualities in increasing measure, they will keep you from being ineffective and unproductive in your knowledge of our Lord Jesus Christ.
2 Peter 1:5–8

Lyman Beecher was a Presbyterian minister during the first half of the nineteenth century. He was the founder of the American Bible Society and Lane Theological Seminary and the father of Henry Ward Beecher.

When Henry was a young boy, a man, red in the face with anger, visited the Beecher home. As Henry tells it, "He had, or supposed he had, a grievance to complain of. My father listened to him with great attention and perfect quietness until he had got it all out, and then he said to him, in a soft and low tone, 'Well, I suppose you only want what is just and right?' The man said, 'Yes,' but went on to state the case over again.

"Very gently my father said to the man, 'If you have been misinformed, I presume you would be perfectly willing to know what the truth is?' The man said he would. Then my father very quietly and gently made a statement of the other side; and when he was through the man got up and said, 'Forgive me, Doctor. Forgive me.' My father had beaten him by his quiet, gentle way. I saw it and it gave me an insight into the power of self-control."

Are you growing in faith, goodness, knowledge, self-control, perseverance, godliness, brotherly kindness, and love? Today pray that you will grow in Christ.

> He who reigns within himself and rules his passions, desires, and fears is more than a king.
>
> —John Milton

Day 348
THE LIFE TO COME

And this is the testimony: God has given us eternal life, and this life is in his Son. He who has the Son has life; he who does not have the Son of God does not have life.
1 John 5:11–12

Charles E. Fuller, the radio evangelist and founder of Fuller Seminary once received a letter: "Next Sunday you are to talk about heaven. I am interested in that land because I have held a clear title to a bit of property there for over fifty-five years. I did not buy it. It was given to me without money and without price. But the donor purchased it for me at a tremendous sacrifice. . . .

"There is a valley of deep sorrow between the place where I live in California and that to which I shall journey in a very short time. I cannot reach my home in the City of God without passing through the dark valley of shadows. But I am not afraid, because the best friend I ever had went through the same valley alone long, long ago and drove away all the gloom. He has stuck by me through thick and thin. . .and I hold His promise in printed form, never to forsake, nor to leave me alone. . . .

"I hope to hear your sermon on heaven next Sunday from my home, but I have no assurance that I shall be able to do so. My ticket to heaven has no date marked for the journey—no return coupon—and no permit for baggage. Yes, I am ready to go and may not be here while you are talking next Sunday, but I shall meet you there some day."

Today, breathe a prayer of relief and praise that Christ is with you both on earth and in heaven.

> I am yet in the land of the dying, but I hope soon to be in the land of the living.

> —John Owen

Day 349
HE CARES FOR THE LIKES OF US

Nevertheless, there will be no more gloom for those who were in distress. In the past he humbled the land of Zebulun and the land of Naphtali, but in the future he will honor Galilee of the Gentiles, by the way of the sea, along the Jordan.
Isaiah 9:1

In 1865 the East End of London was a very depressed area. In Whitechapel, the center of this churchless slum, William Booth and his wife Catherine started a mission. Their tent meetings used lively music and fiery preaching to reach the toughest characters of that neighborhood. They preached in the taverns, the jails, and in the open air.

The mission in Whitechapel was the first of what was to become the many stations for the Salvation Army. By 1879 there were eighty-one stations with 127 full-time evangelists holding seventy-five thousand services a year. By 1884 there were over four thousand workers in the Army. By 1891 there were ten thousand officers ministering in twenty-six countries.

When William Booth died his funeral was held in West London. Queen Victoria slipped in to attend the ceremony. Sitting next to her was a woman who quietly confessed to the queen that she had been involved in a life of prostitution. "What brought you here to the service?" asked the queen.

"Well," the woman replied, "he cared for the likes of us."

When Christ started His earthly ministry He chose the rough region of Galilee and for His disciples he chose tough fishermen. Christ went to the lost to save them. If you see the Salvation Army this Christmas season with their handbells and red kettles, remember "Christ cared for the likes of us." Be willing to bring the light of Jesus Christ where it may have never shined before.

> I am convinced the world is more eager to hear our message than we are to deliver it.
> —Howard Hendricks

Day 350
SHARE OTHERS' BURDENS

Carry each other's burdens, and in this way you will fulfill the law of Christ. If anyone thinks he is something when he is nothing, he deceives himself. Each one should test his own actions. Then he can take pride in himself, without comparing himself to somebody else, for each one should carry his own load.
Galatians 6:2–5

Since 1991 Kathy Morrissy has worked closely with ten mothers in Southern California penal institutions and halfway houses by caring for their babies in her home. Her work with pregnant inmates is her full-time ministry. She cares not only for the baby but for the entire family. She prays and fasts for them; takes the child to visit the mother; and helps the inmate with family relationships, parenting skills, discipline, money management, and in finding God's healing forgiveness.

Morrissy demonstrates the love of God by giving babies a good start in life and helping mothers improve their lives. "The women are hungry for a new way," she said. "Once they have made a commitment to Christ, they want to know what to do and how to do it. They're willing to do it within the [prison] bars. Mothers who have reunified with the babies I have cared for have not regressed. They are not just reformed; they are born-again Christians, caring for their children and serving the Lord." She calls her ministry of mercy "Baby Blessings" and is training other women to become Baby Blessing Moms.

When life's burdens become too heavy for people to carry alone we can demonstrate Christ's love by helping them. Do you listen for God's whisper directing you to help someone? In prayer thank Jesus for the people He has sent to help you when your burden was too heavy. Ask Him to show you someone who needs your loving support.

> There is a kind of burden which comes to a man
> from the chances and the changes of life; it is fulfill-
> ing the law of Christ to help everyone who has such
> a burden to carry.
>
> —William Barclay

Day 351
A HASTY WORD

Do not be quick with your mouth, do not be hasty in your heart to utter anything before God. God is in heaven and you are on earth, so let your words be few.
Ecclesiastes 5:2

Milton Wright was born in a cabin in Rush County, Indiana, in 1828. He made a profession of faith in Christ at age eighteen, graduated from Hartsville College, and went on to teach at country schools. He then taught at a seminary, pastored a small church, went to Oregon as a missionary, and became the principal of a college. In 1859 Wright returned to Indiana to marry Susan Koerner. Soon they had two sons, Reuchlin and Lorin.

More children followed, and in 1869 he became the editor of the United Brethren weekly *Religious Telescope*. He moved his family to Dayton, Ohio, where the magazine was published. In 1878, he became a bishop in the Church of the United Brethren in Christ. He was often called upon to be an itinerant preacher and guest speaker in small churches in the Midwest.

Despite all his accomplishments and hard work, Milton Wright would best be remembered for a hasty remark. During the 1870s someone told him, "Why, in fifty years I believe it may be possible for men to soar through the air like birds!" Milton was shocked. He replied, "Flight is strictly reserved for the angels and I beg you not to repeat your suggestion lest you be guilty of blasphemy!"

On December 17, 1903, Wright received a telegram from his two youngest sons, Orville and Wilbur. They had accomplished the blasphemous! Manned, powered flight.

Today in prayer, ask Christ to give you wisdom and discernment before you speak.

Our words have wings, but fly not where we would.
—George Eliot

Day 352
TIMELY WORSHIP

But Mary treasured up all these things and pondered them in her heart. The shepherds returned, glorifying and praising God for all the things they had heard and seen, which were just as they had been told.
Luke 2:19–20

This is a Russian fable entitled "Babushka (Old Woman) and the Three Kings":

A long time ago on a cold winter's night during a snow storm there came a knock on a Babushka's door. At the door were three kings who were half-frozen. "We are following a star to find the Christ child. We are bringing him gifts but we have lost our way in the snow. Come with us, Babushka, help us find the child and let us worship him together."

The shivering old woman replied, "Dear sirs, please come in and warm yourselves. It will be better to look for him in the morning. It is a dreadful night to be outside!"

"There is no time to waste, we must continue on and find the Christ child." And the kings turned and walked away into the darkness.

The next morning Babushka desperately tried to follow the kings but was unable to find their tracks. She asked everyone she saw, "Have you seen which direction the three kings have gone?" No one knew who she was talking about. "Have you seen the Christ child?" Again no one knew who she was talking about. To this day she continues to roam about looking for the three kings and the child they sought to worship.

There is no time like the present to worship Jesus Christ. He came to us so we may have life in Him. Today in prayer consider the Scriptures and give thanks that Christ came to this earth to save sinners.

> But thanks be to God that His Son gave Himself to the World in condescending love and became Man, bringing a perfect revelation of God as the Holy and merciful Lord.
>
> —Norval Geldenhuys

Day 353
THE RIGHT KIND OF FAITH

The apostles said to the Lord, "Increase our faith!" He replied,
"If you have faith as small as a mustard seed, you can
say to this mulberry tree, 'Be uprooted and
planted in the sea,' and it will obey you."
Luke 17:5–6

The nineteenth-century Russian novelist Leo Tolstoy tells the story of "The Three Hermits":

A bishop was traveling by ship when he heard that three hermits lived on a nearby island. He decided to stop and instruct them in the faith.

The bishop asked them how they prayed. One answered, "We pray thus: 'You three have mercy on us three.'" He told them they should not pray that way and so labored to teach them the Lord's Prayer. He repeated each word a hundred times until they learned the prayer by rote. The bishop said farewell and returned to the ship while the hermits repeated the Lord's Prayer with loud voices.

The ship sailed away. The bishop looked back toward the island and saw the hermits running over the sea as if it were dry land. They came on board and said, "We have forgotten, servant of God, we have forgotten what thou didst teach us. While we were learning it, we remembered it; when we ceased for an hour to repeat it, we have forgotten it. Teach it to us again." The bishop bowed to the hermits and said, "Acceptable to God is your prayer, ye hermits. It is not for me to teach you. Pray for us sinners." They paused, turned, and went back over the sea to their island.

The amount of faith is not as important as the right kind of faith—trust and dependence on our all-powerful God. Today ask Jesus to help you to trust Him completely for everything.

Don't be afraid to take a big step if one is indicated.
You can't cross a chasm in two small jumps.
                                        —David Lloyd George

Day 354
DRAMATICALLY CHANGED

If we have been united with him like this in his death,
we will certainly also be united with him in his resurrection.
For we know that our old self was crucified with him
so that the body of sin might be done away with,
that we should no longer be slaves to sin.
                                        Romans 6:5–6

In December 1832 Charles Darwin arrived at the
southern tip of South America—Tierra del Fuego. He wrote of
the inhabitants: "These wretched looking beings had no proper
clothes, no fit language, and no decent homes or property. . . .
The Fuegians are in a more miserable state of barbarism than
I had expected to have seen a human being." The Fuegians
menaced Darwin's camp and stole incidental possessions.
There was strong evidence that during times of famine they
resorted to cannibalism. When faced with this prospect the
would-be missionary Richard Matthews decided not to remain
and stayed with Darwin's party aboard the *Beagle*.

Years later a small outpost was established on Tierra del
Fuego to secure English shipping around Cape Horn. At the
outpost were members of the South American Missionary
Society. Darwin made regular donations to the Society with
the hope that the natives would one day be civilized.
Lieutenant Bartholomew Sulivan had been with Darwin on
his visit to Tierra del Fuego. Sulivan believed that no man was
beyond the simple saving message of the gospel. In 1869

Sulivan returned to the island and mailed pictures of the natives to Darwin. They were dramatically changed, not by evolution, but by the Word of God.

Humans can only rid themselves of sin by surrender to Jesus Christ. Have you ever been a slave to sin? Today praise Christ that He has conquered sin through death and resurrection. Thank Him that your life is transformed by faith and the Word of God.

Grace reigns only through the mediation of Christ.
—John Murray

Day 355
THE LIGHT OF LIFE

The God of peace will soon crush Satan under your feet.
The grace of our Lord Jesus be with you.
Romans 16:20

*D*uring the nineteenth century Absalom Backus (A. B.) Earle visited the Bunker Hill Monument and recorded these thoughts: "A few years ago, I visited Bunker Hill Monument. . . .After paying the small fee to the man who has the care of the monument he gave me a small lamp to light my steps. I took the lamp and stepped inside on the stone floor. . .I looked far up its rugged steep steps as far I could and at once called the attention of the man in charge to my small lamp. I said: 'This won't do. It doesn't light a quarter of the steps. Look up there!'

"He smiled. . .and said to me, 'You are not up there yet. Why do you want it lighted there until you get there? Is it not bright enough on the first step where you want to put your foot?'

"'Oh, I see, I see! It is all right. My lamp is large enough. I only need one step lighted at a time.'

"So I started on, . . .my lamp lighting each step as I went upward, until it had lighted every one of the two hundred and ninety-five steps. Then I began to inquire how much love to Christ I needed to start with. Like the little lamp's shining. . . so I needed enough love to take the first step in the Christian journey."

"I am the light of the world," said Jesus. Are you walking in faith with the Lord? Today thank Christ that he is your light.

> You will find that the amount of time you spend alone with the Lord and with your own soul will have much to do with your present comfort and strength and with your future fruitfulness!
>
> —Alexander Whyte

Day 356
MY INDIVIDUAL RESPONSIBILITY TO GOD

So the Twelve gathered all the disciples together and said, "It would not be right for us to neglect the ministry of the word of God in order to wait on tables. Brothers, choose seven men from among you who are known to be full of the Spirit and wisdom. We will turn this responsibility over to them and will give our attention to prayer and the ministry of the word."

Acts 6:2–4

Daniel Webster graduated from Dartmouth University in 1801, studied law, and then entered public service. He was a member of the U.S. House of Representatives from both New Hampshire and later Massachusetts, a senator from Massachusetts, and served as Secretary of State under three presidents. One of his crowning achievements was the Webster-Ashburton Treaty which settled the boundary between Maine and Canada. He was known as one of the best orators of his age and few people could keep up his fast pace of life.

Webster saw individual responsibility and duty as an everyday, omnipresent reality. In a speech reminiscent of Psalm 139, he said, "A sense of duty pursues us ever. It is omnipresent, like the Deity. If we take to ourselves the wings of the morning, and dwell in the uttermost parts of the sea, duty performed or duty violated is still with us, for our happiness or our misery. If we say the darkness shall cover us, in the darkness as in the light our obligations are yet with us."

Late in life Webster was asked, "What is the most important thought you ever entertained?" After reflecting he replied, "The most important thought I ever had was my individual responsibility to God."

Are you taking full responsibility for your life and work? Give thanks to Jesus Christ for what He has given you to do and for the strength and wisdom to do it well.

> It is easy to dodge our responsibilities, but we cannot dodge the consequences of dodging our responsibilities.
>
> —Sir Josiah Stamp

Day 357
WHERE IS YOUR FOCUS?

Therefore we do not lose heart. Though outwardly we are wasting away, yet inwardly we are being renewed day by day. For our light and momentary troubles are achieving for us an eternal glory that far outweighs them all. So we fix our eyes not on what is seen, but on what is unseen. For what is seen is temporary, but what is unseen is eternal.
2 Corinthians 4:16–18

Christmas, 1968—two-year-old Charlotte King was diagnosed with an incurable genetic disease called cystic fibrosis.

Her frail body produced a thick, sticky mucus that clogged her lungs and impeded her digestion. Daily medication, treatment, therapy, and frequent hospitalization only slowed the progress of this cruel disease.

Charlotte came to know the love of Jesus as a child and committed her life to Christ at age thirteen. She loved God's Word and promises. Her faith was simple yet unshakable—if God said it she believed it regardless of the circumstances. Her faith and joy inspired everyone who knew her.

Charlotte loved to study the Bible, worship, fellowship with believers, and share God's love. In her journal she recorded her trust in the loving Father, her longing for more of Him, and her anticipation of a glorified body like her Savior's. Charlotte's health deteriorated but her spirit was renewed daily.

Three days before she died Charlotte prayed, "I want to be healed Father, but I also want Your will, so I give You my body, my soul, and my spirit. They're Yours now, Father, to do with as You wish. I trust You to keep me until that day." On June 9, 1985, Charlotte went home to be with the Lord whom she had come to know so intimately.

Where is your focus—on the temporary or the eternal? Today thank the Lord that His promises give you strength for today and hope for tomorrow.

> We ask less of this life because we know full well that more is coming in the next. The art of living with suffering is just the art of readjusting our expectations in the here and the now.
>
> —Joni Eareckson Tada

THE POWER OF PRAISE

But when the time had fully come, God sent his Son,
born of a woman, born under law, to redeem those under law,
that we might receive the full rights of sons.
Galatians 4:4–5

During the French and Indian War the French incited the Indians to attack non-French colonists. In 1755, at the French fort Duquesne, now the city of Pittsburgh, colonists suffered a bitter defeat from French and Indian forces. Then, in Pennsylvania's Lehigh Valley, the Conestoga Indians wiped out the Moravian mission at Mahanoy. The Moravian colonists at nearby Gnadenhutten fled to the neighboring fortified village of Bethlehem. Christmas was fast approaching and everyone in Bethlehem fully expected the Indians to attack. Night after night war cries could be heard and fires burned brightly on the surrounding heights.

On Christmas Day, despite imminent attack, the colonists gathered together for worship. Fearing for their lives they sang praises to Christ with more feeling than ever before.

The fighting men had hardly returned to their posts after worship when they saw the Indians break camp and leave. There would be no bloody fight.

When peace was made years later, the Indians told why they had not attacked. Their war council was preparing for the attack when they heard the sweet sound of Christmas carols. Those blessed tunes soothed the angry warriors. So in the songs of praise to Jesus Christ the colonists found deliverance.

Today in prayer, praise the Lord!

Jesus is God spelling himself out in language that men can understand.

—S. D. Gordon

JESUS, LORD AT THY BIRTH

The Spirit of the LORD will rest on him—
the Spirit of wisdom and of understanding,
the Spirit of counsel and of power,
the Spirit of knowledge and of the fear of the LORD.
Isaiah 11:2

In 1818, when Joseph Mohr wrote the words to "Silent Night" he was a priest in the Church of St. Nicholas in Obernorf, Austria. Mohr's close friend was Franz Gruber, the church organist. The church's organ was broken and Gruber feared that the Christmas Eve service would be a disaster. Mohr set out to write a simple hymn to be presented Christmas Eve. Upon reading the words, Gruber proclaimed, "Friend Mohr, you have found it, the right Christmas song. God be praised." Gruber used a guitar to add the sweet music we now sing to this beautiful text.

The parishioners were deeply moved by "Silent Night" and through the years the carol has gained in popularity. It has been translated into every major language and brings a reverence for Christ to all who sing it.

Before He had preached a sermon, before He had healed a person and before He rose from the dead, Jesus Christ was Lord. All that is God was in Jesus from birth. This Christmas season, in the midst of the hurry of buying presents and visiting relatives, remember that we are celebrating the coming of the Son of God with His redeeming grace.

> Silent night! holy night! Shepherds quake at the sight; glories stream from heaven afar, heavenly hosts sing alleluia, Christ the Savior is born! Christ the Savior is born!

> —Joseph Mohr

A Thought of Someone Miles Away

For this reason, ever since I heard about your faith
in the Lord Jesus and your love for all the saints,
I have not stopped giving thanks for you,
remembering you in my prayers.
Ephesians 1:15–16

Jonathan Goforth and his wife Rosalind were about to leave their native Canada and become missionaries in Honan, China. But Jonathan was making painfully slow progress in learning the Chinese language. Even after many long hours of study and practice people had difficulty understanding him.

A year after arriving in China, Jonathan was on his way to chapel. He said to his wife, "If the Lord does not give me special help in this language I fear I shall be a failure as a missionary." That day at chapel his sentences flowed as never before. People approached him after the service to converse further. That chapel service was a turning point in Goforth's ministry.

Ten weeks later a letter arrived from a student attending Knox College in Canada. He related that he and several other students prayed one night for the Goforths. Seeking encouragement, the student asked if anything special had occurred because of their prayers. Goforth realized that at the time the students were praying for him, he broke through in speaking Chinese.

The Lord answers prayer. He also prompts us to remember people who are not in our everyday lives. Do you remember others in prayer? Today pray for those who minister far away.

I cannot tell why there should come to me, a thought of someone miles and years away, in swift insistence on the memory, unless there is a need that I should pray.

—Rosalind Goforth

TAKE OUT THE GARBAGE

But among you there must not be even a hint of sexual
immorality, or of any kind of impurity, or of greed, because these
are improper for God's holy people. Nor should there be obscenity,
foolish talk or coarse joking, which are out of place, but rather
thanksgiving. For of this you can be sure: No immoral, impure
or greedy person—such a man is an idolater—
has any inheritance in the kingdom of Christ and of God.
Ephesians 5:3–5

In 1898, J. Milton Eckerd invested $600 and opened his first discount drugstore in Erie, Pennsylvania. Eckerd's low prices and high level of service attracted loyal customers. In 1951 his son Jack took over the business. By 1959 he had a chain of ten stores. Eckerd Drugstores went public and by the time J. C. Penney bought the chain there were 1,724 stores throughout the country.

In 1971 a grandmother wrote Jack Eckerd complaining that there were risqué books sold at Eckerd Drugstores and that they posed a danger to her fourteen-year-old grandson. Eckerd was shocked. He took immediate action and had all such books and magazines removed from all seventeen hundred stores. Business associates said he would lose over three million dollars in business. Instead sales increased. When asked what motivated him to take this action Eckerd replied, "God wouldn't let me off the hook!"

If your town's garbage collector went on strike you probably would wonder how you would get rid of all your accumulated trash. In the same way we need to examine our thoughts, our words, and our actions that do not bring glory to Christ. Do you need to take out the garbage? Today give thanks to Christ. He can take away immorality and impurity in our lives.

Purity and cleanliness belong to the Christian.
—Harold F. Pellegrin

Day 362
OUR TRIUMPHANT LEADER

But thanks be to God, who always leads us in
triumphal procession in Christ and through us
spreads everywhere the fragrance of the knowledge of him.
2 Corinthians 2:14

On October 30, 1899, during the Boer War in South Africa, the Boers besieged the township of Ladysmith. The British garrison under the command of Sir George White came under fire from Boer guns situated on the surrounding hills. British forces quickly suffered 300 casualties. Nearly six weeks later Sir Redvers Buller was assigned this task: Break through the Boer lines to reach White.

Buller's first attack was quickly repulsed. But he was determined to win in what seemed to be an impossible situation. He continued to assail the hills surrounding the town until he finally captured them two months later. Buller lost almost ten percent of his men in liberating Ladysmith.

When Buller's army marched triumphantly into Ladysmith, Sir George White and his staff sat on emaciated horses in parade formation. White's men had endured four months of starvation, bombardment, and disease. But one obstacle almost defeated them—discouragement. Though most of White's men were fiercely loyal, there was a man who was convicted of being a "discourager." This soldier had lost all hope and used discouragement as a weapon to wear down his friends. This soldier looked in fear at his circumstances and not in trust to his leaders.

Jesus Christ is a victorious leader. Do you get discouraged by circumstances? Today praise Christ—He leads us in triumph.

I've never been one who thought the Lord should
make life easy; I've just asked him to make me strong.
—Eva Bowring

Day 363
THE MOST HONORED GUEST

The LORD says to my Lord: "Sit at my right hand
until I make your enemies a footstool for your feet."
Psalm 110:1

Queen Victoria of England ascended to the throne at age
eighteen. At her coronation she was presented with a Bible
inscribed with these words:

"Our gracious Queen, we present you this Book, the most
valuable thing the world affords. Here is wisdom; this is the
royal law; these are the timely oracles of God. Blessed is he that
readeth and they that hear the words of this Book; that keep
and do the things contained in it. For these are the words of
eternal life, able to make you wise unto salvation, and so happy
forever more, through faith in Christ Jesus, to whom be the
glory forever and ever. Amen."

Victoria sometimes visited the cottages of her subjects.
Once she entered the home of a poor widow and enjoyed Christian
fellowship with the woman. Later the widow was taunted
by unbelieving neighbors. "Granny, who's the most honored
guest you have ever entertained in your home?" They expected
her to say Jesus. The woman replied, "It was Her Majesty
the Queen." "Did you say the Queen? Ha, we caught you this
time. What about that Jesus you are always talking about? Isn't
He the most honored guest you have ever entertained?"

"No, indeed!" said the woman, "He's not a guest. He lives
here!"

Christ is the King of Kings. He doesn't just visit us, He

has made us part of His family. Today give thanks that our King not only rules in heaven but also lives in our hearts.

It is not just that we should strive to live like Jesus, but that Jesus by his Spirit should come and live in us. To have him as our example is not enough; we need him as our Savior.

—John R. W. Stott

Day 364
THE WAY OF ESCAPE

No temptation has seized you except what is common to man. And God is faithful; he will not let you be tempted beyond what you can bear. But when you are tempted, he will also provide a way out so that you can stand up under it.
1 Corinthians 10:13

Ehrich Weiss was famous for his escapes. In Essen Rhur, Germany, he even picked the lock at the local jail. Once the employees of a local linen factory challenged Weiss: "If we nail you in this packing case like we do our linens you will never be able to get out." Ehrich's joking response: "Oh! That would be easy."

The next day the morning newspaper printed a public challenge for Ehrich to escape from a packing case. The linen workers purposed to tie him with ropes and nail the case shut. Ehrich remembered how, a year earlier, he had disassembled a packing case for firewood. So he accepted the challenge, successfully escaped, and launched his career as Houdini, the great escape artist.

Throughout his career, Houdini offered rewards to anyone who could successfully restrain him. He escaped from handcuffs, leg irons, straightjackets, jails, a mail pouch, packing crates, and milk cans. He originated the underwater packing crate escape, the upside down straightjacket escape, and the buried-alive escape.

Houdini debunked magic. He considered himself a performer and always knew how he would escape before entering seemingly impossible situations.

Does temptation sometimes feel as though it has you locked in a submerged trunk? Today in prayer ask Christ to keep temptation from crouching at your door. And when you face a struggle ask God for the way of escape and follow it.

> Now God helps us in two ways so that we will not be overcome by the temptation: He supplies us with strength, and He sets limits to the temptation.
>
> —John Calvin

Day 365
THANK THE LORD FOR A FRESH START

They were also to stand every morning to thank and praise the LORD. They were to do the same in the evening.
1 Chronicles 23:30

When Thomas A. Edison was twenty-one he invented an electric vote recorder which is still being used in some states to record votes of legislators. In 1869, he designed the Edison Universal Stock Printer, a vast improvement on the stock tickers of the time. With the finances from that royalty Thomas Edison moved to Menlo Park, New Jersey, where he could devote himself full-time to inventing. In 1876 he formed the Edison Electric Light Company—before he invented the light bulb.

The Menlo Park laboratory was quite productive with sixty workers working on up to forty projects at a time. Edison invented the light bulb, the phonograph, the motion picture camera and projector—he held 1,093 patents, more than any other person in U.S. history.

Edison eventually built a huge laboratory complex in West Orange, New Jersey. Over five thousand people were employed there. Then in December, 1914, a fire blazed through the laboratories. Edison walked among the ashes and rubble of his projects and said, "There is great value in disaster. All our mistakes are burned up. Thank God we can start anew." He then rebuilt the West Orange facility and continued working to the day he died at eighty years of age.

Each morning is a gift from the Lord; as is each new year. In Christ all of your mistakes are burned up and buried. Thank God tonight for his faithfulness to give you each day of a new year to live in Christ.

> The best thing about the future is that it comes only one day at a time.
>
> —Abraham Lincoln

Day 366
THE JOY OF FELLOWSHIP

For what is our hope, our joy, or the crown in which we will glory in the presence of our Lord Jesus when he comes? Is it not you? Indeed, you are our glory and joy.
1 Thessalonians 2:19-20

John Fawcett was born in Yorkshire, England, in 1740. He was ordained at age twenty-six and received a call to pastor a small, poor church congregation at Wainsgate in Northern England. After seven years there, where his salary barely paid for the necessities of a growing family, he received a call to pastor the large and influential Carter's Lane Baptist Church in London. On the day of the scheduled departure from Wainsgate, saddened parishioners, who had grown to love the Fawcetts as family, gathered around the wagons.

Mrs. Fawcett broke down and cried, "John, I cannot bear to leave. I know not how to go!"

"God has spoken to my heart too," said John. The order was given to unpack the wagons and the Fawcetts stayed.

Inspired by the love that had developed between his congregation and his family, he wrote a poem about the experience. Today, we know it as the hymn "Blest be the Tie that Binds." Fawcett continued his ministry at Wainsgate for more than fifty years at a salary of two hundred dollars a year. Though he received other ministry opportunities for more money and prestige, he forfeited it all to minister to the people he loved.

The joy of Christian fellowship is like no other. The shared experience of knowing that Jesus Christ is our Savior is a wonder that carries through eternity. Are you experiencing the joy of Christian fellowship? Today in prayer, if you do not have a church home, ask the Lord to lead you to a body of believers who will encourage and strengthen you.

> Blest be the tie that binds our hearts in Christian love. The fellowship of kindred minds is like that to that above.
>
> —John Fawcett

A

Abrahams, Harold-Day 128
Adams, John Quincy-Day 10, Day 336
Adams, Samuel-Day 185
Adkins, Donna-Day 247
Akers, Michelle-Day 83
Aldrich, Joe-Day 320
Alexander the Great-Day 42, Day 247
Alexander, Archibald-Day 226
Alkamaar-Day 200
Allen, David-Day 262
Andersen, Hans Christian-Day 197
Anderson, Gary-Day 315
Andre, John-Day 61
Antony-Day 286
Aristotle-Day 6, Day 119
Arnold, Benedict-Day 61, Day 280
Arsenev, Nikolai-Day 136
Asbury, Francis-Day 282
Athanasius-Day 286
Augustine-Day 19, Day 151, Day 213, Day 228

B

Bach, T. J.-Day 45, Day 57
Baillie, John-Day 305
Ballou, Hosea-Day 195
Bannister, Roger-Day 121
Barclay, William-Day 23, Day 44, Day 65, Day 71, Day 152,
        Day 183, Day 302, Day 314, Day 347, Day 350
Barnes, Albert-Day 76, Day 258
Barrett, David-Day 233
Bartlett, Allen E.-Day 343
Barton, Clara-Day 258
Basil of Caesarea-Day 2
Bassham, Lanny-Day 315
Beck, Fred-Day 215
Beecher, Henry Ward-Day 55, Day 190, Day 195, Day 222,
        Day 327
Beecher, Lyman-Day 80, Day 347
Beecher, Thomas-Day 55
Beethoven, Ludwig Van-Day 188
Bell, Gary-Day 313
Bennett, Arnold-Day 95
Bernard of Clairvaux-Day 96

Bibesco, Elizabeth-Day 205
Biederwolf, William-Day 224
Bilney, Thomas-Day 226
Bjorn, Thyra F.-Day 326
Black, Matthew-Day 291
Blaikie, W. G.-Day 102
Blondin, Charles-Day 160
Blum, Edwin A.-Day 104, Day 315
Boice, James Montgomery-Day 227
Bojaxhiu, Agnes Gonxha-Day 199
Bonaparte, Napoleon-Day 107
Booth, Ballington-Day 225
Booth, Catherine-Day 62, Day 225, Day 323, Day 349
Booth, Emma-Day 225
Booth, Evangeline-Day 225
Booth, Herbert-Day 225
Booth, Lucy-Day 225
Booth, Marian-Day 225
Booth, William-Day 225, Day 323, Day 349
Bounds, E. M.-Day 82, Day 126, Day 324
Bowring, Eva-Day 362
Bradbury, William-Day 255
Bradford, John-Day 314
Bradford, William-Day 331
Brand, Paul-Day 201
Brewster, David-Day 189
Brewster, William-Day 331
Briscoe, Stuart-Day 177
Britten, Benjamin-Day 261
Broadus, John-Day 289
Brodie, Benjamin-Day 89
Bronstein, David-Day 272
Brooks, Phillips-Day 27, Day 62, Day 139, Day 342
Brooks, Thomas-Day 35, Day 158
"Brother Lawrence"-Day 78, Day 94
"Brother Thanks be to God"-Day 279
Brotman, Manny-Day 243
Brown, Joe E.-Day 11
Browning, Elizabeth Barrett-Day 149
Bruce, F. F.-Day 83, Day 244, Day 290, Day 321
Brunelleschi, Filippo-Day 172
Buckler-Dollins, JoAnn-Day 53
Buller, Redvers-Day 362
Bunyan, John-Day 48, Day 157, Day 187, Day 188
Buonarotti, Michelangelo-Day 70
418

Burgoyne, John-Day 280
Burke and Wills-Day 293
Burleigh, Celia-Day 89
Burnett, Frances Hodgson-Day 191
Burns, James D.-Day 69
Burns, Robert-Day 278
Burr, Aaron-Day 244
Burton, Robert-Day 191

C

Calvin, John-Day 33, Day 75, Day 188, Day 273, Day 364
Campbell, James Montgomery-Day 288
Cantril, Hadley-Day 105
Card, Michael-Day 39
Carey, William-Day 188, Day 292
Carlyle, Thomas-Day 318, Day 339
Carmichael, Amy-Day 58
Carroll, Maggie-Day 257
Cartwright, Peter-Day 173
Carver, George Washington-Day 117
Cato, Marcus-Day 256
Cerutty, Percy-Day 227
Chaffee, Roger-Day 27
Chalmers, James-Day 147
Chalmers, Thomas-Day 16
Chambers, Oswald-Day 260, Day 312
Chapman, John Wilbur- Day 60, Day 198
Chase, Salmon P.-Day 317
Chaudhari, Anand-Day 163
Chesterton, G. K.-Day 328
Cho, David-Day 265
Churchill, Winston-Day 152
Cicero, Marcus Tullius-Day 108, Day 148
Clark, Adam-Day 62
Coffelt, Leslie-Day 305
Cole, Nathan-Day 14
Coleridge, Samuel Taylor-Day 180
Colgate, Samuel-Day 212
Collazo, Oscar-Day 305
Collingwood, Admiral-Day 32
Converse, C. C.-Day 81
Coolidge, Calvin-Day 154
Copernicus, Nicolaus-Day 311
Cornwallis-Day 185
Cowper, William-Day 156, Day 166

Cranfield, C. E. B.-Day 131
Crawford, Daniel-Day 310
Crosby, Fanny-Day 29, Day 62, Day 84, Day 188
Crowell, Henry P.-Day 56
Cruz, Nicky-Day 127
Cuyler, Theodore-Day 122
Cyril-Day 209

D

da Vinci, Leonardo-Day 35
Dale, R. W.-Day 269
Damien, Joseph-Day 39
Darwin, Charles-Day 354
Davis, Grace Weiser-Day 171
Davy, Humphrey-Day 283
De Pree, D. J.-Day 304
de Requesens, Don Luis-Day 200
Deck, James G.-Day 15
Defoe, Daniel-Day 182
Delitzsch-Day 7
Descartes-Day 6
Deyneka, Peter-Day 202, Day 233
Dickens, Charles-Day 72, Day 234
Dickson, H. R. P.-Day 241
Dilworth, Thomas-Day 252
Diocletian-Day 205
Dixon, Francis W.-Day 159
Doan, Eleanor L.-Day 66
Dobson, James-Day 41
Douglas, Michael-Day 236
Downey, Steven-Day 281
Doyle, Arthur Conan-Day 206
Dravecky, Dave-Day 34
Duff, Alexander-Day 346
Duke of Wellington-Day 68
Duke, Doris-Day 248
Duke, James Buchanan-Day 248
Dulles, John Foster-Day 130
Durer, Albrecht-Day 113

E

Earle, Absalom Backus-Day 355
Eckerd, Milton J.-Day 361
Edison, Thomas A.-Day 16, Day 365
Edward, Duke of Kent-Day 19
420

Edward, Prince of Wales-Day 122
Edwards, Jonathan-Day 186, Day 244, Day 270
Einstein, Albert-Day 6, Day 53
Eliot, George-Day 351
Elliott, Charlotte-Day 1
Elliott, Herb-Day 227
Emerson, Ralph Waldo-Day 37, Day 322
Emperor Charles V-Day 108
Emperor Franz-Josef-Day 47
Erickson, Millard J.-Day 18, Day 47
Euripides-Day 308

F

Faraday, Michael-Day 283
Farel, William-Day 273
Farrar, Steve-Day 41
Fawcett, John-Day 366
Felix of Nola-Day 45
Felix-Day 279
Fenelon, Francois-Day 323
Fermat-Day 6
Fields, James T.-Day 224
Flavel, John-Day 250, Day 301
Fleece, G. Allen-Day 55
France, R. T.-Day 341
Francis of Assisi-Day 203
Francis, Debbie-Day 66
Franklin, Benjamin-Day 259
Frederick the Great-Day 30
Frere, Henry Bartle Edward-Day 154
Frost, Henry W.-Day 49
Fuller, Charles E.-Day 348
Fuller, Thomas-Day 170

G

Gajowniczek, Franciszek-Day 299
Galileo-Day 311
Galsworthy, John-Day 114
Gambrell, J. B.-Day 153
Garfield, James-Day 183
Garibaldi, Giuseppe-Day 137
Geldenhuys, Norval-Day 352
George, David Lloyd-Day 353
Gerber, Henry-Day 155
Gibson, H. R.-Day 98

Gilbert, William-Day 28
Goforth, Jonathan-Day 321, Day 360
Goforth, Rosalind-Day 360
Goodwin, Thomas-Day 295
Gordon, A. J.-Day 4
Gordon, Charles G.-Day 340
Gordon, S. D.-Day 358
Gorges, William-Day 17
Graham, Billy- Day 23, Day 56, Day 173, Day 204, Day 221
Gray, Jock-Day 167
Griffith, Harold-Day 89
Grimaldi, Joseph-Day 338
Grissom, Gus-Day 27
Gruber, Franz-Day 359

H

Haldane, James-Day 335
Haldane, Robert-Day 112
Hale, Sarah Josepha-Day 324
Halley, Edmund-Day 301
Hamlin, Cyrus-Day 235, Day 341
Handel, George Frideric-Day 44, Day 125
Harris, Murray J.-Day 21, Day 271
Harrison, Everett F.-Day 198
Hatfields and McCoys-Day 269
Havergal, Frances Ridley-Day 254, Day 267
Hawthorne, Nathaniel-Day 224
Haydn, Franz Joseph-Day 44
Hearst, William Randolph-Day 295
Heinz, Henry John-Day 80, Day 298
Hendrick, George R.-Day 3
Hendricks, Howard-Day 130, Day 349
Henry, Matthew- Day 31, Day 128, Day 142, Day 219,
        Day 293, Day 307
Henry, Patrick-Day 179
Herbert, George-Day 107, Day 165
Herman, Nicholas-Day 78
Herod-Day 65
Hess, Rudolf-Day 299
Hsi-Day 254
Hodge, Charles-Day 232
Hodges, George-Day 28
Holladay, Carl R.-Day 223
Holland, Josiah Gilbert-Day 67
Hollings, Michael-Day 109

Holmer, John Andrew-Day 253
Holyfield, Evander-Day 313
Hoover, Herbert-Day 50
Hoste, Dixon-Day 254
Houdini-Day 364
Hubbard, Elbert-Day 168
Hudson, Kathi-Day 211
Hulsapple, Cornelius-Day 290
Hume, David-Day 238
Humel, Charles E.-Day 276
Hunt, William Holman-Day 145
Huxley, Aldous-Day 36
Huygens, Christian-Day 6

I

Ibsen, Henrik-Day 248
Ibycus-Day 135
Ingalls, John J.-Day 183
Ingersoll, Robert G.-Day 36
Ironside, H. A.-Day 14, Day 119, Day 212, Day 289, Day 346

J

Jackson, "Shoeless" Joe-Day 20
Jackson, Andrew-Day 164, Day 173, Day 181
Jackson, Thomas "Stonewall"-Day 325
Jefferson, Thomas-Day 168
Jennings, James E.-Day 12
Jerome-Day 273, Day 335
Johnson, Enid-Day 89
Jones Sr., Bob-Day 70, Day 333
Jones, Mary-Day 12
Jowett, J. H.-Day 343
Judson, Adoniram-Day 189
Julian of Norwich-Day 280
Julius Caesar-Day 71

K

Keil-Day 7
Keller, Helen-Day 257
Kelsey, Morton T.-Day 251
Ken, Thomas-Day 176
Kepler, Johann-Day 93
Khalif-Day 223
Kidner, Derek-Day 329
King Alfonso XIII-Day 330

King Edward VI-Day 302, Day 314
King George II-Day 125
King George III.-Day 162
King Henry VIII-Day 72, Day 193
King Netzahualcoyotl-Day 79
King Philip-Day 200
King, Charlotte-Day 357
Knight, G. L.-Day 306
Knigstein, Franz-Day 113
Knox, John-Day 302
Koerner, Susan-Day 351
Kolbe, Maximilian-Day 299
Koop, C. Everett-Day 230
Kuhn, Isobel-Day 126, Day 174

L

Laidlaw, Robert-Day 220
Lambright, Mary-Day 256
Landry, Tom-Day 134
Lange, Johann Peter-Day 8, Day 91
Latimer, Hugh-Day 72, Day 226
Laubach, Frank-Day 13
Lee, Mark-Day 118
Lee, Robert E.-Day 190, Day 317
Lee, Robert Greene-Day 285
Lenyoun, Estean-Day 146
LeTourneau, Robert G.-Day 241, Day 300
Leupold, H. C.-Day 144
Lewis, C. S.-Day 51, Day 92, Day 201, Day 268, Day 288, Day 344
Lewy, Alfred J.-Day 342
Liddell, Eric-Day 128, Day 332
Lincoln, "Tad"-Day 114
Lincoln, Abraham-Day 114, Day 208, Day 264, Day 284,
    Day 324, Day 328, Day 365
Lincoln, Willie-Day 284
Lintner, Robert Caspar-Day 325
Littauer, Florence-Day 296
Little, Paul E.-Day 160
Livingstone, David—Day 133, Day 310, Day 332
Lloyd-Jones, D. M.-Day 176
Logan, Katherine-Day 163
Longenecker, Richard N.-Day 32
Lord Lucan-Day 271
Louis-Day 169
Lowell, James Russell-Day 101

424

Lowry, Robert-Day 334
Luther, Martin-Day 26, Day 38, Day 74, Day 99, Day 108, Day 188, Day 297, Day 299

M

MacArthur II, Douglas-Day 130
MacArthur, Douglas-Day 115
Macartney, Clarence E.-Day 141
MacDonald, George-Day 208
Machiavell-Day 284
Machnick, John-Day 5
MacLaren, Alexander-Day 197, Day 240
MacLaren, Ian-Day 22
Madison, Terry-Day 233
Mahal, Mumtaz -Day 69
Malan, Cesar-Day 1
Mallon, Mary-Day 232
Marshall, I. Howard-Day 88
Marshall, John-Day 164
Marshall, Peter-Day 279
Martin, Curtis-Day 194
Martyn, Henry-Day 10, Day 177
Martyr, Justin-Day 119
Masih, Ayub-Day 240
Matthews, Richard-Day 354
Mays, Willie-Day 260
McAuley, Jerry-Day 52
McCartney, Bill-Day 213
McCartney, Lyndi -Day 213
McCheyne, Robert Murray-Day 278
McCluskey, George-Day 41
McConville, J. G.-Day 262
McDowell, Josh-Day 11, Day 73
McGee, J. Vernon-Day 6, Day 200
McKinley, William-Day 98, Day 101
Mears, Henrietta C.- Day 134, Day 196
Menninger, Karl-Day 235
Methodius-Day 209
Meyer, F. B.-Day 54, Day 132, Day 155, Day 196, Day 207, Day 250
Mickelsen, A. Berkeley-Day 220
Miller, Donald G.-Day 17
Miller, Emanuel-Day 256
Miller, J. R.-Day 77
Milton, John-Day 46, Day 62, Day 347

Moelders, Werner-Day 13
Moffat, Robert-Day 303, Day 332
Mohr, Joseph-Day 359
Moll, Carl-Day 75
Monroe, Harry-Day 76
Montague, J. J.-Day 327
Montgomery, Bernard Law-Day 90
Montgomery, James-Day 171
Moody, D. L.-Day 56, Day 106, Day 111, Day 147,
    Day 172, Day 178, Day 202, Day 238, Day 241,
    Day 254, Day 255, Day 259, Day 304
Moody, Dale-Day 164
More, H.-Day 192
Morgan, G. Campbell-Day 26, Day 42, Day 155
Morgan, John Pierpoint-Day 319
Morison, Frank-Day 181
Morrissy, Kathy-Day 350
Morse, Samuel-Day 148
Mote, Edward-Day 345
Mother Teresa-Day 129, Day 199
Moule, C. F. D.-Day 41
Moule, H. C. G.-Day 143
Mozart, Wolfgang Amadeus-Day 44
Müller, George-Day 22, Day 50, Day 306
Murray, Andrew-Day 140, Day 322
Murray, John-Day 354

N

Nathan, George Jean-Day 9
Neander, Joachim-Day 94, Day 162
Needham, George-Day 263
Neff, Patrick-Day 18
Neighbour, Ralph-Day 265
Nelson, Horatio- Day 32, Day 175
Nero-Day 294
Newton, Howard W.-Day 124
Newton, Isaac-Day 6, Day 301, Day 311
Newton, John-Day 117, Day 156, Day 247, Day 274, Day 281
Nishida, Shuhei-Day 221
Nommensen, Ludwig-Day 87
Norman, Robert-Day 28
Novykh, Grigory-Day 136

O

Oe, Sueo-Day 221

Olshausen, Hermann-Day 20
Olson, Milton-Day 253
Oppenheimer, Robert-Day 307
Owen, John-Day 348

P

Paderewski, Ignacy-Day 50
Patton, George-Day 214
Paxton, Catheryn-Day 103
Pearce, Mark G.-Day 88
Peary, Robert-Day 28, Day 96
Pellegrin, Harold F.-Day 361
Peltz, Esther-Day 272
Penn, William-Day 77
Penney, J. C.-Day 361
Penn-Lewis, Jessie-Day 146
Phillips, J. B.-Day 237
Pierce, Bob-Day 98
Pink, A. W.-Day 169
Pippert, Rebecca Manley-Day 298
Plantinga, Jr., Cornelius-Day 34
Plato-Day 119
Playfair, William-Day 46
Plutarch-Day 249
Polo, Marco-Day 24
Pope, Alexander-Day 31
Prince Rostislov-Day 209
Prochnow, Herbert V.-Day 79
Proctor, William-Day 175
Publilius Syrus-Day 193

Q

Quarles, Francis-Day 48
Queen Elizabeth I-Day 216
Queen Mary-Day 302, Day 314
Queen Victoria-Day 122, Day 349, Day 363
Quintilian-Day 103

R

Rainey, Dennis-Day 86
Raleigh, Walter-Day 216
Ramabai, Pandita-Day 57
Ramsay, William-Day 120
Rasputin-Day 136
Ravenhill, Leonard-Day 113

Redmond, Derek-Day 214
Richardson, Bobby-Day 260
Richie, David-Day 256
Richter, Jean Paul-Day 338
Rickenbacker, Eddie-Day 211
Riddle, M. B.-Day 115
Rieu, E. V.-Day 243
Rimmer, Harry-Day 218
Rinkart, Martin-Day 275
Robert of Bruce-Day 344
Robinson, Don-Day 236
Rockne, Knute-Day 180
Romaine, William-Day 287
Romero, Luis-Day 281
Rommel, Erwin-Day 90
Roosevelt Jr., Theodore-Day 15
Roosevelt, Franklin D.-Day 179, Day 287
Roosevelt, Theodore-Day 85, Day 96, Day 138, Day 258
Rubens, Peter Paul-Day 210
Ruskin, John-Day 203
Russell, D. S.-Day 218, Day 310

S

Saint Nicholas-Day 205
Saint, Nate-Day 2
Samoset-Day 331
Sanders, Oswald-Day 116, Day 217, Day 225
Sankey, Ira-Day 255
Schlier, J.-Day 209
Schwab, Charles M.-Day 141
Scofield, Cyrus Ingerson-Day 38
Scott, Walter-Day 62, Day 188
Scriven, Joseph-Day 81
Searfoss, Geraldine-Day 337
Sekhen-Day 7
Semmelweis, Ignaz-Day 334
Seward, William-Day 324
Shackleton, Ernest-Day 64
Shah Jahan-Day 69
Shakespeare, William-Day 43, Day 142, Day 242, Day 245,
    Day 264, Day 326
Shaw, George Bernard-Day 116
Sheridan, Richard B.-Day 111
Simeon, Charles-Day 10, Day 63
Simpson, A. B.-Day 24, Day 158, Day 329

428

Singletary, Mike-Day 150
Slessor, Mary-Day 123, Day 188, Day 316
Smith, Amanda-Day 174
Smith, Charles-Day 195
Smith, Cornelius-Day 60
Smith, Mary-Day 303
Smith, Rodney "Gipsy"-Day 60, Day 151
Smith, Roy L.-Day 257
Smith, Samuel Francis- Day 132, Day 184
Smith, Wilbur-Day 234
Socrates-Day 28, Day 170
Soper, George-Day 232
Sorenson, Flora-Day 336
Southey, Roberty-Day 300
Spafford, Horatio-Day 178
Spinola, Ambrogio-Day 210
Spoelstra, Watson-Day 251
Spurgeon, Charles-Day 37, Day 40, Day 43, Day 88,
        Day 136, Day 145, Day 178, Day 292, Day 309
Spurgeon, Thomas-Day 37
Squanto-Day 331
Stamp, Josiah-Day 356
Standish, Miles-Day 331
Stanley, Charles-Day 261
Stanley, Henry M.-Day 133
Stanley, Roger-Day 339
Stanton, Edwin-Day 208
Steeves, David-Day 129
Stevenson, Robert Louis-Day 62, Day 166
Stoeckhardt, George-Day 266
Stott, John R. W.-Day 363
Stowe, Harriet Beecher-Day 54
Stubblefield, Nathan-Day 276
Studd, C. T.-Day 59
Sulivan, Bartholomew-Day 331
Sullivan, Annie-Day 257
Sunday, Billy-Day 282
Swift, Jonathan-Day 63
Swindoll, Charles-Day 57, Day 187, Day 204, Day 230,
        Day 286
Swinnock, George-Day 30, Day 210

T

Tada, Joni Eareckson-Day 188, Day 357
Tallmadge, Benjamin-Day 61

Taylor, Edward-Day 242
Taylor, Hudson-Day 137, Day 254, Day 263
Taylor, James-Day 254
Taylor, Jeremy-Day 58
Taylor, William-Day 100
Temple, William-Day 78, Day 206
ten Boom, Corrie-Day 161
Teresa of Avila-Day 84
Theodulf-Day 229
Thomas à Kempis-Day 25, Day 52, Day 316
Thomas, W. H. Griffith-Day 138
Thompson, Francis-Day 51
Thompson, James W.-Day 68
Thomson, James-Day 311
Thoreau, Henry David-Day 4
Thrasamund-Day 223
Tolstoy, Leo-Day 149, Day 353
Torresola, Griselio-Day 305
Torrey, R. A.-Day 87, Day 217
Townsend, William Cameron-Day 303
Tozer, A. W.-Day 40, Day 228
Traubel, Horace-Day 249
Trench, Richard Chenevix-Day 246
Trouvelot, Leopold-Day 309
Truman, Harry-Day 305
Twain, Mark-Day 82
Tyrtaeus-Day 249
Tyson, Mike-Day 313

U

Upton, Francis-Day 16

V

Van Dyke, Henry-Day 105, Day 229, Day 340
van Rijn, Rembrandt-Day 99
Vanderburgh, C. W.-Day 127
Varley, Henry-Day 272
Vazeille, Mary-Day 73
Verwer, George-Day 265
Vespasian-Day 294
Vitellius-Day 95
von Zieten, Hans-Day 30

W

Wanamaker, John-Day 231
Warren, Frank F.-Day 64
Warren, William Henry-Day 232
Washington, Booker T.-Day 138, Day 143
Washington, George-Day 8, Day 97, Day 123, Day 185,
    Day 215, Day 324, Day 330, Day 331
Watkinson, M. R.-Day 317
Watson, Thomas-Day 135
Watts, Isaac-Day 167
Webster, Daniel-Day 194, Day 356
Webster, Noah-Day 62
Wedel, Theodore O.-Day 239
Weiss, Erich-Day 364
Wesley, Arthur-Day 68
Wesley, Charles-Day 277, Day 285, Day 294
Wesley, John-Day 62, Day 73, Day 109, Day 110, Day 144,
    Day 153, Day 165, Day 319
White, Ed-Day 27
White, George-Day 362
Whitefield, George-Day 318
Whittier, John Greenleaf-Day 139
Whittle, Daniel W.-Day 121
Whyte, Alexander-Day 118, Day 124, Day 216, Day 355
Wiersbe, Warren W.-Day 245
Wilkerson, David-Day 127
Williams, George-Day 150
Williams, Walt-Day 320
Willis, N. P.-Day 74
Wilson, George-Day 164
Wolsey, Thomas-Day 193
Wright, J. Stafford-Day 5
Wright, Milton-Day 351
Wright, Orville and Wilbur-Day 351
Wurmbrand, Richard-Day 59

Z

Ziglar, Zig-Day 184

Inspirational Library

Beautiful purse/pocket-size editions of Christian classics bound in flexible leatherette. These books make thoughtful gifts for everyone on your list, including yourself!

When I'm on My Knees   The highly popular collection of devotional thoughts on prayer, especially for women.
     Flexible Leatherette $4.97

The Bible Promise Book   Over 1000 promises from God's Word arranged by topic. What does God promise about matters like: Anger, Illness, Jealousy, Love, Money, Old Age, and Mercy? Find out in this book!
     Flexible Leatherette $3.97

Daily Wisdom for Women   A daily devotional for women seeking biblical wisdom to apply to their lives. Scripture taken from the New American Standard Version of the Bible.
     Flexible Leatherette $4.97

My Daily Prayer Journal   Each page is dated and features a Scripture verse and ample room for you to record your thoughts, prayers, and praises. One page for each day of the year.
     Flexible Leatherette $4.97